A
PROFESSIONAL
CAREER
IN
PHYSICAL
EDUCATION

PRENTICE-HALL INTERNATIONAL, INC.
London • Tokyo • Sydney • Paris

PRENTICE-HALL OF CANADA, LTD.
PRENTICE-HALL DE MEXICO, S.A.

A
PROFESSIONAL
CAREER
IN
PHYSICAL
EDUCATION

Laurence A. Pape
Professor of Physical Education
Frenso State College

Louis E. Means
Associate Executive Secretary
American Associate for Health,
Physical Education and Recreation

PRENTICE-HALL, INC., *Englewood Cliffs, N.J.* 1962

Preface

This book is written primarily for the "major" or "minor" in physical education as he begins his undergraduate program. It is hoped that the school administrator, the experienced teacher in the field and others who seek to understand the role of physical education may also find this book of value.

For more than 500 years education has exalted the intellect. The academician, ascribing to this view, has a difficult time visualizing physical education as an integral part of education. The challenge of communism has produced many new critics of our schools who would join forces with those who believe that the sole responsibility of the school is the intellect.

Analysis of recent developments suggests that we are undergoing a renaissance of intellectualism in education spurred on by Sputnik. Present practices in our schools are being challenged. The drive behind these efforts to reconstruct the school curriculum stems from the belief that our schools are not measuring up to the needs of the times. Changes in curricula have been made and more are contemplated.

Most of the critics of present practice are working to obtain more school time for such subjects as mathematics, science, English, and language. Their efforts have resulted in crushing pressure, curtailing other areas within the curricula. Physical education in many places has already suffered modifications.

In order to maintain and improve its position in the curriculum teachers of physical education must answer the challenge. Academic people and the public must be helped in understanding that there is no dichotomy between mind and body. The most fundamental fact regarding the human being is that he functions as a unity. There is no stronger argument for the place of physical education in the curriculum.

The tremendous advances occurring on all fronts in the current space age are having far reaching effects on the lives of most people. Sedentary living characterizes work and leisure to the extent that the health and well-being of our population is in serious jeopardy. Physical education has never been more urgently needed than now. Men of science and of medicine know the vital role physical education can play in the education of the youth of the land.

Physical education is at the crossroads. The status quo is destroyed. Either it will fulfill its potential role and become firmly entrenched within the curriculum as a vital subject or it will have to be satisfied with second class citizenship. The years immediately ahead are crucial. Programs must be improved now or those who are following in the beliefs of the academic tradition will have their way. This improvement calls for well-informed, talented, and dedicated physical educators. The future of physical education depends upon the caliber of young men and women now preparing or soon to be preparing for careers in the field. They must close the gaps, eliminate the cleavages, and fashion programs which are educationally significant.

In examining most collegiate departments of physical education that include teacher education, one finds that the first theory course in the professional sequence is usually of an orientation or of an introductory nature. This course is normally the only one offered in the lower division. The remaining work is in fundamental or activity courses and in the required general education pattern.

The authors believe that this first theory course is the key which may successfully launch the new student into his professional undergraduate career. The plan of organization and the selection of material for this book were made with the belief that the beginning student must be given an insight into the challenges and opportunities associated with leadership in physical education. Here the beginning student must be given the opportunity to visualize the wide horizons of physical education as a profession. Course content resembles a smorgasbord, cutting across subject matter usually presented in upper division courses in order to present the new student with a picture of the entire program.

The course should function as an integrating vehicle as the student proceeds on his academic path in the first two years. He has great need to see the relationships which exist between courses within the physical education pattern, as well as to understand the significance of the required courses in general education. The sequence of courses in many departments permits the student to flounder ahead with little effort made to help him gain perspective. The new student must quickly be brought to that point where he sees physical education as education of the individual through the physique. Armed with this awareness he is able to assimilate in much finer fashion the material to which he is exposed in the work associated with the lower division.

This volume is written with these thoughts in mind and attempts to satisfy at least these purposes:

1. Orient the new student to the opportunities and obligations associated with becoming a major in the area of physical education.

2. Provide the student with a basic understanding of the task ahead of him as it relates to the general education, professional education, and professional physical education courses he is to take.

3. Provide the student with a general understanding of the field of physical education as a profession.

4. Provide the student with a sound concept of the scope and the role of school physical education.

The authors have endeavored to be practical. An honest blending of realism with inspiration has been attempted. They were mindful of the points of view of the many students who have participated in discussion in their own classes through the years.

They are appreciative of the counsel and suggestions from contemporaries as the book was developed. They hope that those students who work through its pages will emerge subsequently as professional leaders better equipped to help shape America's future citizens.

Laurence A. Pape

Louis E. Means

Table
of
Contents

ix

A
PROFESSIONAL
CAREER
IN
PHYSICAL
EDUCATION

Part I

PHYSICAL EDUCATION
AS A CAREER

Physical Education and You

What we are born is God's gift to us. What we become is our gift to God.

Ralph Waldo Emerson

1

The fundamental purpose of the opening chapter is to present the kind of information which will help you appraise yourself as a prospective teacher of physical education. A panoramic view of physical education as a career is offered so that you may evaluate your abilities, aptitudes, and attitudes as they relate to the responsibilities associated with physical education. Physical education is a broad field; it demands a great deal from its leadership. The material in this chapter should help you make a good start toward career competency.

FROM THE STUDENT'S POINT OF VIEW

As a student embarking upon a course that ultimately leads to the challenging and exciting profession of leadership through physical education, you should begin now to seek answers to such questions as:

Do I really understand the nature and the kind of work associated with teaching physical education?

Is the field of physical education appealing enough to make it my life work?

Do I really like people and do they appear to like me?

What are the qualifications I need in order to be successful in the profession?

What courses must I take to help obtain these qualifications?

What are the job opportunities that will be available when I graduate?

What salary level may I expect as a physical education teacher, supervisor or coordinator, department head, or teacher of future teachers?

What are the opportunities for advancement?

Is there reasonable security in the field of physical education?

A great deal of thought and planning should be devoted to your career. Many students find that their attitudes change as they begin to discover answers to the questions listed. The selection of your life's work is one of the most important tasks facing you in your lifetime. It should not be undertaken casually. It is only prudent to be realistic in evaluating the desirability of teaching as a career. This important decision should follow considerable exploration and serious deliberation. The student's original choice needs to be constantly re-evaluated in early semesters of professional preparation. Continual analysis and planning help to insure against preparation for a career where interests are temporary or merely recreational in nature. It is not disastrous for the student to reach the conclusion, after a semester or two, that a wrong choice has been made. The student who has not done extensive thinking about a future career before arrival at college must question his aptitude for the unusual challenge ahead. Collegiate life presents many new fascinating experiences. The thoughtful student keeps an open mind and evaluates the worthiness of the many new ideas which are suddenly thrust upon him.

Must Interests and Competencies Be Diversified?

The fact that you are taking this introductory course in physical education suggests that you are, at least tentatively, considering physical education as your future vocation. Perhaps you are intensely interested in sports and already participating in intercollegiate athletics, taking part in intramural sports, or engaging in men or women's athletic activities and physical recreation. If this is true, you have made a good start. A desire to participate in sports, coupled with the ability which enables you to excel to some degree, is evidence that you have potentialities which, with the kinds of experiences you will receive in the undergraduate program, may very well qualify you for the physical education profession. However, it takes much more than basic sports interest and skill to qualify you for this career. You will soon discover that physical education is much more than competing on varsity teams or being expert in the dance.

If your desire either to coach or to specialize in one of the specific areas within the program has led you to major in physical education, you should realize that a great number of graduates may not at once have an opportunity to coach their favorite sport or teach exclusively in their specialty. It is possible that you may not do so for some time. The athletic coach must be trained as a competent educator.

To be a successful physical educator you must be reasonably skilled and have an interest in a wide variety of physical activities before the undergraduate program is completed. A casual glance at the variety of teaching assignments people in the field carry out will readily verify this statement. A small group of physical education teachers attending a recent summer school graduate course was asked to list the activities which they taught in their first year of service. The one who taught the least number of different activities reported that she was involved in five; the one who taught the most actually taught sixteen different activities. The average number of activities taught was nine. One young man reported that he had taught twenty-three different activities in three different school districts over an eight year period. The physical education program at any age level would be most ineffective unless a varied number of activities was used.

Perhaps those of you who thus far have had only one or two interests in the wide range of activities which make up the tool kit of physical education should give careful thought to what lies ahead. Leaders in physical education believe that undergraduates most likely to become successful should possess a high degree of skill in at least three areas, and should be reasonably skilled in a great number of motor activities. Those of you who have already demonstrated considerable skill in two or three activities and who indicate an eagerness to participate in all activities that are important to the physical educator have chosen this career wisely. And it is not too late to develop these competencies if you have the inclination and desire. On the other hand, as you move through the wide sweep of activities that are a part of the undergraduate program, if you discover that you do poorly in a number of them you may have reason to doubt whether you should continue in physical education. You are not expected to excel in all phases of the activity program, but a certain standard of performance must be reached in order to teach physical education.

It should be remembered that there is much more to physical education than motor skills. Activities are but inert vehicles which are used to educate youth through the physical. They are not ends in themselves. They are the medium through which children and youth can learn, and grow to intellectual, emotional and physical maturity. The serious student of physical education also exhibits a genuine interest in other subjects, designed to help him in understanding and interpreting his own field.

Is Physical Education a Suitable Career for Women?

There are parents who object to their daughters selecting physical education as a career because they have come to believe that teaching and participating in physical activities is unladylike. The idea that sports participation may cause the development of mannish characteristics and hyper-development of musculature still persists. It takes only casual observation of the successful women in the field to disclose that this fear is unfounded. The girl who participates in physical recreation regularly is healthier, happier, and better adjusted to life's responsibilities. One is more apt to find that young women develop richer personalities and enjoy fuller lives because of the stimulating environment in which they work, and the wholesome experiences that are a part of this career. Young women who possess reasonable skill and interest in physical activity and who enjoy working with boys and girls find that physical education offers an exceptionally fine career opportunity. The personal benefits derived from participating in sports and recreational activities suggest that teaching physical education is excellent preparation for home and community living for a young woman.

Public Schools of Norfolk, Virginia

Skills taught in sports, like golf, prepare and equip youth for a lifetime of exercise and healthful use of leisure time.

What Makes Teaching Satisfying?

First you should ask yourself if in your past experience you have shown any inclination toward helping others enjoy participation. If you must admit that your only satisfaction has come from personal participation in sports and activities, you may find that you do not have the desire or the patience to assume the role of teacher. At this stage in your program you may not be able to answer this question, but sooner or later you must do this. The answer will be found as you take part in the fundamentals and methods courses that make up your curriculum.

The beginning student often sees only the more glamorous and exciting aspects of physical education. Experience discloses that teaching physical education could become a drudgery for those who have little interest in teaching others or who lack enthusiasm for the activities they must teach. It is to your advantage to analyze your own feelings early. You would do well to carefully think through your ambitions, abilities and personality in order to determine whether you believe that you could enjoy success in a career in physical education. In the event that you find your choice is doubtful, it would be wise to immediately consider another area of specialization.

What Do Administrators Seek in Teaching Applicants?

Although you are just beginning the undergraduate program, now is the time to find out what elementary and secondary school administrators in your locality are seeking in physical education personnel. You can be sure that they carefully examine academic preparation. Grades are important. You must work to maintain a good grade point average. The problem of earning good grades in college is one of the important tasks facing the student. In Chapter 3 a brief discussion dealing with methods of studying effectively is presented to help you understand the best ways to approach these responsibilities. You will discover that most administrators hire the teacher who makes the best impression during the personal interview. Candidates with poor grades rarely are fortunate enough to reach the interview stage of job procurement.

Administrators usually are concerned with the courses taken by applicants in their undergraduate programs. You will be wise to go beyond minimum requirements and attempt, with assistance of your major adviser, to build a broad educational background. Electives should be used to select courses that will enhance your ability to handle non-school problems and activities related to general functions of the teacher. Do not seek the easy course, the one that fits your schedule most conveniently, or the one with the sympathetic professor. This kind of schedule-making leads to a weak transcript and often seriously dilutes professional preparation.

Plan to make college days yield career dividends. Seek out and utilize all possible counselling to help you chart a course most effectively. You then have a chance to qualify as a superior teacher, an active productive member of the profession, and a cultured citizen in the community.

In many states the beginning physical education teacher is required to teach academic subjects as well as those in his major field. This frequently involves teaching assignments in social studies or biological sciences. The applicant may find that his minor area of preparation determines whether he is to be hired for the position sought. Counsel with your adviser on this point. Visit the placement office. Personnel in the placement office are in direct contact with school administrators and are in a position to give you the best current information.

FROM THE VIEWPOINT OF THE PHYSICAL EDUCATION STAFF

Curriculum planners at the college level are concerned with the quality of graduates from their programs. The wise student attempts to learn, as quickly as possible, what staff members in his department expect from their students.

The primary task of professional physical education departments is to prepare students to perform the variety of functions which fall within the broad scope of school and agency physical education. The competent staff recognizes that physical educators, as all other teachers, are citizens first, then teachers and leaders, and finally, specialists in physical education. This concept influences staff members as they select candidates for admission and eventual job placement. More than that, all the experiences provided for students majoring in physical education reflect this purpose. Once candidates are selected, the department has a specific obligation toward those who are successful in meeting graduation requirements. This obligation is met most effectively by helping those students secure positions that match their respective abilities. Physical education department members thus make commendable contributions to the quality of school physical education while at the same time successfully launching the professional careers of graduates.

Curriculum planners are recognizing that undergraduate professional preparation is more than merely successfully passing required courses. For a long time educators in teacher education institutions have known that meeting pre-determined requirements is no guarantee of competence in any particular area of education. This concept may be applied to teacher education in physical education. For example, the physical education major is required to "take" a methods course in swimming or aquatics to satisfy departmental requirements. The purpose of this course may be primarily to equip the student to teach swimming. Most students pass this course. As far as course work is concerned the student has met the departmental requirement in swimming, but it is doubtful if from this course alone he will be qualified to teach swimming satisfactorily. The ability to teach swimming, or any other physical activity, is based upon considerable knowledge about the activity, ability to perform creditably in it, and an understanding of the teaching-learning process. It would seem logical, therefore, that there is more to becoming qualified to teach physical education than to complete successfully the required pattern of courses.

A growing number of college physical education departments involved in teacher education recognize that as long as graduation from college and certification for teaching are based upon the passing of courses alone, ineffectual teaching will continue in the schools. These departments have begun to fashion evaluating criteria which go beyond specified courses and accumulated credits. Snyder and Scott[1] suggest an effective approach to the problem when they urge that plans should be developed to delineate the specific competencies which the student ought to acquire before he can function effectively as a professional person. Achieving these competencies should become the primary purpose of the student and the department. In other words, to prepare more adequately, the professional student must demonstrate the mastery of selected competencies before he can complete an area of instruction, irrespective of the time required.

Selected References

Davis, Elwood C. and Earl L. Wallis, *Toward Better Teaching in Physical Education,* Englewood Cliffs, N. J.: Prentice-Hall, Inc., 1961, Chapter 1.

Downey, Robert J., *et al., Exploring Physical Education,* Belmont, California: Wadsworth Publishing Company, Inc., 1962, Chapters 2 and 3.

Duncan, Margaret M. and Ralph M. Johnson, *Introduction to Physical Education, Health Education and Recreation,* Englewood Cliffs, N. J.: Prentice-Hall, Inc., 1954, Chapters 1, 2, and 3.

Evans, Ruth and Leo Gans, *Supervision of Physical Education,* New York: McGraw-Hill Book Company, Inc., 1950, Chapter 2.

Fraley, Lester M., *et al., Physical Education and Healthful Living,* Englewood Cliffs, N. J.: Prentice-Hall, Inc., 1954, Section II, pp. 39-71.

Jenny, John H., *Physical Education, Health Education, and Recreation,* New York: The Macmillan Company, 1961, Chapter 13.

Johnson, Granville B., *et al., Your Career in Physical Education,* New York: Harper & Brothers Publishers, 1957, Chapters 1 and 11.

Nash, J. B., *Opportunities in Physical Education, Health and Recreation,* New York: Vocational Guidance Manuals, Inc., 1950.

Nixon, John E. and Florence S. Frederickson, *An Introduction to Physical Education,* Philadelphia: W. B. Saunders Company, 1959, Chapters 1 and 2.

[1] R. A. Snyder and H. A. Scott, *Professional Preparation in Health, Physical Education and Recreation,* McGraw-Hill Book Company, Inc., New York, 1954, pp. 76-78.

Palmer, Chester L., "Physical Education as Your Career," *JOHPER* (March, 1953), pp. 17-19.

Scott, Harry A., *Competitive Sports in Schools and Colleges,* New York: Harper & Brothers, 1951, Chapter 7.

Snyder, Raymond A. and Harry A. Scott, *Professional Preparation in Health, Physical Education and Recreation,* New York: Mc-Graw-Hill Book Company, 1954, pp. ix, 421.

Uhler, William P., "On Being a Teacher of Physical Education," *JOHPER* (March, 1950), pp. 21 and 65.

Van Dalen, Deobold B. and Marcella M. Van Dalen, *The Health, Physical Education and Recreation Teacher,* Englewood Cliffs, N. J.: Prentice-Hall, Inc., 1956, Chapter 1.

City Schools of Seattle, Washington

The Undergraduate Program

Thought and theory must precede all salutary action; yet action is nobler in itself than either thought or theory.

Wordsworth

2 The first days on a college campus are usually somewhat hectic and bewildering. Freshman Week is packed with new experiences arising at a pace likely to leave new students in a temporary state of confusion. The first reaction of awe at the buildings and spacious grounds might give way to frustration as the new student strives hard to keep up with assignments that appear endless. Adjustment must be made to new techniques and methods. It is no wonder that some students feel homesick and lost as they are hurried from one test to another, through auditorium sessions and orientations, frantically trying to be on time for scheduled meetings with counselors, and rushing to find the proper place at the right time for medical examinations and physical education classification tests. Fortunately, this period is of short duration. Even though it presents a discouraging introduction to campus life, the many tests and examinations offer valuable information to those who will guide the student's progress during the next few years.

As order emerges from chaos the time is at hand to take stock of all that has occurred and begin the process of getting your feet on solid ground. It is time to evaluate what lies ahead. Study the catalog to find what courses you are expected to take. No doubt you already have had one meeting with your major adviser. Go back to him again and ask the questions which will set you straight on your way. Do not hesitate to seek this kind of help in clarifying your thinking about things you do not understand. Your adviser is available to help you in your professional preparation. He will willingly devote the time and effort necessary to satisfy your needs.

In the event that you have not had the advantage of good counseling in high school, it may come as a surprise to learn that subjects in such broad areas as the natural sciences, social science, literature, the communicative arts, and philosophy are part of your course of study. In any event, it behooves you right from the start to find out what you must take and why. Psychologists tell us that motivation plays an important role in academic success in college work. You are more apt to be genuinely interested in courses which seem far afield from physical education if you know they relate to the demands of your future profession. The first few semesters in college are largely devoted to such courses. Most of these are part of the broad area of general education. Professional leaders recommend that approximately one-half of all college work should be devoted to well-rounded general education courses. An understanding of general education may contribute to your enthusiasm for taking courses which, on the surface, appear to have little relationship to your career objectives. Let us, therefore, consider this matter.

General Education

General education is an important part of the course work of all students. To secure a general understanding of the role it plays in higher education it seems advisable to trace briefly its evolution.

The traditional college function was an intellectual one. Until the middle of the nineteenth century there was a definite pattern, characteristic of most colleges. All graduates had much in common. This unity was disturbed when President Elliot of Harvard University introduced the elective system. The times were ripe for change. The elective system spread like wild fire. The natural sciences began to grow in color and extent, and started to compete on a fairer basis for the student's time. Emphasis was still intellectual but unity was destroyed and the flood gates opened for specialization. The emergence of graduate schools at this time, specializing in subject matter, brought a change in faculty members. They became intensely interested in subject matter. The focus of attention was toward knowledge rather than on use of that knowledge.

The elective system seemed to answer the needs for higher education at the beginning of the twentieth century to meet the demands of industrialization, capitalism, and individualism. It seemed to answer the problem of the great additions of knowledge in the physical and social sciences and, at the same time, to meet the demands for more and more young people entering higher education. With the expansion of colleges to meet these practical needs, many criticisms of the system were heard. The critics seemed to arrange themselves into two opposing groups. On the one hand were the conservatives who wished to preserve the traditional concept of a liberal education. They insisted that the university's function was to improve the intellectual quality of scholarly traditions. On the other hand, the experimentalists argued that, since modern society is complex and rapidly changing, the college must give the student an integrating and unifying experience in order to prepare him more directly for living in an interdependent society. Thus, both groups agreed that the free elective system which led to highly specialized courses and narrow subject matter was educationally unsound. Their proposals for reform differed. They favored more prescription, but of different kinds.

The general education movement, which proposed greater integration by stressing common bodies of knowledge, ranged from the proposal by President Hutchins of the University of Chicago to that of progressive educators, often called experimentalists, following Dewey's philosophy. The vast majority of college educators fell between these two extremes. They seemed to attempt a revision of the curriculum by making compromises between the principles of prescription and election; sometimes following the conservative position and sometimes that of the experimentalists.

It is obvious that general education is still controversial. Differences of opinion stem from the variety of accepted philosophical views found in higher education. On some very general points there is little disagreement. Few would deny that general education is an important function of all collegiate programs. It is that phase of higher education considered to be necessary for all students—in varying degree. It is a movement designed to establish a better balance between the liberal and the vocational elements in education. It attempts to provide a more coherent and adequate introduction to those acts by which men attempt to understand reality and to meet life's problems. Attempts to be more specific lead at once to disagreement.

Several fundamental characteristics of general education can be noted: (1) The most obvious characteristic is a reaction against specialization; (2) It attempts to provide a more adequate integration of subject matter in related fields; (3) It is the tentative answer to the inadequacies of the free elective system. In attempting to balance the necessary diversity in higher education it proposes to teach a common body of ideas, skills, and attitudes which all students should possess; (4) It is concerned with a wider range of objectives. Proponents of general education agree that the cultivation of the ability to think clearly, logically and cogently plays an important part in the program. The experimentalists also view it as an opportunity for the student to learn to integrate the various activities of his life into a meaningful pattern; and (5) the experimentalists state that general education must be mainly concerned with the immediate problems of life because all students do not intend to pursue each subject area into its upper branches.

It is interesting to note that as the general education movement continues it has become increasingly clear that the nature and scope of the program is expanding to include co-curricular activities as essential to the purposes of higher education. These areas are gaining equal status with well established academic subjects. This view immediately singles out physical education as a most important part of the program of general education. Most colleges and universities require all students to take several semesters of physical education activities, although some still hesitate to consider physical education seriously as an integral part of the general education program. Each decade more firmly establishes the value and place of physical education.

In view of the trend in general education it seems certain that the professional attitude of faculty and administration toward physical education on each campus, and the resultant stature of the department, will be shaped by the quality of the entire physical education program organized and conducted by the department.

It is well to point out that faculties normally formulate their own opinions on the department of physical education by the kinds of students who major in the area. The point is clear enough. The status of physical education on your campus rests, to a considerable degree, upon your shoulders. Your behavior on campus and in academic courses reflects directly upon your physical education department. You have, therefore, an important role to fulfill in your years on campus to help maintain the educational integrity of your department.

Professional Education

This is that vital area within your requirements designed to acquaint you with the broad scope and function of education. The fundamental concepts in the educational courses you will take will provide you with basic understandings of the scope and task of the teacher.

Professional education endeavors to provide the background of information which will enable you to develop a philosophy of education that will work, regardless of any specific teaching situation. Unfortunately, there are teachers in every area who, when faced with the limitations and obstacles found on the job, lose sight of the major purposes of education. Along with the many fine teachers who are doing commendable work there are those who fail to achieve the kind of results desired. Some even fail to reach the level of mediocrity.

A number of teachers, soon after entering the profession, cease striving to do a good job. They find it more convenient to relax in their teaching situation and go along with existing practices within their school even when these practices are woefully inadequate. They do not feel it essential to work to achieve acceptable educational results. They are content with their own inertia. There are other teachers who become irritated by the myriad details of their tasks. They soon fall into a pattern of action that leads them to discard theory as unworkable. Their endeavors are more apt to be prompted by expediency. There are other teachers who become set in their ways and resist new ideas. These teachers seldom vary their procedure. They are content to follow old patterns year after year. Experimental design is unknown to them. Woe be the newcomer who dares to suggest changes.

To become a good teacher you must thoroughly understand educational philosophy, possess a keen insight into the nature and needs of the individual, grasp a comprehensive understanding of child growth and development, and have a clear notion of the teaching-learning process. If the student fails to acquaint himself with these major tenets, he is courting professional disaster. He becomes prey to the numerous, always present, pressures which lead to ineffective results. Like a rudderless ship the poorly prepared teacher lacks direction. Conversely, the well prepared and ambitious physical educator develops and employs a set of principles which helps him to become a successful educational leader.

A casual look at college and university catalogues discloses many different patterns of professional education. Whatever the policy of an institution may be, the required professional education courses usually cover the following areas:

Introduction or orientation to provide the student with a broad overview of education.

Child growth and development to familiarize the student with forces and factors which shape behavior patterns at each developmental level from conception through adolescence.

Foundations of education, involving social, philosophical, psychological, and biological aspects.

Organization, administration, and supervision of public education.

Techniques of guidance and counseling.

Audio-visual education and instructional materials.

Evaluation, covering methods and techniques. The student is given opportunities to be critical in self-evaluation of effort as well as in the evaluation of program results.

Principles of teaching and learning. Experiences in this area are brought into focus when the student serves a period of internship in an actual teaching situation.

Recent years have seen a revolutionary approach to the teaching of professional education courses. The older subject matter-centered pattern is giving way to the student-centered functional approach to professional education.

The traditional pattern, belonging to the academic tradition, organized curricular areas into rigid compartments. Education courses under this arrangement frequently fail to include direct experiences and contacts with children and youth, or, if included, such contacts are so fragmentary that the professional student is left with only a vague notion as to the relationship that exists between theory and practice. In some instances little relationship exists between courses. It is then difficult for the student to assimilate the information to which he is exposed in his course work. A growing number of educators believe that a more effective method of general professional education lies in the functional approach.

The functional approach centers attention upon providing experiences that contribute to the development of competencies needed by teachers. When this approach is used the required courses are rich in laboratory experiences which include direct contacts with schools, children, and communities. Careful planning of course content enables the student to assimilate the information from each course. College and university education departments using the functional approach seek to develop patterns of organization designed to meet the demands of each situation. However, each will seek to integrate theory and practice.

Specialized Physical Education

The pattern of courses required of all students majoring in physical education is constructed to provide the prospective teacher with specialized knowledge essential for the successful performance of his ultimate duties. In other words, the area is designed to prepare the professional student to teach in the total area of physical education. You will learn in later chapters that the broad functions of the physical educator include instruction in required and voluntary courses, organization and supervision of intramural and extramural sports, leadership in many phases of school physical recreation, coaching of interschool athletics, and some community responsibilities.

The basic aims which guide staff members in the teacher education program are:

1. To provide experiences enabling the student to develop a working philosophy;
2. To create experiences which enable the student to develop a wide variety of physical skills;
3. To help the student develop an appreciation and an understanding of the contributions each phase of physical education makes to the total program.

Physical education, as all other specialized areas, supplements general education and general professional education through its extensive offerings. Authorities believe that approximately one-third of the total academic credit time of the physical education major should be spent in his specialized area. Most institutions of higher education require from 24 to 40 hours for a major. The exact number of credits necessary is normally determined by a combination of state certification laws and college requirements.

The specialized area of physical education has requirements grouped into three categories; namely, orientation, activity, and academic. During the first semester in college the student should thoroughly familiarize himself with the requirements in each division or category, thereby gaining a clear perspective of that which lies ahead.

Orientation

The new student begins the process of orientation during Freshman Week. For all practical purposes the process continues throughout undergraduate years. How well the student plans his total activities and the degree of motivation he possesses toward college work may determine whether or not he becomes adjusted to college, and to the profession of his choice.

During Freshman Week the new major usually has his first contacts with members of the physical education department. Most departments take advantage of this period by trying to make the new major feel at ease. A tour of the physical plant provides the opportunity to issue lockers and uniforms, and generally acquaint the student with proper procedures for using the physical education facilities and equipment. Some departments, wishing to hasten the development of good fellowship among students and faculty, set aside a few hours for recreational use of the plant for freshmen.

Many departments use this week to begin the process of individual and group counseling. Each student is assigned to a physical education faculty member who is to serve as his major adviser. Usually a conference is immediately arranged so that the adviser may help the student work out his schedule for the first semester. The major adviser is a person the beginning student should soon

Skills instruction will span many sports and activities, indoors and outdoors.

come to know. He can be most helpful in orienting the major to his obligations and responsibilities. To supplement the adviser's efforts most departments require the beginning student to take an orientation or introduction course the first semester. This is the first physical education theory course, the purposes of which usually are:

To provide the beginning student with a basic understanding of his relation to general education, professional education, and professional physical education courses he is to take. Attention is directed to the problem of general guidance in order that the student may work more effectively with his adviser.

To provide the beginning student with a general understanding of the field of physical education as a profession.

To present the program in such a way that the beginning student will develop a sound concept of the scope and the role of physical education.

Activities

Departments of physical education are vitally concerned with the level of skill attained by their majors in motor activities. Competencies in each of the following areas are important: a wide variety of games; normal range of athletic activities; gymnastics; fundamental patterns of movement and rhythms; outdoor activities; and aquatics including life saving. To this list for boys and girls should be added combatives for boys. It is well for you to realize from the very beginning that you must seek to develop skill and interest in a number of these physical activity areas, and that you should not graduate with a real deficiency in any of them. Proficiency in only one or two activity areas is not enough when you will undoubtedly be called upon to direct all aspects of the school physical education program.

Many departments, utilizing the functional approach, have developed techniques of discovering and evaluating the measure of skills their students possess in each activity area. These departments establish achievement tests in each activity which attempt to measure the minimum standard of skill that majors should attain by the time they graduate. Students who believe they already possess the degree of competency desired may request permission to take the tests to determine whether they meet the required standards. The content of achievement tests of this kind vary to serve the purposes of the specific department. They usually involve performance skills and written knowledge. A number of departments find that standardized achievement tests serve their purpose very well; others seem to be better satisfied with locally designed tests. The latest sports and activities skills test developed nationally has been made available by the American Association for Health, Physical Education and Recreation, with national norms developed by the AAHPER Research Council.

When the student successfully passes an achievement test in an activity area the course requirement at the fundamental level for that activity is usually waived. Departments organized in this way demonstrate their desire to focus attention on competencies rather than limiting their evaluating techniques to course requirements alone. Obviously, this procedure of challenging fundamental activity courses does not apply to the methods courses which may be related to that activity area.

Academic Courses

The academic phase of the physical education curriculum usually includes the following courses: methods of teaching and learning activities; organizing, conducting and evaluating programs for the several age-grade levels; organizing and conducting competitive sports of both intramural and interschool nature; administration of public school physical education; programs for the atypical; and specialized and applied science courses relating to physical activity and movement.

You already know that maintaining a certain grade point average is necessary to remain in college. In addition, you should begin to appreciate the vital role that good grades play in securing your first teaching position. Some students have the erroneous idea that physical education theory courses are relatively easy and that they do not require as much study time as other academic courses. This, indeed, is a fallacy. They have fully as much content as courses in other areas. Although good grades should be of prime consideration to you in all your courses, maintaining a good record in your physical education classes is doubly important. You may be sure that your physical education faculty is more inclined to recommend students for the better job opportunities who do well in work within their area. To further verify the need to devote considerable time to physical education course work you should visit the college placement office and ask about the relative importance of recommendations from your major department when job placement is sought.

Selected References

Armstrong, W. Earl, "Basic Elements of a Teacher Education Program," *64th Proceedings CPEA,* 1961, pp. 21-26.

Bucher, Charles A., *Foundations of Physical Education,* St. Louis: C. V. Mosby Company, 1960, Chapters 19 and 20.

Duncan, Margaret M. and Ralph M. Johnson, *Introduction to Physical Education, Health Education and Recreation,* Englewood Cliffs, N. J.: Prentice-Hall, Inc., 1954, Chapter 6.

Esslinger, Arthur A., "Improving Professional Preparation," *JOHPER* (October, 1960), Part I, pp. 44-46 and 58.

Galligan, Glen E., "An Experimental Project in Evaluating A Professional Undergraduate Physical Education Program," *62nd Proceedings CPEA,* 1958, pp. 72-77.

Jenny, John H., *Physical Education, Health Education and Recreation,* New York: The Macmillan Company, 1961, Chapters 14, 15, and 20.

Johnson, Granville B., *et al., Your Career in Physical Education,* New York: Harper & Brothers, 1957, Chapter 9.

Knapp, Clyde and Ann E. Jewett, *Physical Education: Student and Beginning Teaching,* New York: McGraw-Hill Book Company, 1957, Chapter 2.

Smith, Hope M. and Marguerite A. Clifton, *Physical Education: Exploring Your Future,* Englewood Cliffs, N. J.: Prentice-Hall, Inc., 1962, Chapter 13.

Snyder, Raymond A. and Harry A. Scott, *Professional Preparation in Health, Physical Education and Recreation,* New York: McGraw-Hill Book Company, 1954, Chapters 1-8.

Van Dalen, Deobold B. and Marcella M. Van Dalen, *The Health, Physical Education and Recreation Teacher,* Englewood Cliffs, N. J.: Prentice-Hall, Inc., 1956, Chapter 2.

San Francisco's Fleishhacker Pool

Getting
Off to
a Good
Start

> If you want to create some-
> thing, you must be something.
>
> *Goethe*

3

In the preceding chapters you have been urged to give some thought to your qualifications and interests in physical education as a career. An overview of some of the basic factors, including the demands placed upon you by physical education requirements, has been presented to guide your thinking. There are still many things for you to consider before deciding finally that your future is to be in physical education. This chapter and other sections of this book, will present additional information to assist you in clarifying your intentions.

During your college career you will undoubtedly encounter many problems. You will be able to handle most of them by yourself, but it is not always possible to get the answers to all questions without assistance. In most cases your major adviser is the person who can help you.

The Major Adviser

Departments of physical education which prepare teachers are organized so that individual counseling and guidance is an integral part of the responsibilities of each staff member. Your departmental administrator knows that best results are achieved when the instructor has ample opportunities to learn to know his advisees. With this thought in mind he attempts to limit the number of advisees assigned to each staff member.

No doubt your adviser will set up some counseling meetings with you for the purpose of arranging your schedule. Your adviser can help you in many other ways. Take the initiative in seeking him out. Make a point of dropping into his office occasionally. Keep him up to date on your progress in classes and other campus activities. Following this procedure it will not be long before you begin to know him as a person and, perhaps more important, he sees you as an individual. At this point counseling usually becomes meaningful. Once this rapport is established you will feel able to request his help whenever needed. At the same time, since he will know you better, he will be in a position to provide you with the guidance required.

Experience discloses that benefits derived from this guidance, beyond the usual information obtained during scheduled meetings, depends upon the degree of mutual respect created. To encourage the development of this respect you should take the initiative. You may gain a good friend, and receive the personal and professional guidance from an adviser who takes a genuine interest in your individual and professional progress.

Professional Organizations

No doubt you will be given opportunities to join the professional physical education organizations active on campus. By all means associate with these organizations. Active participation in these groups will help you to develop the kind of broad professional point of view expected of leaders in the field. Contact opportunities with professional workers, and observation of their work, is important to prepare for the day when you assume major leadership roles. If there is doubt in your mind about organizational relationships, staff members are always ready to counsel on this point.

The best preparation for future membership in professional organizations is to study each organization while still in college. Become familiar with the purposes and services of leading organizations in the field of physical education. Visit the library and read their official publications. Additional information may be obtained by writing to their headquarters.

It is not practical here to describe in detail all of the professional organizations related to the field of physical education. A brief discussion of a few of them might be helpful.

The Physical Education Major's Club

Most departments of physical education sponsor an undergraduate major's club. It may or may not be affiliated with our most important national professional organization, the American Association for Health, Physical Education and Recreation (AAHPER—NEA). In some institutions the clubs are separate for men and women, while in others they are co-educational. Many departments require all majors to belong to this club because they do not want students to miss the professional experiences provided by them. If membership is optional in your department it is to your advantage to join as early as possible. Participation in club activities brings you into close contact with your fellow students, the faculty of your institution, and frequently with professional leaders in the local area. The purposes of your student organization are social and professional. Do not miss this opportunity to grow professionally.

National Professional Fraternities

Many departments provide opportunity for their students to qualify for membership in the national professional societies. Phi Epsilon Kappa is the national professional fraternity for men; and

Delta Psi Kappa and Phi Delta Pi are the national professional fraternities for women. These groups promote the interests of physical education and work to develop close professional and social relationships among those in the field. An examination of their publications will familiarize you with their work. Phi Epsilon Kappa publishes *The Physical Educator;* Delta Psi Kappa— *The Foil,* and Phi Delta Pi—*The Progressive Physical Educator.*

American Association for Health, Physical
Education and Recreation

Most physical education major clubs hold student membership in AAHPER. If your club is not directly affiliated, ask your adviser what steps you would have to take in order to become a student member of AAHPER. One of the important immediate benefits a student membership provides is a monthly copy of *The Journal.* For an additional small sum members may receive *The Research Quarterly,* the publication dealing with scientific testing and investigation carried on by research specialists. These publications provide the reader with a continuing awareness of programs, facilities, and professional viewpoints of leaders in the field across the nation and in foreign lands. All majors should read these publications. From time to time they may be a part of your reading assignments.

Membership may provide many other supplementary benefits such as early professional identification, special rates on insurance and hotel accommodations, free printed materials, announcements from time to time, and eligibility to attend and participate in local, state, district and national conventions and conferences. Student section meetings, planned by students, are a regular part of the annual association conventions. Through this organization, major national efforts in fitness have taken place, and new materials are constantly available. The professional stimulation you will receive by mingling with well known professional leaders in working conferences becomes a tremendous motivating factor toward the profession.

Plan to join your colleagues in attending as many of the con-

ferences in your area as possible. You will then have many opportunities to meet and talk with respected leaders, many being authors of the professional textbooks you are using. It is surprising how much more meaningful the theory discussed in your classes becomes when you take part in professional conferences. Your physical education courses become significant as you observe the

demonstrations of activity teaching techniques and skills, participate in panel discussions on important aspects of physical education, or listen to leaders discuss the way they do things on the job.
More than that, the materials and information you receive at these
conventions make excellent current additions to your growing professional library.

Learning to Study

You are no doubt beginning to realize that doing good work in
college courses is much more difficult than it was in high school.
You may have done well with a minimum of effort previously.
You are now probably discovering that much more work is required of the college student. New techniques of study must be
developed. Taking notes during lectures and discussion, taking
essay examinations, writing term papers, and using the library assume new proportions. New skills must be learned. Individual
initiative is now more important. High school teachers were more
apt to prod students who began to falter. The college student is
not so closely supervised. It is important for you to realize early
that you alone will be responsible for your study habits. Under
the circumstances it is no wonder that the transition from high
school to college takes its toll. Only the more able students complete their higher education. Statistics disclose that the greatest
number of college casualties due to poor grades occur in the first
semesters.

Sub-standard work on the part of a heavy percentage of college
students constitutes one of the most difficult and persistent problems encountered by college faculties. The problem is a common
topic of conversation among faculty members. The usual conclusion in these discussions is that students are poorly prepared for
college work. Professors are often appalled at the number of students who are weak in spelling and use of the English language,
and who seem to be unable to cope with normal assignments. The
gap between high school and college is often poorly bridged. Poor
study habits appear to be at the heart of the problem. In many
cases the student falls far behind in his work and never seems to

be able to adjust to new requirements and the new environment. It is obvious that a good start must not be delayed.

Students who experience difficulty in earning good grades may conclude that they lack general intelligence to do college work. This is not necessarily the case. It is true that higher intelligence increases the possibility of graduation from college. However, there is no guarantee that intelligent students will complete their work. There are many factors that affect academic results. Colleges using follow-up procedures with students find that intelligence alone does not correlate with grades obtained in college. Some of these colleges find that, on the basis of psychological aptitude tests given during Freshman Week, almost as many students from the top one-third of test results find themselves on probation as do students who are in the lower one-third group.

Abundant evidence accumulated by research specialists proves that actual success in school is not a matter of intelligence alone; but that it depends to a considerable extent on the degree to which the student is motivated, the attitude the student has toward his own ability, and the methods of study he has learned.

How are your study habits? Can you concentrate? Do you know how to complete reading assignments effectively in a reasonable length of time? Determine the amount of time you waste the next time you sit down to study. Are you aware of every minor disturbance that occurs? Does your mind wander? While you are making an analysis of your own study habits it might be revealing to you to observe others to find out how well they concentrate. The best place to do this is in the library. What happens when someone walks into the room? Does the slightest noise distract many? How long does it take the student to settle down once he has been disturbed? What is the first thing the student does when he opens his book? Does he leaf through to see the length of the assignment and then place a book mark at the place marking the end of the assignment? If he does this, you can almost be sure he feels he is facing a chore and the most important thing is to finish the pages. Best results cannot be gained if the student is thinking of the number of pages he has left. If you note any of these examples of poor concentration, your obvious conclusion is that motivation is weak.

A good student does not waste time in carrying out responsibilities. He knows how to get started and how to complete his task successfully in a minimum amount of time. Many of the best students follow a detailed daily time schedule. You may find later that you do not require a written guide in order to keep abreast of your obligations. It is not difficult to work out a daily schedule. America's greatest business and corporate executives follow such a plan. Simply keep in mind that the daily schedule is an organizational device that enables the individual to budget his time so that important tasks are not neglected. The schedule should be developed around the things that must be done during the day such as sleeping, eating, attending class, and studying. By closely following such a plan even the busiest student, one who has much to do beyond his classwork—athletics, part-time employment, campus activities—finds that there is time for recreation, weekend dates and relaxation.

The good student has also learned the most efficient ways of getting the most out of time spent in the classroom and in completing assignments. He has learned the cues offered by textbook organization, classroom lectures, and examinations. From these three sources the student can get much help in improving his reading and listening efficiency.

You may wonder at this point what you can do if you find yourself with faulty study habits. Perhaps the first thing is to talk the matter over with your adviser. He will know if the institution provides opportunities for correcting study deficiencies. A number of colleges, cognizant of the difficulties encountered by beginning students in adjusting to college work, offer remedial English courses and other opportunities to learn effective study habits. Many beginning students would profit greatly by enrolling in one of these classes. There is no stigma attached to taking such remedial courses. It is worthwhile to do all you can to increase your chances for doing successful academic work.

Selected References

Bucher, Charles A., *Foundations of Physical Education*, St. Louis: C. V. Mosby Company, 1960, Chapter 21.
Downey, Robert J., *et al.*, *Exploring Physical Education*, Belmont,

California: Wadsworth Publishing Company, Inc., 1962, Chapter 11.

Duncan, Margaret M. and Ralph M. Johnson, *Introduction to Physical Education, Health Education and Recreation,* Englewood Cliffs, N. J.: Prentice-Hall, Inc., 1954, Chapters 4 and 11.

Hepner, Harry W., *Psychology Applied to Life and Work,* Englewood Cliffs, N. J.: Prentice-Hall, Inc., 1957, Chapter 10.

Jenny, John H., *Physical Education, Health Education, and Recreation,* New York: The Macmillan Company, 1961, Chapter 17.

Johnson, Granville B., *et al., Your Career in Physical Education,* New York: Harper & Brothers, 1957, Chapters 9 and 13.

Miller, Ben W., "The Role of the Professional Organization," *JOHPER,* (December, 1943), 16:551.

Morgan, Clifford T. and James Deese, *How to Study,* New York: McGraw-Hill Book Company, 1957.

Nixon, John E. and Florence S. Frederickson, *An Introduction to Physical Education,* Philadelphia: W. B. Saunders Company, 1959, Chapter 3.

Robinson, F. D., *Effective Study,* New York: Harper & Brothers, 1946.

Smith, Hope M. and Marguerite A., *Physical Education: Exploring Your Future,* Englewood Cliffs, N. J.: Prentice-Hall, Inc., 1962, Chapter 10.

Solomon, Ben, "So You're Going to a Convention," *JOHPER* (March, 1949), 19:179.

Van Dalen, Deobold B. and Marcella M. Van Dalen, *The Health, Physical Education and Recreation Teacher,* Englewood Cliffs, N. J.: Prentice-Hall, Inc., 1956, Chapter 5.

Williams, Jesse F., *The Principles of Physical Education,* Philadelphia: W. B. Saunders Company, 1959, Chapter 8.

Kenneth Miller, Florida State University, Tallahassee

Professional Qualifications

The wealth of a nation consists more than anything else in the number of superior men that it harbours.

William James

4

The reason most people don't get what they want out of life is because they don't know what they want. They settle for whatever comes along. They never really clearly define their objective, even to themselves. Is it any wonder the wishful arrows they shoot in the general direction of their target seldom make a bull's eye?

It requires great stamina to withstand the sacrifices necessary for achievement. It may sound ridiculous to some, but there is ample evidence to prove that a person can reach the status he seeks. He must first know what he wants and then concentrate all his thoughts and actions on it. A man's powers, often unrecognized, have a way of matching his dreams; but his aims cannot be achieved just by dreaming. All his efforts must be concentrated on his goal and he must forego everything that stands in his way.

You are no exception. You can reach your aim in life if you are prepared to pay the costs. However, be sure in your own mind that the goal you have chosen is worth the struggle, or select a better one.

The preceding chapters dealt with the immediate problems the student will encounter. An analysis of necessary courses also was presented to familiarize him with the academic nature of preparation. This chapter will seek to project the student's thinking to that time when he takes his place in the profession. It is concerned with an appraisal of the personal and professional qualities that seem to contribute best to success.

Thus these first chapters should do much to enable the student to ascertain whether he has the qualities and the viewpoints necessary for a career in physical education. Ample information is presented to help the student determine with reasonable accuracy whether the challenge and opportunity in school physical education opens the door to his career.

DESIRABLE QUALITIES OF THE
UNDERGRADUATE MAJOR

Physical education as a profession has passed the period when confusion sometimes characterized programs. Leaders today are in general agreement on the purposes the program is to serve, and much is known about the kind of leadership which is desirable. Effective ways have been found to determine the calibre of students who are involved in the teacher education aspects of the program. College and university departments, together with their professional organizations, are delineating specific competencies required of the professional physical education student to enable him to function effectively as an educated citizen and a professional person.

You should seek to determine these competencies early in your major program. The sooner you become familiar with both the personal and professional requisites, the more time you will have to work at improving areas of weakness before entering the field as a graduate.

All teachers have much in common. Physical educators are not a distinctive breed, for regardless of the area of specialization, teachers are expected to meet the same educational background requirements. In education today the focus of attention is on the individual. The efforts of teachers are directed toward the task of providing students with experiences which contribute to the attainment of well-defined goals. The content of each subject within the curriculum simply represents the variety of tools used by teachers to educate the individual. Physical education is one of the indispensable mediums that must be used. The teacher of physical education is in partnership with his colleagues in seeking the same ultimate goals, although through use of different tools.

As the several broad areas in education are considered—English, mathematics, science, industrial arts, music, physical education and others—it becomes clear that teachers must have specialized education in the content of their particular field. You are gaining your specialized education through the physical education courses required for all majors. Teachers occasionally become so involved in their own specialization that they tend to forget they are only a part of the total educative process. Sometimes this happens to teachers of physical education, especially those who may become engaged in athletic coaching. As you proceed through the preparatory process it is advantageous for you to be cognizant of the fact that the physical educator is a member of a well integrated team with a specific job to do. Team success always depends on how well each member does his job in harmony with his teammates. No other teacher should know the values of teamwork better than you. If you persist in this view upon entering your first job situation, you will augment your chances of being respected by your colleagues and administrators.

Let us now proceed to a more detailed discussion of competencies that are desirable and necessary. Study them carefully and be as objective as possible in analyzing your own strengths and weaknesses. Remember that weaknesses can be corrected:

1. Excellent health, abundant vitality, and skill in motor activities are basic requirements for the physical educator.

The work of the physical educator is physically demanding. The instructor is constantly "on the go"; one class of active youngsters quickly follows another. There is no rest between classes for the conscientious teacher. Meeting the physical demands and tensions which characterize this profession calls for a person who is physically fit. This is an asset as well as a requisite, and accrues as a dividend for healthy and prolonged living.

To obtain best results the instructor must demonstrate often, and occasionally be an active participant. The "sideliner" and "dry deck" aquatics instructor is not usually effective. Youth is eager to participate when the instructor can perform well. It is not necessary to be highly skilled in all the activities that one is called upon to instruct, but demonstrated skill in several activities quickly establishes rapport with students. Have you been assigned to a teacher who obviously has little ability in any activity? How did you feel about his leadership?

It is not necessary for older instructors to be as active as the younger person in order to be effective. Such a person, having demonstrated a high degree of proficiency in the past, can participate less vigorously and still retain the ability to demonstrate when needed. Students will know and respect the capable leader.

As a beginning student you are probably taking one or two fundamental activity courses. Your adviser and instructors are already appraising your physical fitness and skill level. Perhaps you have taken a land and water skills test during Freshman Week. You may be certain that your physical abilities will be constantly appraised by your instructors. They are looking for majors who are reasonably skilled in a variety of activities and who are above average in strength, endurance and health. The department looks with approval on the major who is well coordinated and learns new skills easily. You will have many opportunities in the next few semesters to demonstrate your ability in a wide range of activities. You should accept the fact that your performance ability is to play a large part in your ultimate success as a major.

Most departments encourage or require participation in intramural sports and, if possible, in the intercollegiate athletic program. Some require all majors to participate in at least one sport, while others insist that those who do not participate must become managers of at least one team. These departments recognize that varsity participation provides men majors with experiences which best prepare them for future teaching-coaching assignments. Lettermen are given preference for positions in many parts of the nation. Participating athletes carry more saleable assets into the personal interviews which usually precede job procurement.

No one will deny the fact that skill in physical activities is an important asset for the physical educator, but people sometimes fail to recognize that skill in sports must be coupled with many other attributes in order to qualify as a good teacher and leader. Unfortunately, some school administrators will hire the outstanding athlete to coach and instruct in the physical education program with little consideration given to his other qualifications. This practice helps to explain why teachers are sometimes employed who do not have the necessary qualifications to teach in the diversified physical education program. These administrators are influenced by community interest in winning teams. The public sees the athletic program and, for the most part, has only a vague notion as to what takes place in the other phases of the total program.

School administrators are not under this kind of pressure in communities which are aware of what goes on in sound physical education programs. Citizens in a community who have seen and known, and who understand the values of sound diversified programs demand and support instructional and intramural programs as well as the interscholastic athletic program.

This is not a problem in women's physical education, since most school programs do not place emphasis on interschool sports. They do not cater to the spectator, and intense and often inappropriate interest does not deter sound program development for girls and women. Administrators are not encouraged to seek the specialist because of community pressure. This helps to explain why fewer women enter the physical education field with interests and skills confined to one or two activities.

Since skill and energy in participation are assets for the teacher, you should consider the following questions: Am I reasonably skilled in a variety of games and sports? Do I learn new skills quickly? Do I like to participate in a variety of activities? Do I enjoy good health? Do I usually have abundant energy and stamina? If your answer is negative to these questions, you should seriously consider changing your major.

2. A sincere belief that physical education is a broad program, involving more than playing games and participating in athletics is a prerequisite for success as a physical educator.

The staff constantly evaluates the major in terms of demonstrated professional growth and philosophy. Your department seeks to help you to a mature awareness of the responsibilities and obligations facing the teacher. Physical education is effective when it serves the interests and needs of youth as a way of education achieved through participation in physical activities. This central thesis is emphasized throughout this book and by your faculty members who strive to develop high level leadership to attain this objective.

Many secondary schools have yet to develop this ideal in their programs. Think back to your own program. Was it appealing to all students? Were the classes small enough for good instruction? Were students grouped according to skill levels? Was there a definite program for the handicapped student? Was there a strong intramural program which magnetized the attention of students and involved most of them frequently? Was the required program poorly organized and dominated by the highly skilled? Did you feel that the program was "instructor centered," or did students have a chance to express their ideas? Take the opportunity to visit and observe classes in action in nearby secondary schools, keeping these questions in mind.

You should know that the physical education profession has not succeeded in widely achieving its ideal of effectiveness for all students. Perhaps this is true of all specialized areas of education. Great strides forward have been made. Programs here and there are beacon lights of real leadership and initiative. Physical education has progressed from the traditional concept of physiological outcome alone. The need for dedicated and soundly trained teachers and leaders will grow more acute each year. Their services will be in demand. This is your great opportunity for service in a field which cries out for real leaders. Too many teachers talk a good program. Too few demonstrate a willingness to put forth the effort necessary to rise from mediocrity to excellence. Make no mistake, there are many problems in the way of upgrading the quality of physical education in a specific school situation. Your sincerity of purpose, the quality of your training, your skills and equipment, and your perseverance will all determine your ultimate success on the job.

The calibre of physical education programs during the next decade will depend upon the kind of new teachers now being prepared for entrance into the profession. Future physical educators must be helped to grow in stature and effectiveness. You must develop a strong belief which cannot be shaken in the vital role a dynamic program can play in education, in the school, and in the lives of future citizens. The responsibility for introducing majors to this concept rests upon the shoulders of those involved in teacher education. If this job is done well, it is inevitable that an increasing supply of teachers who possess sound philosophy, needed skills, and dedicated purpose will enter the field.

Careful measures to screen new students entering the field in many institutions is concrete evidence that the profession is aware of its responsibilities. Students may be asked to change their major even when grades are adequate. The usual reasons center around the lack of skill in motor activities or personality deficiencies. It is not uncommon, however, for students to be asked to withdraw from the program who obviously lack an appreciation of the function of physical education.

Even at this early stage in your undergraduate years, ask yourself if you are beginning to understand the role of school physical education. Can you recall what led you to this major? What did you think about the program before you started college? Are you beginning to see physical education in a somewhat different light? From time to time, as your work progresses, you should attempt to determine whether you have developed any new convictions about the role of the program. Be critical of your own varying point of view; you may be certain that your adviser and instructors will be aware of these changes.

3. Eagerness to learn while an undergraduate marks the major as one who desires to develop a professional point of view.

The immediate problem facing the new major is to do well in undergraduate work. Earlier it was pointed out that making a satisfactory record in courses is dependent largely on the degree to which the student is motivated. Your faculty soon recognizes those

students who are seriously motivated toward the profession. They
see the signs in their contacts with the major; his interest in becoming involved in departmental activities, the attitude he expresses with faculty and students, and in many other ways.

Instructors in fundamental skills and methods classes quickly
determine the degree of coordination, skill, and interest in activities possessed by the major. They also learn much about the major
as a person. Instructors in physical education theory courses discover how seriously motivated each student may be toward the
field. The student whose interest is limited to coaching athletic
teams or teaching a certain activity usually discloses his lack of
professional direction early and constantly. He may pick up interest only when his favorite sport is emphasized; and show his lack
of concern in other necessary areas of leadership. Unless drastic
changes in viewpoint take place this student is a poor professional
prospect.

The faculty expects men and women majors who enter the program with a background of sports participation to be very much
interested in athletics. There is nothing wrong in a highly developed interest in one or more activities. The athlete and the
special interest student is encouraged to major in physical education because highly skilled performers are needed in the profession. However, the department expects to observe a broadening
viewpoint as the "specialist" is exposed to the variety of activities
normally taught in fundamental and methods courses, and to the
principles and philosophies espoused in theory courses.

Physical educators realize that many of their majors, while in
high school, have experienced inferior programs which were narrow in scope. They also know that in many situations the varsity
high school athlete has not been required to take regular physical
education courses with other students. Whatever the background,
the department anticipates that many majors may have missed the
opportunity to learn and enjoy such activities as gymnastics, volleyball, handball, swimming, tennis, golf, archery, boating, shooting, angling, and the dance. Staff members expect and anticipate
that these highly skilled students will learn to enjoy and appreciate the new activities to which they are introduced.

Usually, a student active in one or more sports readily acquires
new skills. Many, having little opportunity to learn a variety of

skills earlier, are amazed to discover that keen competition and real enjoyment can be derived from a great number of activities. The few specialists who fail to broaden their interests are judged to be poorly qualified to teach in the full program of physical education. The only place for these individuals is in the few situations where they might be called upon to do nothing beyond coaching or instructing in their specialty. Their future is often limited.

It is now time for you to do serious thinking about the part you will want to play in the profession upon graduation. Will you attempt to influence only a select few in the years ahead, or will you project your leadership contribution into the lives of thousands of future citizens? Do you find yourself looking forward to each class you are now taking? Do you detect any quickening of enthusiasm to learn more? You may find yourself forming an entirely new and healthy outlook toward the many things you are learning, and the many experiences possible in departmental affairs.

4. Physical education leaders are seeking undergraduate majors who possess desirable leadership traits.

By definition, a leader is one who consistently influences the behavior of others. Instruction in physical education involves leadership and develops it. Although a wide range of different personality types become successful in physical education, they all share one ability—to help students achieve good results. Beginning teachers occasionally attempt to be a carbon copy of a teacher they admired very much. This is seldom possible because each individual is unique. An effective procedure might be for the new teacher to study the techniques and personal qualities of others, and adapt the usable ones on a trial basis. He should always remember to be himself in his relations with others.

Leaders in the field of human relations have directed much attention to the study of successful people. Case studies reveal that of all the qualities which seem to contribute to success in any line of work, none is more valuable than to feel a genuine respect for others. A respect for all people, a real interest in those who have not yet achieved recognition, and a genuine recognition of the worth of every individual are important attributes of the young physical educator.

Good teachers are well liked by others. They have developed a kind of solid interpersonal relationship with people that set them apart as leaders. Just as successful people differ in many respects, the teacher evidences uniqueness of personality. However, within the personality of all good instructors, certain important similarities are detected. The respect for the integrity and worth of each student stands out as a basic element for success as a physical educator.

The clean cut, wholesome and dynamic leader, genuinely interested in people, and displaying enthusiasm for the things he teaches, is very apt to engender the kind of respect from youth that culminates in meaningful results. Perhaps you can recall teachers who were sincerely and completely absorbed in their teaching responsibilities and opportunities. If you do remember such a teacher, you will recall that his enthusiasm tended to be quite contagious. You and your fellow students were very likely to have shared his enthusiasm, and you probably enjoyed the subject taught. Perhaps you can also recollect a teacher who appeared to be bored with his work. What effect did he have on the students? It takes little more than casual observation to discover the impact of a teacher's attitude and personality on the learning process. Those who are sincere, confident, and enthusiastic contribute to an easy relationship, conducive to good learning; and those possessing a colorless, negative personality tend to destroy motivation, creating an atmosphere charged with tension which characterizes a poor learning climate.

There are many attitudes or qualities which seem to lead to effective leadership in physical education or any other field, but two seem to be of particular significance. They are a *vigorous curiosity* and a *sincere desire for improvement.* The major should strive to develop an attitude questioning whether accepted answers and solutions are actually adequate. The desire to know *why, where, how, when,* and *what* leads to professional growth; although it should be remembered that dogmatism must be avoided. This outlook, plus the desire to improve status quo contributes to a professional behavior pattern necessary for leaders in the field.

Probing deeper into action patterns of successful leaders, the astute observer or student may see additional attributes that most good teachers possess. The more one considers the problem, the more apt he is to see four elements of good leadership which stand out in the behavior of outstanding teachers. First, to be a truly good teacher one must be sensitive to the problems in both physical education and total education. The physical educator who is not sensitive to countless numbers of opportunities for constructive action, who cannot see things that are wrong, will be no more effective than the football coach who has not grasped the importance of teaching fundamentals of blocking and tackling to his players. Being sensitive, being aware, and having knowledge is not enough. Secondly, the good teacher must possess a heightened sense of personal responsibility to work for the elimination of imperfect and undesirable situations. Being aware, and having a feeling of responsibility to work for betterment is still not enough. Thirdly, the teacher must know how to analyze the situation, and how to plan an appropriate course of action. Then, of course, fourthly, the most important element of all is for the teacher to have practical ability to act on the plan.

The undergraduate student is constantly given opportunities to demonstrate leadership traits. Many students seem to be naturally endowed with qualities which encourage others to follow, while some must seek every opportunity to gain practical experience which will develop them. Those of you who may wonder whether you have an appropriate degree of leadership potential, should realize that leadership is a form of behavior and can be acquired. As you begin to acquire each desirable trait, your total behavior changes and you begin to evidence a higher degree of leadership potential. It is sound procedure to rate yourself in terms of leadership traits as you move along the preparation trail.

5. Good manners and a well-groomed appearance contribute to the individual's social stature and should be cultivated by the physical education major.

People who seem to be most attractive to others usually are pleasant and well mannered. Etiquette is a combination of good taste, common sense, and consideration for others. Perhaps you have not thought of it as such, but good manners are basic to good sportsmanship. Participation in sports and physical activities is at its highest level when the performers combine fair play and consideration for opponents with maximal effort. Leadership in physical education is achieving desirable results under such circumstances. For this reason, the physical educator should avoid conspicuous behavior that marks one as crude or unmannerly. Good manners should be cultivated until they become spontaneous attributes.

Psychologists tell us that the knack of getting along well with others and of displaying characteristics which tend to create a pleasant feeling of friendliness are qualities of social intelligence. Thus it is reasonable to propose that the physical educator establishes the most effective learning situation when he contributes to the social ease of his students. Some students have this ability naturally; others must strive to develop it through constant practice. Some important behavior aspects observed in effective leaders are listed here. Study them carefully and put them into daily practice. You will be rewarded by developing added resourcefulness in social and instructional situations.

1. Encourage others to talk about their interests, hobbies, friends, and experiences. Be attentive and indicate interest.
2. Remember a new friend's name and his interests. Try to find out beforehand about his interests, his ambitions, and his experiences. Show clearly that you regard these things highly.
3. Show respect for the other person's wishes, his peculiarities, and his idiosyncracies by adjusting yourself to them.
4. Put yourself in the other person's place. We often are too self-centered to forget our own wishes, interests and opinions.
5. Refrain from trying to allocate motives to what others do and say. We react favorably to those who trust us; to those who expect the best from us.
6. Recognize the good points in the endeavors of others and comment on them favorably.
7. Express opinions without becoming argumentative.
8. Be a good member of a group. Give leaders the cooperation that is merited—that you would appreciate if the positions were reversed. Good leaders are good followers.
9. Consult with others and accept worthwhile suggestions when you are in charge of a group. Responsibility is an honor. Do a good job without becoming dictatorial or overbearing.
10. Influence rather than drive others into cooperative action. Influencing others is 99% leading, not driving. They will follow someone they like—someone who offers a way of attaining the things that are valuable to them.

Your general appearance makes an impression on others. Most personal contacts are with people at close range; therefore, it is of vital importance to achieve good grooming and the atmosphere it creates. People like to be associated with others who are clean and neat. Being well-groomed makes a person feel better and more confident. Careful attention to one's appearance pays dividends in better relationships with friends, family and colleagues. Attractiveness is more than good features, nice figure, good physique, or expensive clothes. To be attractive one must take advantage of his best qualities. Cleanliness, good posture, well-pressed and appropriate clothes, and a pleasant expression mark the person who uses good judgment in personal appearance.

Women majors of physical education should take care to dress and act in a feminine manner. It is not expensive to keep the hair attractively styled, to wear well designed, appropriate clothing, or to use good taste in make-up. Men majors should practice good grooming just as conscientiously as women. Regular haircuts, care of nails, a clean shave, and clean, well-pressed clothes contribute to lasting impressions. By exercising reasonable care the informality of campus attire becomes casual, rather than slovenly. The major, as well as the teacher, should maintain an appearance on a par with others on campus. The soiled and smelly sweat shirt is not the costume of the successful physical educator.

6. To be a successful teacher of physical education the major must show evidence that he is reasonably intelligent.

The old cliché "brawn and brains do not mix" is as inaccurate as the concept held by some, that athletic ability is all that is necessary to qualify as a good teacher of competitive sports. A dull person is not effective in any phase of the total program. It takes above average intelligence to develop skills and to understand and work toward the fulfillment of education. An alert instructor is needed to mold individuals into a harmonious team, or to cope with the ever changing series of events that accompany class teaching. The ability to organize, to provide inspirational leadership, and to be expert in human relations are prerequisites for success in the field.

Two vitally important attributes needed for effectiveness in the profession are: (1) the ability to speak well, and (2) the ability to write reasonably well. These are skills one associates with above average intelligence. There are countless occasions when the physical education teacher is called upon to speak before groups. Undoubtedly the coach is called upon to speak before groups more frequently than those engaged in the instructional program. And yet, more important than speaking engagements is the ever present need to be effective in communicating with students. Every day in each class the instructor's facility to communicate plays an important role in determining the results he will achieve with his students. It is difficult to visualize continued success for the teacher who expresses himself poorly, or who fails to handle written communications satisfactorily because of lack of competency.

Do not feel discouraged if it is difficult for you to be at ease in speaking before a group or if your English themes displease your instructor. These skills can be acquired. If you lack these capabilities, you should have an added incentive to master them since skill in the communicative arts is vital. Take every possible opportunity to talk before groups, no matter how difficult it may be at present. Purchase a pocket dictionary. Exercise real care whenever you write, whether a required paper or a letter home. Only through practice can these arts be developed.

7. The ability to control one's behavior is a distinguishing characteristic of the successful physical educator.

The very nature of physical education activities enables the teacher to create a setting which helps young people to develop emotional behavior characteristic of the mature personality. A more complete discussion of emotional maturity may be found in chapter seven. For the present, a brief analysis of some of the salient ways this trait serves the physical educator should be sufficient to demonstrate the importance of controlled behavior in competent leadership.

The serious nature of college work, with its exacting demands on student time and energy, causes some students difficulty in recognizing the need to maintain enthusiasm and be cheerful in contacts with others. A confident manner is characteristic of the individual who makes good adjustments to situations and to people as he encounters them. The well-adjusted person has learned to control his own emotions under stress and strain so that they work for him, rather than against him in most situations. The job of teaching physical education is physically and mentally exacting because the entire experience has a tremendous potential for tension. For this reason the teacher of physical education must have easily accessible and satisfying outlets for emotional energy in order to prevent tension from accumulating. He or she must learn how to relax and to teach others its value.

The physical education program is a great laboratory for teaching the skills in satisfying activities which will enable students to develop wholesome outlets for tension. Exercise itself is a great stabilizer—the balance wheel of adjustment. At the same time it must be recognized that participation in physical pursuits could become frustrating and detrimental to some if not intelligently controlled. The calibre of leadership is the determining factor as to whether the program is to be beneficial or harmful.

It is well established that the lives of many people are cluttered with tensions to the point of neuroses. The pace of modern living has brought an entirely new area in medical research—psychosomatic medicine. Meninger[1] pointed out that there are approximately one thousand patients per day entering mental hospitals. He emphasized that there are more patients in hospitals today due to nervous disorders than all other causes combined. Another leading psychiatrist originated the phrase, "we are becoming a race of neurotics." The industrial age ushered in a whole new set of problems to bewilder mankind. The ever increasing pressures and tensions that characterize the life of the modern American has progressed to the point that the term "neurosis" is used freely in ordinary conversation. Mental health has become the number one health problem in the United States. The conclusion is obvious. People have urgent need to get rid of tensions associated with daily living. The physical educator now becomes associated with therapeutic remedies never before realized. Total fitness becomes more than just a slogan.

The sports, dances, games and activities that comprise the physical education program should be sources of enjoyment, not anxiety; of fun, not anger; of anticipation, not frustration. Programs should not be so demanding that they contribute to tension. With good leadership the physical education program provides the laboratory within which youth have ample opportunity to grow emo-

1 Carl Meninger, AAHPER, Annual Convention, Los Angeles, April 1952.

tionally. Learning skills in physical education can be stimulating and exciting. Class activity should lead to satisfying participation on a continuing basis. Through this medium emotions are always aroused and motivation reaches a high peak. Capable leadership is alert to see that these activities are a source of pure joy to participants. In qualified hands the total program of class instruction, intramurals and athletics is structured to maintain an atmosphere of good will; an atmosphere that is conducive to the expenditure of nervous tension. Here activities are taught as *great sport*. The key note is maximal effort in satisfying activity. Enjoyment is derived from the activity itself, not from outside inducements. In this setting participants are encouraged to exercise proper self-control, even in the most intense situations. This kind of physical education far transcends the purely physical, and is of great value in helping students achieve emotional maturity. It is the product of dedicated professional people.

Concluding Statement

This chapter has presented you, the undergraduate major, many sources of encouragement, and many guide posts to avoid disappointment and disaster. It has also frankly tried to show you some divergent points of view. Attention thus far has been directed toward your work as a student with physical education emphasis, and upon qualities that contribute to vocational and professional competency and success. It is strongly suggested that you pause periodically for self-analysis. Refer to the seven desirable qualities discussed in this chapter to help evaluate your progress. Use them to chart your professional growth. They are not the only qualities that are important; others are perhaps equally valid. However, by checking your personal habits and attitudes according to this criteria, you can keep a running evaluation of progress. The ability to measure yourself in this way can be a potent incentive to improvement and growth. As one of America's early college presidents once said: "the world stands aside for the man who knows where he wants to go." The inscription on one of the state government buildings in Sacramento, California, speaks eloquently to all who would pause to see: "Give us men to match our mountains." This expresses so well the great need today for dedicated and well trained leadership in the field of physical education.

Selected References

Bucher, Charles A., *Administration of School Health and Physical Education Programs,* St. Louis: C. V. Mosby Company, 1958, Chapter 8.

————, *Foundations of Physical Education,* St. Louis: C. V. Mosby Company, 1960, Chapter 18.

Davis, Elwood C. and Earl L. Wallis, *Toward Better Teaching in Physical Education,* Englewood Cliffs, N. J.: Prentice-Hall, Inc., 1961, Chapter 3.

Emery, Donald B., "The Physical Educator—A Mental Hygienist," *JOHPER* (January, 1953), p. 27.

Jenny, John H., *Physical Education, Health Education, and Recreation,* New York: The Macmillan Company, 1961, Chapter 13.

Johnson, Granville B., *et al., Your Career in Physical Education,* New York: Harper & Brothers, 1957, Chapter 10.

Nixon, John E. and Florence S. Frederickson, *An Introduction to Physical Education,* Philadelphia: W. B. Saunders Company, 1959, Chapter 4.

Scott, Harry A., *Competitive Sports in Schools and Colleges,* New York: Harper & Brothers, 1951, Chapter 7.

Smith, Hope M. and Marguerite A. Clifton, *Physical Education: Exploring Your Future,* Englewood Cliffs, N. J.: Prentice-Hall, Inc., 1962, Chapters 2, 3, 4, 5, 6, and 12.

Louisville, Ky. Courier-Journal *and* Times, *and Ellis Mendelsohn*

Economic
Status
and
Security

There may be luck in getting a good job—but there is no luck in keeping it.

J. Ogden Armour

5

Attempting to present accurate salary statistics at this point is difficult and somewhat unreliable. The situation differs greatly in various sections of the nation; from one type of position to another. You should become familiar with present salary practices and trends in your particular area and in other states where you might want to teach.

As a young man you will doubtless marry and raise a family. Prudence suggests that you plan your needs when that time comes, and match them against your possible salary level at that time and later. As a young woman the situation may be somewhat different.

Most of you will marry sooner or later and at least temporarily accept a different career. Even with marriage you may decide to continue your teaching career. In light of the great and continuing need for trained and able women leaders in the field, it is hoped that marriage plans may include teaching. This kind of dual career is entirely possible, and is being followed by an increasing number of women.

In seeking answers to your inquiries regarding salary potential it would be well to keep two factors in mind: (1) salary schedules are constantly being revised upward; and (2) teaching opportunities and salaries vary a great deal in various sections of the nation.

Present Status

Historically, teaching has never ranked among the highest of professional careers in salary potential. Following World War II teaching salaries in some areas were below subsistence levels. Increased wages in industry triggered an unusual exodus from education. This occurred simultaneously with a sharply increased school population. The outcome was a critical shortage of teachers. To make matters worse, fewer students entered professional education. Young people entering higher education found that the other professions held greater financial promise.

The situation grew to such proportions that it resembled, in impact on the American people, a national tragedy. Finally, complacency gave way to real concern by leaders in all walks of life. The press, state and federal government, groups of aroused citizens, and others, helped create an awareness of the problem. The public became aware of the necessity for more teachers and the value of better trained and higher paid teachers for the public schools. Consequently, in the 1950's a steadily increasing salary scale accompanied by better teaching conditions and added security was the rule for most public school teachers. In 1950 the average salary of public school teachers in the United States was $2,886. In 1960 many communities were paying teachers more than $8,000 per school year. New school district salary schedules now provide upper steps well above $10,000 in some areas.

In this same decade school administrators have rapidly moved from low levels of compensation to salaries up to $35,000 per year. Here and there some form of merit system holds hope for even greater recognition of the worth of leaders in this field who are willing to produce real results.

The undergraduate major who completes his program and moves into the field is certain to find and enjoy a much higher standard of living than did his predecessor of a few years ago. There will be continuing salary increases, and growing respect for the worth of educational leaders. Coming with this is better tenure, welfare benefits, more jobs, and better retirement features.

Improved teaching conditions and better compensation has not eliminated the shortage in trained teachers. Inadequately prepared teachers, hired on a short term basis are found in great numbers in school districts across the country. Population statistics indicate the trend will continue with shortages more pronounced in the years immediately ahead. These alarming facts contribute to a situation wherein a future in teaching is most promising to those of you contemplating such a career. Better salaries and improved working conditions will continue to increase. You are entering the profession at the best time in the nation's history.

The problem of recruiting sufficient numbers of capable high school graduates to prepare for teaching is not easy to solve. Lawyers, dentists, and physicians command somewhat higher salaries. But not all of these professional people succeed. Teachers normally reach their maximum earnings within approximately fifteen years; while successful businessmen may surpass the teacher in the same length of time, and continue advances in later years. At the same time, businessmen may have a high failure rate. Teachers may later advance to positions in administration, supervision or coordination, accompanied by much higher salaries, even equal to or exceeding the other professions mentioned.

The teaching profession will never be a profession suitable for those who attach a dollar value on everything. Teaching attracts people who place greater values on considerations other than financial. It attracts those who are interested in living full lives themselves, and who enjoy contributing to others by helping to enrich the lives of young people. In the decades ahead physical educators will have favorable salary compensation and there will always be other rewards not found in most occupations.

When adding the advantages of teaching, high on the list would be the nine- or ten-month working year, supplemented by several short vacations. Improved salary schedules enable many teachers to travel extensively during the summer months and to take advantage of countless other opportunities for satisfying experiences. Also on the positive side is the degree of permanency teachers with tenure achieve. The peace of mind in always knowing that one's income is secure is worth a great deal to many people. Mild disturbances in the economy, when money becomes tight, have very little effect upon the teacher's paycheck or security. This is not true in industry. The level of national prosperity has much to do with salary increase patterns, but teachers are always among the last to receive pay cuts during economic stress.

Most public school systems have a definite and fixed salary schedule for various levels of employment—administrators, supervisors and teachers. Usually these schedules provide additional increments for years in service and earned academic and professional preparation. The practice of adopting a basic single-salary schedule for both men and women is a recent development of administrative policy. Some forms of merit compensation are becoming more common. This kind of information should help the student in determining his future prospects.

As a major attempts to determine his probable salary range, it is practical to find out the kind of teaching load to be anticipated. A few well directed inquiries locally will help determine what to expect. To be happy on the job the teacher must be satisfied and competent to handle the subjects assigned to him. This is equally true of the physical educator and the subject area teacher. Many physical education teachers are required to teach other subjects as part of their total work load. The beginning teacher of physical education is almost certain to find that he will spend at least part of the day in the classroom in some areas of the nation. Combination teaching responsibilities may be stimulating and valuable.

Public schools normally adopt a formula for teacher work load in accordance with the type of responsibility involved. The traditional argument that physical education requires little or no preparation continues to lead some administrators to consider physical education as different from other subjects. Therefore, physical education teachers assume a heavier teaching schedule than other teachers in some school districts. This practice is deplored and tends to produce overworked teachers who may let some of their responsibilities suffer. Qualified physical education teachers do prepare. They administer and interpret tests and grade papers. They have a multitude of responsibilities associated with planning, organizing, and conducting the program of activities. Details such as keeping student records, counseling, and taking care of equipment and facilities require many hours of work each week beyond student contact hours.

Job Opportunities

The kind and number of positions available in physical education depend upon the section of the country. There are more positions available to inexperienced teachers of physical education today than ever before. Qualified graduates from recognized physical education departments should have little difficulty in securing positions. There will continue to be a shortage of trained physical education men and women in most states. Colleges in some states are unable to provide sufficient numbers for their state. Examination of enrollment trends in teacher education institutions fail to disclose any significant factors which might change this situation in the years ahead.

Although the prospects for securing positions are excellent, this does not mean the beginning teacher will step right in to the kind of position ultimately desired. He might enhance his opportunities, however, if he is willing to change localities. In most areas of the nation the beginning teacher may find it easier to enter the profession at the elementary level. Here the demand far exceeds the supply. In many localities successful teaching experience is required as a prerequisite before qualifying for a position in a city system. Those who want to locate in a metropolitan area or large school district might first expect to serve in a smaller school system.

Due to the rapid turnover of women teachers there is little difficulty for the woman physical education major to secure the kind of position she seeks. The shortage of women teachers is so acute that many undergraduate upper division majors are lured away from their preparation. The opportunity to secure good paying positions, even though on an emergency basis, is too strong for some students to resist.

Young men who wish to coach should recognize that graduates with outstanding athletic records usually have the best chance to secure head coaching positions. The widespread expansion of sports in recent years has led to an increased number of coaching positions in school and college.

Coaching positions are sometimes linked with classroom teaching rather than physical education. Unfortunately, many administrators have adopted the policy of hiring the specialist to coach and teach in the classroom. Schools that follow this practice are creating a situation which leads to virtual separation of athletics from physical education. This practice is deplored because of its tendency to narrow the scope of a properly conceived program.

A number of leading college and university physical education departments regularly have available a few graduate assistantships. The graduate assistant usually is assigned to teach activity courses in the service program. He or she may have a one quarter or one half teaching load, and is permitted to take graduate courses leading to the Master's or Doctorate degree. This kind of opportunity is valuable to the physical education major who has ambitions for professional advancement. He receives valuable teaching experience in addition to partial salary. Students with outstanding undergraduate records accompanied by strong faculty recommendation, are chosen. It is not too early in your career to make inquiries in this direction. Know the qualifications attached to this opportunity early and set your target. Preliminary work associated with applications for graduate assistantships must be completed early in one's senior year in order to be considered for the fall semester following graduation.

TENURE

Teaching is a stable profession. Steadiness of employment in the teaching profession is assured for those who achieve tenure. This is a very important factor to take into account when considering one's future vocation. Today, all but a few states have adopted some type of tenure program designed to protect teachers from dismissal as long as they render efficient service. For the most part, tenure protects the teacher against loss of employment due to political change or clashes of personality which could occur between the teacher and administrator. Security of this kind is seldom obtained by the worker in industry or business. Therefore, tenure is an important factor on the positive side of the ledger as the merits of teaching are weighed.

There are a variety of plans governing teacher contracts and dismissals. The student should find out the plan followed in his own neighborhood or area. The teacher must usually serve a probationary period before permanent tenure is earned. The number of years of probation varies considerably. In most cases the teacher must serve three to four years before earning permanency.

During the period of probation most school boards utilize one of the following kinds of contracts: (1) annual contracts, with security given for a period of one year; (2) permissive contracts, covering a period of more than one year; (3) continuing contracts, with automatic employment each year unless notified to the contrary before a specified date each spring. After successfully meeting the specified probationary period, the teacher is given tenure, hence security on the job.

There are two types of permanent contracts in wide usage today; namely, the protective type continuing contract, and the permanent tenure contract. They are quite similar. The major difference occurs when dismissal is contemplated. Under the protective type continuing contract the teacher has the right to demand a hearing. In most cases the school board permits the teacher to have the benefit of counsel and witnesses. Under the permanent tenure contract the teacher has similar rights, and in addition is assured added objectivity by the fact that some agency other than the school board reviews the case.

Justification for dismissal occurs only when the teacher is proven to be inefficient, insubordinate, neglectful of duty, unprofessional in conduct, or physically or mentally disabled. On rare occasions a school board may dismiss teachers who hold tenure due to decreased enrollment or territorial change. The latter is not very likely in the years ahead in most places.

Teachers as well as school boards must meet certain obligations under most tenure laws. The teacher who signs a contract agrees to fulfill the stipulations contained therein to the best of his ability. The school board also incurs responsibilities it must respect.

There are certain positions that do not receive tenure. In most states school administrators hold tenure only as teachers, and not as administrators. Coaches of athletic teams, particularly at the college level, may not receive tenure. In some states secondary school coaches receive teaching contracts on a permanent basis, but their contracts do not include coaching responsibilities.

RETIREMENT

Most college students in early stages of career development rarely give much thought to what lies ahead of their productive years. Old age is too far away to think about very seriously. And yet, the time for the student to consider old age security is when career decisions are being made.

The favorable trends noted in regard to salary expectation and job security are also observed in teacher retirement benefits. Early retirement plans were often ineffective or non-existent. Their basic weakness lay in the fact that they were voluntary and local in character. Fortunately, these shortcomings no longer exist. Most teachers can now look forward to a measure of security during their years of retirement. Compulsory, state-wide plans have been adopted in all states. In all but two states the teacher, the state and possibly the local school district contribute toward the retirement fund. In these two states a pension plan is utilized whereby the state and the local school system provides all funds. This would permit teachers to devote a portion of their regular paycheck to other additional retirement accumulations if desired.

In 1950 the Federal Security Act of 1935 was extended to permit educators to participate in social security. As a result, further beneficial changes in retirement plans took place. A number of states abandoned previous retirement systems entirely; others established supplementary programs to provide additional old age benefits.

An overview of the various retirement plans now in operation across the nation discloses many important differences. Major variations occur as follows: service and age requirements for retirement; plans for receiving retirement payments; disability and death payments; and, payments upon withdrawal from teaching or moving out of state. The prospective teacher should study the provisions of the plan operating in his state. It is well to recognize the fact that teacher retirement allowances represent a form of insurance and, as in the case of all other forms of insurance, should be given careful consideration.

It might be well to point out another factor. If the present trend continues, and there is every indication it will, the undergraduate who plans to teach may anticipate considerably more advancement in retirement benefits to take place long before he will reach retirement age. A life of professional service in physical education will provide very satisfactory retirement security at the proper time; a bulwark against worry and privation when earning days are over.

You have now been provided considerable information to enable you to firmly determine your future career. A life devoted to educational leadership can now and in the future provide a modest but secure economic status. It can provide thrilling experiences in working with youth; in helping to shape the future destiny of the nation.

Selected References

Bucher, Charles A., *Foundations of Physical Education,* St. Louis: C. V. Mosby Company, 1960, Chapters 3 and 23.

Davis, Elwood C. and Earl L. Wallis, *Toward Better Teaching in Physical Education,* Englewood Cliffs, N. J.: Prentice-Hall, Inc., 1961, Chapter 18.

Duncan, Margaret M. and Ralph H. Johnson, *Introduction to Physical Education, Health Education, and Recreation,* Englewood Cliffs, N. J.: Prentice-Hall, Inc., 1954, Chapter 10.

Jenny, John H., *Physical Education, Health Education, and Recreation,* New York: The Macmillan Company, 1961, Chapter 9.

Knapp, Clyde and Ann E. Jewett, *Physical Education: Student and Beginning Teaching,* New York: McGraw-Hill Book Company, Inc., 1957, Chapter 1 and Part III.

Van Dalen, Deobold B. and Marcella M. Van Dalen, *The Health, Physical Education and Recreation Teacher,* Englewood Cliffs, N. J.: Prentice-Hall, Inc., 1956, Chapters 3 and 4.

Part II

THE ROLE
OF PHYSICAL EDUCATION
IN EDUCATION

Ted Abel and Allegheny High School, Pittsburgh, Pa.

Physical Education in Secondary Schools

I keep six honest serving men;
They taught me all I know.
Their names are What and
    Where and When
And How and Why and Who.
Rudyard Kipling

6

The material presented in Part I should help you to see the nature of the profession. The purpose of Part II is to clarify the role physical education plays in the total school program.

The best preparation to become a competent professional leader is to gain a clear understanding of the contributions physical education may make to participants. The undergraduate needs to begin to develop a set of sound principles to guide future actions as a teacher. Obviously, the degree of success the new teacher enjoys upon entering the field depends upon many factors. None is more significant than the viewpoint he holds toward his responsibilities. If he has established a sound, workable *blue print* which serves to guide professional endeavors he will qualify as one who is capable of maintaining and upgrading the quality of the program. The fundamental task is to acquire a solid concept of the purposes which can be served by the program. What one believes regarding physical education has a great deal to do with what one does as a professional worker.

It is hoped that the material in these chapters will help the student develop a deep pride in physical education as a career and that it will lead to the kind of thinking which will enable him to develop a sound philosophy of physical education.

PURPOSES OF SECONDARY EDUCATION

To understand the role physical education plays in the secondary school one must first be aware of the purposes of secondary education. In the professional education requirements for students preparing for a career in physical education the sequence of course offerings provide an opportunity to become familiar with the diversified aims and objectives of the school. It seems unnecessary here to go into detail concerning educational philosophy. It is appropriate, however, from the very outset that the major be given an opportunity to comprehend the scope of the task facing the secondary school. Armed with a general concept of the functions of the school the student may grasp more readily the highly significant role physical education may play in the curriculum. This kind of awareness serves as a valuable integrating vehicle as the professional student moves through the undergraduate years.

Secondary Education in a Changing World

In recent years the school has been forced to take on additional important responsibilities. Fundamental changes in the structure of home, family, and society dictate new demands on the school.

In the early days of American colonial life the family was the primary unit in the social order. The strong family structure of European nationalities transplanted in sparsely populated frontier areas served to weld the family into the central factor in our culture.

This was the America of the first 300 years; an America with vast frontiers, great natural resources, and unlimited opportunities for work. Those who sought work found it in abundance. This agrarian life is now declining. The United States is industrial, and work is specialized. The rapid increase in the population doomed rugged individualism. Interdependence is the rule in all areas of life.

No thinking person can doubt that we are living in a decisive moment in human history. The atom bomb ushered in a new era. The vivid publicity given to the constantly growing number of awesome implements for waging global warfare and the incredible victories achieved in mastering outer space has far reaching effects upon people. It is little wonder that young people feel the impact of the uncertainty about the future welfare of themselves and of the world of which they are a part.

Within an almost unbelievably short period of time the task of the school has become acutely more difficult. Automation has drastically changed the situation facing the school. The race for supremacy between the United States and the Soviet Union has created fear in the minds of the American public that Russia might be forging to the front in the battle to control space and to create the power to destroy the world. This fear raised the question as to what caused this possible shifting of world power. Inevitably the school became suspect. Critics of American education sprang up everywhere. Nothing in the curriculum escaped the scathing attacks on present practices in secondary education.

Recommendations by study groups and authorities such as James B. Conant[1] are having an impact upon schools. In the drive to discover the superior student and direct him into a study of the scientific fields the so-called essential subjects of mathematics, science, English, and language began to receive more attention.

To make the task of the school even more difficult experts[2] for some time have attempted to point out that there is urgent need to place more emphasis on cultural, citizenship, and avocational edu-

1 James B. Conant, *The American High School Today* (New York: McGraw-Hill Company, Inc., 1959), pp. 140.

2 *T. C. Topics*, Vol. 6, No. 1 (Columbia Teachers College, Fall 1957).

cation. They predict that education "for earning a living" will be increasingly supplemented by the slower and more difficult education "for service to mankind."

Automation will develop rapidly and continuously; it will speed up the newer social trends and start others, and contribute to the conditions which will drastically change man's habits and the ways he spends his time. Society has arrived at that point where it must reaffirm its beliefs in human values. Education, although painfully slow, is the most effective implement in meeting new social and individual needs. In this setting the school's responsibility to the people as an instrument of social transition is greatly increased.

A major premise of this text is that, as education faces its task today, physical education has a much more important role to play than ever before. As education takes on new directions in an effort to meet it's challenges so must physical education change its emphasis and seek new and better ways to achieve its potential value in the school. Physical educators must re-evaluate their program efforts in terms of today's needs. They have a great potential contribution to make to an education struggling to prepare youth for life in this age of automation. The manner in which physical education meets the challenge depends upon present leadership in the field and upon those who graduate from teacher education institutions in the next few years.

Physical Education: An Important Part of Education

Physical education is a misinterpreted field, misunderstood by many people. Among administrators, faculty, and people in the community are those who think of physical education as athletics, exercise and perspiration, or as play, and a waste of time. One of the crucial problems facing the profession today is to let the public know what physical education can contribute to the fundamental purposes of education.

The problem of communications begins within the ranks of those involved in the program. Physical education is broken into fragments; and, in many instances there is little real relationship existing between the parts. This has lead to intramural discord and disunity. It is difficult for the student or the public to understand the real function of school physical education as they participate in and observe programs in action. Let us here attempt to arrive at proper perspective in considering physical education as it plays its part in the school.

Everything that is derived from the motor world is physical education. The function of school physical education is to organize this world of movement so that all youth may gain experiences that enable them to move on into adult life with habits which will cause them to seek participation regularly in physical activity. Without physical activity there is atrophy and decay. This is the fundamental concern of all those involved in the total program.

The *urge to act* is universal. The phylogenetic origin of activity goes back to the beginning of time. If antiquity is a measure of respectability then physical education is as old as the hills. Man has always had the urge to move as well as the need to move. He has always learned through movement.

In attempting to understand the role of physical education the reader may wonder why it has been given a minor part to play in the curriculum in many states. To understand this apparent paradox one must consider the traditional function of education. Herein lies the crux of the reasons why physical education is given elective status in some states and assigned as a requirement for varying degrees of time in others.

For more than five hundred years education has exalted the intellect. The German Universities in the 1600's set the tune. The early Universities in the Eastern States in this country, Harvard, William and Mary, Princeton, and Columbia followed the European pattern. During the nineteenth century a flood of universities sprang up in the United States, all sharing a single purpose; the cultivation of the intellect. Even today, institutions of higher learning, in the face of all the evidence to the contrary, still persist in believing that the serious business in higher education centers on things intellectual.

The cliché, "a sound mind in a sound body" is still believed. Such a belief indicates a dichotomy between mind and body. Those who believe this, usually believe that physical education is outside the hallowed circle of academic subjects.

Since the mid 1950's a growing fear of Russia and China's military strength has triggered a series of events which has led to a renaissance of intellectualism in our schools. College faculty, teachers, and others who have felt that physical education did not merit basic consideration have gained support. Some institutions, reacting to the general feeling that more time must be devoted to the so-called academic subjects, have eliminated their all-college requirement in physical education. As might be expected this action lead to repercussions at the secondary school level.

In this atmosphere of critical appraisal of all areas of the curriculum, the so-called non-academic subjects were hard pressed to maintain status. However, just when the picture appeared darkest, support for physical education materialized. Oddly enough, as critics of the program appeared, new friends also were gained. Both groups were created out of the conditions associated with the precariousness of the international scene. National concern for the fitness of youth acted as a strong force to create balance and help to prevent serious inroads into the amount of time devoted to the program.

The national fitness movement initiated by President Eisenhower in 1955 and carried forth with renewed vigor by President Kennedy has helped to appraise the nation of the necessity to work to develop fitness. This movement gained momentum under the leadership of the AAHPER's project, "Operation Fitness—USA." Under the able direction of the project team the fitness aim—activity for all—has been carried to every corner of this great nation.

This movement will be discussed in the next chapter. The point that should be raised here is that leadership in the field must be aware of the total situation which faces the profession as it seeks to develop programs in step with the times and which are acceptable to those who follow the academic tradition.

In appraising the present situation it is the conclusion of some thoughtful leaders that physical education is caught in a giant pincer movement. On the one hand are the intellectuals who would like to eliminate the program from the curriculum. On the other hand are those people in physical education who are misunderstanding the basic purpose of the national fitness movement. Some departments of physical education have focused attention in their programs on physical fitness per se. Such activities as calisthenics, weight training, gymnastics, and fitness units dominate these programs. Even the term physical fitness rather than total fitness is used carelessly. The intellectuals then charge that physical education is only concerned with the physical. This is not the sole concept of leaders who are striving to bring more activity into the lives of everyone, but they conceive fitness in a more substantial sense. Wrong emphases tend to stultify the program. The shortcoming of many current fitness programs lies in the fact that strength—organic fitness—is quickly lost after activity is terminated.

The program will continue to fail to receive major attention in education until emphasis is placed on the intellectual and emotional as well as the physical aspects of physical education. Emphasis on muscle alone is not the product of our art. Some would call physical education a craft instead of an educational profession. The problem is to develop a program of education through the use of movement.

Professional groups within the field must unite and agree that their fundamental purpose is education. Any activity has intellectual content when it is directed to the whole man. The first criteria which will lead physical education out of the gigantic squeeze it is in is to focus attention on the totality of the personality.

Great strides toward this concept have been made in recent years. Never has there been greater need for young men and women to enter the field who are well informed and who possess a broad perspective as to the relationship of everything they do in the diversified program of physical education to education. They must be able to recognize program weaknesses and have the ability to eliminate them.

As young people enter the profession in the 1960's they should be aware of the fact that physical education presents three faces to the faculty and the public. The split between physical education and athletics and between boys' and girls' programs clouds the issues and undermines the program. Stability of viewpoint is of the essence. It is essential that the profession demonstrates, for all to observe, that it is a clear, understandable part of the educational scheme.

In considering the diversity that is necessarily a part of the program it is obviously true that commonality of viewpoint on all matters is difficult to obtain. It is possible, however, for all involved in the several aspects of the program to stress common purposes which are acceptable to everyone. Unity of purpose must be found if program weaknesses are to be eliminated. The following five purposes have potent meaning for all and may serve as an integrating force as the profession moves ahead toward solidarity.

1. Physical education contributes to the whole man. It is preposterous to believe that the only result of the tennis match, the badminton game, the basketball game is physical. Man does not exist as a creature of segments. Men of science, medicine, and psychology are well aware of this fact. Actually, college academicians have at times tended to ignore this fact. And, therein lies the difficulty. Physical education must persuade and prove to the academician that its program is educationally significant. Physical educators must join forces with those in the educational ranks who are struggling to destroy the obsolete notion that the human being can be carved up into parts. This means that programs must be developed which demonstrate for all to see that the central consideration is the individual as he lives in his environment. Physical education does just this when it constantly keeps the individual in view as it seeks to teach habits which lead to a persistent desire to be active. Staff efforts center on helping youth to obtain satisfactions through participation. Only when the individual enjoys participation will there be permanency. And, this is a necessary condition which must be met before the program can make a lasting contribution to the lives of people.

2. It is the task of school physical education to prepare youth to be participants in things the American public does during leisure. Physical education has a great deal to do with life in the United States today. Standards of living were never higher. Money for luxuries is available in larger amounts to a larger proportion of the population than ever before. We are living in an era of expanding leisure. Literally millions of people spend time, money, and energy in such activities as boating, fishing, basketball, baseball, golf, skiing, hunting, archery, and bowling. Millions more are spectators of a growing number of sport activities. An entire new audience and an ever increasing number of participants are being created by the television industry as it expands its coverage of sporting events.

The amount of participation is encouraging and on the in-

Julian W. Smith, AAHPER Outdoor Education Project

Instruction in casting and angling provides lifetime utility and pleasure.

crease. Nevertheless, the present generation of adults obviously has received little help from the years spent in school physical education. They simply are not active enough as adults. Somewhere along the line adults erroneously develop the idea that play is for youth and that they must put thought of play out of their mind. Today's physical education must teach youth to live well, be sensible, to play games, and to be active. It must teach the *Why* for physical activity. Youth must be led to see the essentiality of activity in school years and throughout life.

What is the answer? There is no universal prescription. Physical educators must be architects and engineers to design a program that includes a wide selection of activities—the smorgasbord approach. In selecting activities for the program the contemporary sports and recreational world must be taken into account. A study of what people do during their leisure opens up a whole new array of wholesome physical activities.

3. We are living in an age of automation within which man searches and finds ways to save labor. As we look ahead to future technological advances it becomes obvious that increased sedentarianism will be the lot of greater numbers of people. Man must have activity or decay. Physical education is the only area within the school that teaches youth to be active. Diet and proper health

habits are not sufficient. No longer does the person who disdains physical exercise have a case. There are ample scientific facts to explode the snobbishness of the pseudo-intellect.

Everyone involved in physical education has the vital task of teaching people skills in activity. There is now an urgency in the matter of preparing people to deliberately seek activity which will continue to sharpen as automation continues. The facts to substantiate this conclusion are everywhere. Within a very short time these facts will be better understood by everyone; and, physical education will be given the stature it merits in the curriculum.

4. Physical education can make a major contribution in the struggle to curb juvenile delinquency. Reports from many sources indicate that juvenile delinquency is out of bounds. Crime statistics are appalling. They reveal that youth commits most crimes. Physical education does not have the whole answer in combating delinquency; however, authorities recognize the great potential contained within it for helping to meet the problem if youth is given ample opportunity for expression.

The juvenile delinquent needs diverting types of activities. It is the responsibility of physical education to provide *all* youngsters with skills in activities which divert them from fruitless endeavor. It is tragic that there are not enough places for these youngsters to participate in wholesome activities. It is even more tragic to observe excellent facilities unused so frequently. Physical educators should work with school and community recreation groups and other agencies to encourage communities to build facilities and provide physical recreation programs. Planned youth and adult programs should be carried out in the late afternoon and evening periods in every gymnasium and playfield in the country.

Psychologists are discovering that delinquents hold themselves in low esteem. The very nature of physical education marks it as an ideal setting wherein the delinquent may gain the experiences which lead to the development of a positive attitude toward life. This attitude is usually missing from his make-up. Achievement of program objectives provides the participant with skills and satisfactions—prerequisites to the development of self-esteem.

5. Physical education must seek equality of opportunity. Sports participation is a great common denominator. The fact that physical education has given those with limited ability a

chance to participate, as well as the star, is probably one of its greatest glories; and, at the same time, one of its greatest challenges.

Many people feel that democracy will automatically survive. It will not without great effort. This fact is brought home to anyone who has the opportunity to observe the growth of new suburbs. Fields, orchards, and wooded areas disappear. The occasional tree is all that is left to remind us of early landmarks. Democracy, like orchards or fields, must be cultivated in order to survive. It is the responsibility of the school to work to perpetuate and extend our culture. No one in the school gets closer to the people, their hopes, aspirations, feelings, and problems than those involved in physical education. The opportunities to teach democracy is nowhere brighter.

Outcomes Depend Upon Leadership

The values that students receive from their experiences in physical education depend upon the calibre of leadership given to the program. This is far more important than costly facilities. The right kind of leaders are necessary if physical education is to assume its important role in education. In observing superior teachers at work one may detect many differences in mannerisms and in personalities. Among the array of abilities and qualities which mark one as an outstanding teacher of physical education today the following professional viewpoints seem to be shared by all master teachers.

1. The good teacher works diligently to help physical education measure up to the needs of the day. He believes in the values that can flow from participation in physical education. Perhaps the most distinguishing characteristic competent leaders share is a great pride in physical education—a pride which stems from a sincere belief in the importance of the program. Pride in one's profession engenders the kind of enthusiasm which helps carry one over the disappointments and setbacks associated with the work in any program of physical education.

2. The successful leader has perspective. He knows where he

is in relation to where he ought to be. Furthermore, he possesses ingenuity and foresight. The "man with an idea" is a potent force. The basic concept of greatness in teaching is the willingness to push ahead a little further. It has been said that it does not matter what or how one teaches as long as the essential values are there as the central consideration of what is done.

3. The good leader is convinced that he must relate program efforts to that of other areas within the school. As previously pointed out some administrators, teachers, and laymen still believe that there is a line between the physical and the intellectual. There still remains a deepseated conviction that brain and brawn do not mix. The skillful teacher does his part in destroying this misconception. He does this by demonstrating that he is an integral part of the faculty.

4. The qualified leader keeps the individual in view as he functions within the group. He does this as he works in the several areas within the program. Good instruction enables students to learn the skills of activities presented to them. In addition, the learning atmosphere is structured so that students emerge from their physical education experiences with added assets.

The prepared teacher has a thorough understanding of human nature. He recognizes that the deepest urge in human nature is the desire to be recognized. It is a gnawing and unfaltering human hunger. It leads people to want to own the latest model cars, wear the latest styles of clothes, and talk about their accomplishments. Since people hunger for a feeling of importance, imagine what miracles the physical educator can achieve by giving them skills in activities admired by others; and, at the same time, provide the emotional balance which leads them to develop honest appreciations.

A Problem Facing the New Major

The professional student of physical education may have difficulty in absorbing all that he is exposed to in his undergraduate program. His outlook is conditioned by the kind of programs he was exposed to in earlier years. If those programs were poor much of what is discussed in this book and in other courses is theoretical. If this is true in your case you may anticipate that it will take considerable time and much thought before you will be able to fully appreciate the potential contribution physical education may make to the education of youth.

Strive to be open-minded as you study and take part in class discussions. Avoid the error of paying homage to false gods. Stand ready to change your views as new information is presented. Avoid the pitfalls of holding on to pet ideas, biases, and prejudices. You are preparing to enter a profession with unlimited possibilities for doing good. Your task is clear; you must arrive at your own philosophy of physical education. If it is sound and shapes the direction of your professional efforts you will reap the rewards of deep personal and professional satisfactions throughout your career.

Selected References

Bucher, Charles A., *Foundations of Physical Education,* St. Louis: C. V. Mosby Company, 1960, Chapters 2 and 8.

Cowell, Charles C. and Helen W. Hazelton, *Curriculum Designs in Physical Education,* Englewood Cliffs, N. J.: Prentice-Hall, Inc., 1955, Chapter 1.

Cowell, Charles C. and Hilda M. Schwehn, *Modern Principles and Methods in Highschool Physical Education,* Boston: Allyn and Bacon, Inc., 1958, Chapter 1.

Davis, Elwood C. and Earl L. Wallis, *Toward Better Teaching in Physical Education,* Englewood Cliffs, N. J.: Prentice-Hall, Inc., 1961, Chapter 7.

Esslinger, Arthur A., "The Challenge We Face," *CAHPER* (May/June, 1961), pp. 7-11.

Jenny, John H., *Physical Education, Health Education, and Recreation,* New York: The Macmillan Company, 1961, Chapter 1.

Johnson, Granville B., *et al., Your Career in Physical Education,* New York: Harper & Brothers, 1957, Chapters 2 and 3.

Kozman, Hilda C., *et al., Methods in Physical Education,* Philadelphia: W. B. Saunders Company, 1958, Chapters 5, 6, and 7.

Nixon, John E. and Florence S. Frederickson, *An Introduction to*

Physical Education, Philadelphia: W. B. Saunders Company, 1959, Chapters 4, 5, 9, and 15.

Oberteuffer, Delbert, *Physical Education,* New York: Harper & Brothers, 1956, Chapters 1 and 2.

————, "Some Answers to the Challenge," *JOHPER* (September, 1958), pp. 38-41.

Shepard, Natalie M., *Foundations and Principles of Physical Education,* New York: The Ronald Press Company, 1960, Chapters 1, 2, 3, 4, and 15.

Smith, Hope M. and Marguerite A. Clifton, *Physical Education: Exploring Your Future,* Englewood Cliffs, N. J.: Prentice-Hall, Inc., 1962, Chapter 1.

Van Dalen, Deobold B. and Marcella M. Van Dalen, *The Health, Physical Education and Recreation Teacher,* Englewood Cliffs, N. J.: Prentice-Hall, Inc., 1956, Chapter 12.

Vannier, Maryhelen and Hollis F. Fait, *Teaching Physical Education in Secondary Schools,* Philadelphia: W. B. Saunders Company, 1957, Chapter 1.

Williams, Jesse Feiring, *The Principles of Physical Education,* Philadelphia: W. B. Saunders Company, 1959, Chapters 2, 3, 4, and 5.

The Principia, *Elsah, Illinois*

The Contribution of Physical Education

We look to our schools and colleges as the decisive force in a renewed national effort to strengthen the physical fitness of our youth.

President John F. Kennedy

7 Immediate Values

The immediate, easy to see values that result from engaging in physical activities are skill and enjoyment. The success of physical education rests upon the attainment of these outcomes. Competent teachers are well aware of this significant fact. They know that most individuals will stop trying to learn if they fail to achieve some measure of success. Instead of seeking opportunities to participate these individuals will avoid activity. Thus the important biological, psychological, and social values which can be attained through physical education are lost. It follows, then, that the foremost consideration of the teacher is to teach so well that participants gain a measure of skill in the variety of activities which comprise the program.

It is not difficult to understand why physical educators recognize that the attainment of skill is the primary function of the program. Is it not true that increased desire to participate in activity is associated with acquiring skill? The novice begins to enjoy a new activity when he sees that he is making progress. It is fun to play tennis when one can keep the ball in play. It is frustrating to swing ineffectively. People like to do things they can do well. Even an elementary understanding of human nature discloses the validity of the formula: skill leads to interest, and interest leads to participation.

All of the important values that can evolve from participation in physical activities are dependent upon sustained participation. And, participation beyond program requirements depends upon whether the individual has acquired a taste for participation which is normally associated with at least a measure of skill.

As one studies physical education it becomes clear that the achievement of skill beyond the level of the novice is the major task of the instructional phase of the program. This is where all students are involved. So it can be considered that the class period is the heart of the total physical education program.

Although teaching skill in activities is of prime consideration it is not the sole job of instruction. Development of skill does not automatically bring forth the other important values which can be gained through participation. Achievement of skill simply makes it possible to obtain other values. The point to keep in mind is that as the teacher plans his daily lessons he deliberately plans for the attainment of other values along with skill objectives.

Remote Values

Physical education, properly conceived, can serve as a rich laboratory of experiences in which the student is led to develop the characteristics essential for successful living in our times. Beyond the immediate outcomes of skill and enjoyment lie the deeper values obtainable through physical education. Professional physical educators plan their programs so that these values are actively sought. They know that skill and pleasure must come first if there is to be any real progress in reaching the deeper goals.

Physical Fitness

Things are happening in our culture that make it essential for man to seek physical fitness. It does not come as a by-product of one's daily life as it did years ago. Man today needs movement to survive in a different sense. This is an age of ease. Man's work is divorced from strenuous muscle effort. According to many economists the man who works with his hands will be almost extinct by the 1970's.

This way of life is taking its toll, because man is still a biological being who needs to be physically active in order to function effectively. There is no substitute for exercise. It is just as important today as when primitive man roamed the plains of Syria.

Ample scientific facts are known, and more are being discovered daily, to substantiate the statement, "inactivity is not conducive to survival." The American Medical Association is impressed enough with recent research findings regarding the essentiality of exercise to live effectively for its delegates at its national convention in 1960 at Miami Beach, Florida, to resolve that it do everything it can to foster health and physical education programs in schools and colleges.

Authorities in medicine, psychiatry, nutrition, and sociology for some time have been telling the American public that it must seek activity in order to live. For instance, Paul Dudley White,[1] the eminent cardiologist states:

> Evidence of the most important cardiovascular disease-coronary and cerebral atherosclerosis-often appears in middle age, but the actual disease starts earlier. It is undoubtedly due to a slow accumulation of the atherosclerosis and other factors that begin probably in the twenties. . . . We do not have all the information we need about preventive measures, but we are quite sure we do have some clues. One of these is the maintenance of physical fitness, including the avoidance of obesity and the establishment of regular habits of vigorous exercise, especially in the case of men.

[1] Paul Dudley White, "Health and Sickness in Middle Age," *JOHPER*, October, 1960, pp. 21-22.

Let us examine how physical education should go about the task of seeking the biological end point. We know what we are after—physically fit people. The question before us is what are we after in fitness? Is it fitness for today? Is it fitness for next week, or is it fitness for life? That is the question which bears directly on what we should do in our physical education programs. Our mission in life is to teach youth habits requiring action. This cannot be accomplished through programs that feature a few team sports and a minimum of instruction. It cannot be done through calisthenics, gymnastics or physical fitness tests alone.

A program of vigorous activity in calisthenics, rope climbing, and weight training one to two hours each day for six weeks will build a higher degree of physical fitness. But what occurs when this training is terminated? Fitness is a fleeting attribute, it comes with consistent effort, and disappears quickly and easily with lack of movement. We want to build a concept of fitness throughout life. Great emphasis on certain components of physical fitness will bring a degree of fitness closely attuned to those activities. The great challenge to the trained professional physical educator is to provide a structured program for every youth that does not minimize physical outcomes which indeed are our unique contributions to education, but is skillfully deployed to yield a series of desirable outcomes which have lasting impact on youth who later will continue as adults. Perhaps we can best achieve physical fitness which lasts by viewing biological efficiency as one of the important by-products of satisfying activity, and not as an end in itself.

This point of view compels a return to basic concepts. It does not mean that one must concentrate on the very vigorous activities in order to obtain maximum physical fitness. It also does not mean that one must build a curriculum which includes only a few sports and games, heavily sprinkled with doses of skills instruction and little movement in the process. It would be hardly worth the effort and expense if all attention was directed toward golf, tennis, volley ball, basketball, football, and softball if the environment for most graduates will be devoid of golf and tennis facilities, and the other activities are ill-suited for later adult living.

The physical educator with vision will provide a well balanced mixture of individual and team sports instruction and play, with proper time allotment for the very vigorous activities that have real fitness value such as gymnastics, weight training, wrestling, swimming, strenuous running, and jumping activities, all blended to produce high levels of lasting fitness attainment because in the process the very diversity of instruction strikes chords of student interest which will have lifetime utility. He or she will make wise use of physical fitness performance evaluation to identify individual needs, motivate student interest and performance, and will continue testing periodically to chart progress and set goals.

The solution for lifelong physical fitness does not lie in band

Gymnastics as part of a broad and diversified physical education program yields rich dividends to participants.

Northwestern State College, Natchitoches, Louisiana.

wagon crusades for daily calisthenics conducted by anyone who loves to command, intensified because of use of simple but invalid screening tests that determine very little. The solution rather is to be found in the development of the broad and comprehensive program that fashions all elements together into a pleasing and effective combination. Such a program will have achievement grouping, progression in orderly fashion from year to year, marking and evaluation based upon sound use of valid instruments, and skilled instruction that motivates and stimulates each student to a lasting appreciation of values derived.

Progress will come with each intermittent surge of popular but sometimes artificially induced fitness paranoia. The degree and quality of that progress will depend upon how wisely professional leaders and teachers interpret and utilize the current emphasis.

Respect for Others

Experts in the area of human relations have been saying for a long time that no single trait or outlook is more valuable in achieving success in anything than for the individual to honestly feel that everyone he meets is just as capable as he is. The informal, pleasing atmosphere in which physical education activities are carried on with the heavy demands for cooperative action on the part of participants suggests the significant role that the program may play in helping students acquire respect for others. It is important to remember that respect for all people, a real interest in the "little guy" is the key to successful living. Good teachers keep this thought in mind as they go about their varied tasks of instruction.

The physical educator simply cannot afford to lose sight of the student as an individual. Everyone is tremendously important. Program and lesson planning reflect this awareness when efforts are directed toward creating good morale. This kind of planning is recognized when teachers encourage the spirit of fair play, stimulate the development of class and team loyalties, and work to inculcate a sincere regard for others. Under these conditions physical education contributes to the development of the attitudes which lead the student to enlarge his outlook to that point where he can accept views which differ from his own.

The interpersonal give and take on the athletic field, in a class activity, or in learning a fundamental skill leads to acceptance of differences among individuals as a good thing. Teamwork, the essence of good play, develops the group outlook. The close contacts with individuals of all kinds in satisfying activity helps to banish prejudices and discriminations. When the student dynamically interacts with others in a game situation he learns to develop self-discipline, responsibility, and a decent regard for others. Good leadership is aware that these qualities do not come automatically through participation; rather, that they must be consciously implanted.

Perhaps nowhere in the total school curriculum is there more clear-cut evidence that the individual is the great common denominator than in the gymnasium or on the athletic field. The coach has a great opportunity to influence the thinking and behavior of his players. What coach is not aware of the importance of team play, that oneness of purpose that operates in a well-knit team? What coach is not aware of the damage cliques have on his team, or of the harm petty jealousies cause? The all-out effort associated with competitive athletics wherein players, regardless of race, creed, or social standing, are welded together into a cooperative unit is a great source for creating genuine respect for others.

Sportsmanship

Critical examination of well-balanced personalities immediately focuses attention upon sportsmanship as one of the most important qualities an individual can possess if he is to live successfully.

Physical education has a great opportunity to have an impact on morale and ethical judgments of people. Opportunities to teach sportsmanship are available every hour. They occur simply in the normal course of playing the game and in teaching fundamentals. But, they do not occur often enough. The teacher must deliberately set the stage by creating opportunities to teach sportsmanship just as he does in teaching the basic skills involved in the activity.

People in the United States have gone a long way toward making sportsmanship a common pattern of behavior. It is this factor, probably more than any other, that has led American society to a measure of freedom found lacking in many cultures. Certainly the absence of this virtue would make democracy impossible and freedom uncertain.

Secondary education has not placed enough emphasis on this quality, although the real success of modern education in developing citizens for self-government has been training in living by the rules of the game. The American people have demonstrated a considerable measure of honest willingness to be regulated by mutually acknowledged rules, thereby nurturing a democratic form of government.

Well-adjusted, happy individuals have found that it pays to live by the golden rule. They have discovered that there is no merit in cheating, lying, or being dishonest. It is intelligent to treat people fairly and to be loyal to friends. In other words, people who live effectively have learned that it is best to treat others as they would like to be treated.

Although many educators do not clearly recognize the relationship between sportsmanship taught on the playing field and desirable civic behavior, they have the same basic virtue. Sportsmanship of youth must carry on into adulthood, or other traits, such as selfishness, will most certainly be continued into mature life.

Sportsmanship traits—fair play, cooperation, loyalty, honesty, and graciousness—must be deliberately taught and deliberately learned. They are not learned as concomitants of team play, they must be as definitely planned for as are the skills inherent in playing the game. Learning to be a good sport begins when the very young child begins to adjust to his peers. Learning to cooperate with others is no sudden development. It is the result of a long history of experiences, especially those gained during the "gang" years, ages eight to fourteen.

Physical education can, providing attention is focused directly upon the development of the code of ethics consonant with the democratic spirit, offer the student the kinds of experiences necessary to develop habits of sportsmanship which will contribute to his own well-being, as well as his worth as a social group member living in a democratic society.

Democratic Behavior

Physical education has an unparalleled opportunity to teach the true meaning of democracy; one of the fundamental purposes of education. Democracy is misunderstood by many people. There are those who feel cheated when others get ahead of them. They have forgotten that in the days of our first Americans equal rights meant equality of opportunity. There is not one single word in our Constitution or our Bill of Rights which implies that everyone should share equally. When individuals feel that they are entitled to proceed at the same rate of speed as all others they are confused as to the meaning of democracy. In our country we do not want to educate people to want to destroy. Rather, we want to develop people who have the desire to move ahead on their own initiative.

Young people need to be taught that Americanism stands for the open road, with no unfair obstacles placed in the path of any particular individual or group. The teacher offers concrete evidence that he uses democratic precepts to guide him when he seeks to educate youth to admire excellence. It is this attitude, more than any other, that is apt to encourage youth to move ahead vigorously, using the successes of others as their guide.

Physical education provides a dynamic setting in which to educate boys and girls in democratic human relationships. The full program, properly organized and conducted, offers participants rich experiences in the use of the democratic group process. Careful study of the manner in which good programs are carried out readily discloses democracy at work in all aspects of its endeavors. The distinguishing characteristic of the good program is that individual abilities form the basis for program organization. This form of organization suggests that the merit system permeates all activity.

A glance at the interscholastic athletic portion of the program reveals a splendid example of the merit system at work. In the first place the most highly skilled boys and girls are on the athletic teams. The best of these gifted youngsters are on the first team. No favoritism operates here. This is democracy at its best. Secondly, the attention placed upon school athletics by the physical education staff and the enthusiasm engendered in the student body and the community encourages youth to admire the skilled performer. These two factors are potent indications that athletics contribute to the development of democratic behavior.

Democracy is also a central consideration of well-organized classes. Here again the level of skill in an activity has a great deal

Basketball is one of the most universal team sports throughout the nation.

Charles Renfro and Public Schools of Albuquerque, New Mexico

to do with the manner in which the instructor divides the class into smaller groups. The chief aim of instruction is to establish the conditions under which each participant may learn at his maximum rate. Authorities agree that in learning motor skills it is usually best to segregate individuals according to the level of skills they possess. As the program moves along from one activity to another, skillful instructors regroup students according to the level of skill they bring to each new activity. Therefore, one sees again that individual ability (the merit system) is at work. Throughout the required and elective phases of the program capable students should be given leadership responsibilities.

Educators are beginning to recognize more and more that young people cannot learn to live democratically unless they have opportunity in school to experience democratic behavior. Physical education creates these experiences. It calls upon everyone, asking only a contribution in common endeavor.

Emotional Maturity

Authorities agree that the school must be concerned with interpersonal relationships. There is no longer serious debate in educational circles as to the school's obligation to help young people grow to maturity as well adjusted personalities. Very few educators today are unaware that harmonious relations with many people is a decisive factor in determining the individual's ability to make satisfactory adjustments to life.

Education is vitally concerned with the total personality. The addition of counselors and adequate health services helps to shape the school climate in ways which enable students to achieve skill in the area of human relationships. This is one of the major needs which can be met by the secondary school.

In analyzing personality traits which seem to contribute to the individual's attractiveness as a social group member it becomes obvious that happiness hinges on the degree of emotional maturity possessed by the individual. Therefore, in order to determine the part that physical education may play in helping the student attain the degree of emotional maturity that is necessary for effective living, a brief analysis of emotional maturity is indicated.

Although the role of heredity and environment in personality development is still a moot point in the study of human behavior, there are no serious disagreements on some very general points. All would agree that the individual is the result of a fusion of hereditary and environmental factors. Few would deny that environment, unless it stresses inherited qualities, is much more important in shaping the specifics in one's life. Those who are sensitive to recent findings on this point contend that the individual at any given period in his development is the resultant of his life experiences and his reaction to them.

In recent years psychological research has centered upon the practical problems relating to reasons why individuals behave as they do and what can be done about it. Education owes psychology much for what it has learned about the dynamics of human behavior. Findings from its research laboratories are largely responsible for the increasing educational significance given to physical education and other areas long considered to be extra-curricular.

The following observations hold much meaning to the educator in terms of growth and development. On the basis of psychogenetic growth, adjustments are accumulative. The infant, completely dependent upon parents, constantly seeks more and more independence as he grows. Every individual must pass through what is sometimes called *growth hurdles* in order to reach emotional maturity. On the basis of emotional adjustments made at each age level, the individual will attempt to meet the cluster of problems at the next "growth hurdle" in the same manner; and, typical emotional outlets determine the personality and temperament of the individual.

As the individual grows many factors merge in determining how well he meets the problems associated with growing up. The emotional adjustments he makes at each age level is the key to the degree of integration he achieves as a personality.

The emotionally mature individual moves through life with a minimum of tension. He feels at ease in social situations and is well liked and respected by his acquaintances. He is independent; and, quite capable of adjusting readily to new conditions. He fully appreciates the attitudes and behavior of others. His behavior reflects his acceptance of the ways of the group, while retaining his own individuality. He makes intelligent decisions when faced with choices, hence, self-control tempers his actions in most situations. The emotionally mature individual does not waste time and energy in unsuccessful struggling with personal problems; therefore, satisfaction is his reward most of the time.

Physical education, as its best, has much to contribute to the development of emotionally mature young men and women. As previously discussed, modern science and technology has radically changed the life patterns of the majority of individuals in our society. These changes will be more pronounced as automation continues. Almost daily the number of people who need to utilize part of their growing leisure hours in vigorous physical activity increases. Unfortunately, many of them lack the degree of skill in activities necessary to lead them to indulge regularly in vigorous activity. Such individuals have not had satisfactory experiences during their early years, and are not equipped to meet the strains and the tensions of modern life. The principles of good mental hygiene disclose the importance of adequate energy outlets to meet the individual's inner needs. These are not new precepts. More than a decade ago Wolffe expressed the psychosomatic point of view of medical science in these words:

> The effects of trauma, infection, and degenerative processes upon the human system are well known; but the ill-effects of emotional conflicts as a result of poor group or interpersonal relations are not as yet well recognized. Abnormal behavior, moodiness, anxiety states, with their annoying train of symptoms, such as palpitations, pain around the heart, sighing respiration, and digestive disturbances, are but a few of the common manifestations. In later life, peptic and duodenal ulcers, certain forms of hypertensions and angina pectoris, even some types of coronary thrombosis may be added to the list. The increase in all these diseases seems to parallel the increase of abnormal tension resulting from conflict. It matters little what the underlying causes of tension may be, whether induced by social discriminations, by economic inequalities, by racial conflicts, or by conflicts in home or workshop. What matters is its ill effect on the human system. And to this we need only add that social conflicts are on the increase today.[1]

Since social conflicts are on the increase, with a corresponding increase in the diseases which follow in their wake, physical education has an opportunity second to none for rendering an extraordinary public service. Abnormal tensions with their devasting effects are not easily prevented, but they can be curtailed by giving youth wholesome experiences. Physical education geared to meet the physical and social needs of youth can help to produce a citizen with sound attitudes, equipped to live and to help others live.

Seen in this light one must recognize that physical education has a primary responsibility to help prepare youth to make intelligent use of leisure-time. The skills and habits gained through physical education may serve different purposes for individuals. Obviously, activity may have different meanings to the same individual at

[1] Joseph B. Wolffe, "New Horizons in Health, Physical Education, and Recreation," *Journal of Health and Physical Education*, Vol. 18, No. 10 (December, 1947), p. 699.

separate intervals. Its pleasurable possibilities depend upon the degree to which it satisfies a need of the moment. A handball game one day may serve to exercise stagnant muscles, another day it may be a means of escape from an unpleasantness, still another day it may satisfy one's need to build up one's ego by winning a game from an opponent. One may feel the piling up of tension due to long hours of study or work; a game of golf, a session of tennis, or a relaxing swim may prove to be a good outlet.

School physical education, through its breadth of activity offerings, attempts to meet the recreational needs of all students now and later. It is obligated to attune the student to recreational resources and to help him develop methods of utilizing them constructively.

The most significant indication that physical education is approaching maturity is the increasing attention focused on the recreational aspects of its offerings. The trend toward including more of the activities associated with leisure-time pursuits of people, more than anything else, is beginning to impress thoughtful educators with the important contributions physical education may make in the secondary school curriculum.

Physical education contributes to the development of emotional maturity in youth when it seeks to provide students with recreational habits that will not be forgotten as soon as the spur of requirement and the easy availability of facilities are no longer felt. The ultimate criterion of the success of any program of physical education is in terms of the results achieved. The real test of the worth of the program is time. Does the student continue to participate in vigorous activity in his adult years?

Although many physical educators tend to feel that the student must have a variety of experiences in activities, it is more important that he develop enough skill in a few activities to ensure the continued interest in them to motivate participation again and again. Scott[2] is of the opinion that it matters little what worthwhile activity the student enjoys, so long as it serves his need for activity.

Physical education does not necessarily aim to develop the skilled specialist. It does recognize that skill beyond the "dub" stage is

[2] Harry A. Scott, *Competitive Sports in Schools and Colleges* (New York: Harper & Brothers, 1951), p. 199.

essential if the individual is to experience and appreciate the fullest satisfactions in participating in motor activity. The ability to play well contributes to status with one's peers. It feels good to do well; even better when it brings forth approval from others. Under these circumstances the individual is likely to develop a positive, confident outlook on life.

The experienced teacher is well aware of the fact that people tend to avoid things they do poorly and move eagerly toward things they do well. A person who has never played tennis shies away from the tennis court; the novice makes vague excuses when pressed to join a group on the golf course; the girl who plays table tennis poorly finds she has studying to do when invited to play.

A close relationship exists between experience and skill in games and the enjoyment of them by the participant. Experienced teachers of physical education know that skill in sport activity brings pleasure to participation. They have seen how it adds anticipation and zest to the participant's day. These facts make physical education a fertile environment within which youth may be led toward maturity.

The physical education program must be judged successful when youth are led to acquire the habit of participating in pleasurable pursuits that have life-long utility. When it does this it has a lasting beneficial effect. Youth will move on into adult years with adequate energy to cope with the stresses and strains associated with life in these times.

Selected References

Brownell, Clifford Lee and E. Patricia Hagman, *Physical Education—Foundations and Principles,* New York: McGraw-Hill Book Company, 1951, Chapters 7 and 8.

Bucher, Charles A., *Foundations of Physical Education,* St. Louis: C. V. Mosby Company, 1960, Chapters 1 and 7.

Developing Democratic Human Relations, Washington: First Yearbook AAHPER, 1951, Chapters 1, 2, 3, and 4.

Hunsicker, Paul, "AAHPER Physical Fitness Test Battery," *JOHPER* (September, 1958), pp. 24-26.

Irwin, Leslie W., *The Curriculum in Health and Physical Education*, St. Louis: C. V. Mosby Company, 1951, Chapter 3.

Jenny, John H., *Physical Education, Health Education, and Recreation*, New York: The Macmillan Company, 1961, Chapters 7 and 18.

Johnson, Granville B., *et al.*, *Your Career in Physical Education*, New York: Harper & Brothers, 1957, Chapters 4, 5, and 6.

Means, Louis E., "Are We Over the Hill?" *Phi Delta Kappan*, June, 1961.

——, "Why All the Fuss About Fitness?" *The Instructor*, September, 1962.

Nixon, John E. and Florence S. Frederickson, *An Introduction to Physical Education*, Philadelphia: W. B. Saunders Company, 1959, Chapters 6 and 14.

Bauer, W. W., "Facets of Fitness," *JOHPER* (September, 1960), pp. 23-26.

Oberteuffer, Delbert, *Physical Education*, New York: Harper & Brothers, 1956, Chapters 2, 3, 5, and 6.

——, "A Decalogue of Principles," *JOHPER* (January, 1947), p. 4.

Shepard, Natalie M., *Foundations and Principles of Physical Education*, New York: The Ronald Press Company, 1960, Chapters 9 and 10.

"The President's Fitness Program," *JOHPER* (September, 1961), pp. 30-32.

White, Paul Dudley, "Health and Sickness in Middle Age," *JOHPER* (October, 1960), pp. 21-23.

Part III

THE ADMINISTRATION OF PHYSICAL EDUCATION

Photographic Laboratory, Information Services,
Michigan State University

Curriculum Building in Physical Education

> I am indebted to my father
> for living, but to my teacher
> for living well.
>
> *Alexander of Macedon*

8   PHYSICAL EDUCATION TODAY

Physical education is a dynamic field. It passed through a series of interesting decades in the United States as the struggle for agreement on an American concept continued. A great deal of progress has been made since the early years when proponents of European physical education introduced various systems of "gymnastics" into this country. These early programs featured rather rigid formality, and were better adapted to European culture than to the democracy and freedom characterizing life in this young nation. Many elements were included which stressed a *physical culture* program largely bereft of all but the physical outcome. Each type of emphasis of this early day left its impact, particularly upon communities having a heavy European population, but none seemed to possess all of the qualities necessary to guarantee permanence.

The history of the development of physical education in this country is a fascinating study of internal struggle for viewpoint

acceptance. The student should become familiar with the story of
its progress. An understanding of these early conflicts of philosophy and emphasis will enable the major student to better appreciate the controversies, the strange mixture of philosophies, and
the many divergencies found in present day programs.

The twentieth century program evolved to the point where one
could see the real values physical education brings to the growth
and development of all students as they live in today's world. Perhaps the most significant advance made in the last half century is
in terms of purposes sought. In early years attention was directed
to physical outcomes alone. Modern physical education does not
deny the physical contributions which are basic. Indeed this is a
unique contribution. But it does recognize the unity of man and is
concerned with the education of the whole man through the
media of movement. Today's physical education is not physical
culture so accentuated by sensational magazine features of "Mr.
America." It contains but little of the kind of activity found in
slenderizing salons; and it is not sports participation alone. It
helps to produce symmetrical and well-proportioned bodies,
strength, grace and endurance; and yet, it seeks to do far more
than achieve these important physiological objectives.

Modern physical education is concerned with shaping minds,
emotions, and behavior of individuals as well as their physical
bodies. It gives students tools of knowledge, skill and interest in
worthwhile leisure related pursuits. It has post school utility. It
teaches them how to live fully and to adjust in a democratic society. The distinguishing feature of the modern program is simply
that it considers the student as a whole, not as a bundle of muscles,
skills, and postures.

Perhaps there is no other area of education which has greater
variety, more diversified subject matter, more tools with which to
work, or more natural attraction for the learner than physical education. It may be natural to have difficulty in agreeing upon a
fixed pattern of American physical education. And, possibly, it is
very good that we cannot do this.

Present day programs represent a wide divergency at times from
one locality to another; even marked differences between programs within one locality are common. Each state can point with
pride to some programs in action that have attracted attention

and which serve to stimulate others to emulate or surpass them. Magnificent gymnasiums and spacious outdoor areas provide the setting for challenging programs. Sound planning and skillful instruction characterizes the best programs wherever they are found. Unfortunately, far too many school physical education programs are narrow in scope, unimaginative in design and administration, and are conducted with a minimum of real instruction. Too many secondary school programs for boys feature a few balls, three or four sports—and a "loose whistle." Few programs have achieved proper grouping, sound marking and reporting, proper use of evaluation and measurement, and planned progression from semester to semester through the school years. Herein lies a real challenge to you as a potential future leader.

A recent visitation study by one of your authors provided first hand knowledge that mediocrity characterized many secondary school programs today.[1] The study included ninety-two secondary schools in twenty-five states. Obviously, the study involved too few programs to constitute a valid appraisal of physical education in the several states visited; but findings were nevertheless significant.

According to reliable evaluating criteria,[2] only eight of the ninety-two programs visited could be rated as adequate in most important features. Each of the eight possessed excellent indoor and outdoor facilities; featured sound instruction directed toward commendable goals, followed recommended class size per instructor; provided sound administration and good organization; and, presented a varied program of activities for all students of the school. Furthermore, program planning indicated provision for sequence of courses so that any activity taught a second or third time was presented at more advanced levels. These programs also included excellent evaluation procedures to chart pupil progress.

Forty-five schools included in the study were inadequate in more than one phase of a full program of physical education. Context was meager in some; others lacked competent instruction; while others lacked organizational design. Not one school in this group could be said to have a full and balanced program.

1 Laurence A. Pape, "Catalyst for Improved Programs," *JOHPER* (September, 1960), p. 33.
2 California Project on Fitness, "Evaluative Criteria for Physical Education Programs," *California State Department of Education Bulletin,* January 10, 1959.

The remaining thirty-nine programs visited were substandard in almost every respect. Most of these stressed touch football in the fall, basketball in the winter, and track and possibly softball in the spring. What's more, with few additional activities, this meager fare was repeated each year. None of these schools scheduled students in classes according to their grade or achievement level; therefore progression in program content was virtually impossible. Student-instructor ratio in most of these cases was more than sixty to one. In many cases it would have been most difficult to locate the instructor who should have been teaching the class.

Dull, repetitive programs such as these are all too common. Physical education leaders, recognizing that the American public will not and should not continue to support a program in which it does not believe or understand, are sounding the alarm. They are aware that other subject area leaders are exerting pressure for more curriculum time. Attacks upon state and local requirements from time to time emphasize the need for better leadership. Better programs which prove the inseparable value of physical education in the life of every child must strive to maintain status in the face of diminishing confidence in programs which lack perspective. Much professional attention is given in publications and at workshops and conventions to the need for curriculum and instructional upgrading. Daniels,[3] in discussing the serious problems which confront the profession, states that our weakest link is the curriculum. He has found that far too many programs repeat the same uninteresting chapter of monotony from grades five through twelve.

There are a number of plausible explanations for the substandard physical education carried on in many schools. Inadequate facilities and space, large classes with no attempt at homogeneous grouping, overworked staffs, an unsympathetic administration, and many other factors of local nature contribute to the conditions which produce inferior programs. However, one factor, above all others, dominates as the real culprit in producing inadequate programs, that is, the attitude the teacher holds toward his physical education teaching assignments. In the study previously mentioned, interviews with teachers disclosed that many of them

3 Arthur S. Daniels, "Critical Issues in Physical Education," *JOHPER* (September, 1958), pp. 26-27, 66.

felt their athletic coaching assignments and work in their special interest areas were the most important aspects of their job, while instruction in physical education classes was secondary. As one instructor phrased it, "we are an athletic school; gym classes are not considered very important." Another expressed it this way, "we believe that we're doing our job if we see that the kids in physical education classes have a little fun and get some exercise." Interviews with administrators indicated that many shared that view. Interestingly enough, wherever administrators insisted on good instruction in physical education classes, programs were found to be reasonably sound.

Obviously then, regardless of the cause, the negative attitude on the part of some teachers toward total program responsibilities is at the very core of the obstacles preventing the development of worthwhile programs. Unless this viewpoint changes, we will continue to have many narrow and uninteresting programs which stultify the profession. There is no defense for these programs.

These imperfections are no cause for cynicism. The total picture of the present situation brightens as one views, in retrospect, the advances made since the early years of this century. Rapid strides toward functional physical education have been made. There is still much work ahead before physical education wins full acceptance and a respected seat at the educational family table. Never before has the profession had more challenges, or had greater opportunities to forge ahead. There is no time for complacency or discouragement. Existing inadequacies can be eliminated by concerted action of dedicated professional workers. If this can be done, every indication points to even greater forward strides in the years ahead. It is up to the thousands of men and women in the field to put forth more effort to produce the kinds of programs which will elevate the profession to the high stature it deserves in educational circles. The children and youth of America will be the beneficiaries.

Criteria for the Selection of Activities

Activities are a vital part of the physical education program. Through them the values sought can be achieved. The task of making final selection of activities is quite complex. Many factors must be considered by a staff.

Three limiting factors function to reduce the difficulty of choosing activities from the many available. First, the number of available teaching stations is a limiting factor. The size and arrangement of the indoor facilities, the extent of outdoor space and equipment, the kind and quantity of instructional supplies, local weather conditions, and the number of students and instructors involved all shape the program. Second, the ability of the staff to teach activities has much to do with the final selection and course of study development. Teachers skilled in the art of organizing and who know the teaching-learning process are capable of presenting many activities even when their own skills are limited. Nevertheless, staff abilities usually play an important role in activity selection. Third, limitation of time dictates the number of activities that can be taught effectively. Where classes meet only twice each week it is obvious that variety is diminished as compared to the school which provides a daily period. Even in the latter case a department is limited.

The staff is ready to plan a sequential course of study for each year when these conditioning factors are understood. The following criteria may be of value to guide teachers in this process.

1. Each activity must contribute to the stated objectives and goals of the department. Not all activities are of the same value. Those which satisfy the majority of aims should be given highest priority.

2. Activities should be selected so that the total program represents a balance of activities from the several activity areas listed below. Authorities classify activities that are currently used in physical education in several ways. Most activities might be classified into the following groups:

    Individual and dual games and sports.

    Team sports and games of low organization.

    Rhythmic activities including folk, square, tap, modern, and social dance.

    Combatives for boys only.

    Self-testing activities—all activities which permit or challenge students to attempt to better their own previous mark as compared to local, state or national standards.

Gymnastics and physical fitness activities, including tumbling and the trampoline.

Aquatics, including swimming, life saving and water sports.

Outdoor education activities such as camp skills, hunting, angling, field archery, boat handling and boat safety.

Activities which are selected to correct physical defects, or are adapted to meet special individual needs.

3. Activities should be selected in relation to student needs, interests, and abilities. Individuals do differ in many respects. Interest in some activities must be aroused and developed in some students. To do this effectively the teacher must constantly analyze and periodically appraise each student's capacity for performing motor skills.

Many of the shells used for crew at Oregon State University were built by Coach E. A. Stevens and his students.

In addition to this kind of circular study, qualified physical educators are guided by the knowledge that youth shares many needs and interests and abilities that can be met through physical education and must be fully aware of these important facts:

Needs

Teachers of physical education know:

That individuals need a high level of fitness in order to live effectively.

That it is their task to help individuals develop and extend their desire to participate.

That regular participation in pleasurable physical pursuits constitutes a potent outlet for tension.

That leisure is increasing and that the individual needs to be taught how to utilize part of that leisure in vigorous physical activity.

That they are in the business of teaching skills in physical activities that may be used in post school years.

Interests

Teachers of physical education know:

That in many instances they must awaken interest in physical activity.

That interests function as selectors of activity, and that results are best obtained when students are interested, challenged and motivated.

That desires of students should be taken seriously into account, but that they are not reliable guides to program development.

That their programs fail when interests are not aroused and sustained.

Abilities

Teachers of physical education know:

That their approach to groups of students is dictated by the levels of skills possessed by individuals within the group.

That for instructional purposes skill levels should be grouped separately when presenting most activities.

That no matter what level of skill a student has, he can be helped to attain more skill in most activities.

4. A study of community resources and leisure time pursuits enables the teacher to develop a functional program. Physical education leaders for a number of years have urged teachers to enrich program context by looking beyond the confines of the school campus for suitable activity areas. It is strongly recommended that departments of physical education analyze community resources, commercial as well as public recreation facilities, and seek to in-

clude appropriate activities relating to these facilities in their total program. In many instances such activity areas as golf courses, bowling alleys, ice and roller skating rinks, swimming pools, marinas, and riding stables may be used to diversify the program with activities usable for a lifetime—either in the instructional or voluntary school recreation program.

As the staff studies community resources to broaden the program it also becomes aware of the leisure habits and desires found in the community. This information has real meaning for the department and should be considered carefully as the curriculum is structured. A program of physical education, rich in activities regularly used by adults in their leisure, is concrete and meaningful. It should also be remembered that the success of the program is best measured by the degree of utility for post school use.

Facilities for teaching some physical education activities must often be improvised.

Curriculum Guide-posts

There are a number of practices which identify good procedure in curriculum planning. The following suggestions may serve as effective guide posts for this purpose:

1. Curriculum planners in each area within a school must understand the purposes of education so that their efforts best contribute to the goals of the school as a whole. This is as true for the English and science departments as it is for physical education. They should also know, and cause others to know, that physical education can make certain positive contributions no other department can claim.

On occasion, physical education personnel, especially those engaged in athletic coaching, tend to isolate themselves from the rest of the faculty. Teachers resent this and often develop skeptical or negative attitudes toward the program. A continuation of this policy tends to weaken respect for physical education. Common sense suggests that many of the persistent problems and obstacles which prevent physical education from making its best contribution to all students could be solved if the program faithfully supported the general purposes of the school.

Teachers should not minimize this point. They should work diligently to develop harmony with the administration and with all teachers in other subject areas. In most instances proper rapport is established when the teacher of physical education takes a real interest in the work of other departments, seeks membership on faculty committees, and actively participates in school affairs.

2. Curriculum planners must keep abreast of advancements that occur in the profession. Physical education, as in all phases of education, is constantly changing. Changed conditions call for new ways of getting the job done. A program that continues year after year with little or no change may not measure up to its potential. New techniques based upon new evidence are developing. New solutions to old problems continue to be found. You must "keep in step" with progress by attending and participating in professional meetings and conferences, periodically returning to college summer sessions, taking part in clinics, workshops and institutes, and devoting regular periods of time to reading current professional literature. This does not mean that the physical educator must always be a conformist. It is hoped he or she may have the courage to "venture out toward the three mile limit" occasionally with new ideas and pilot or experimental design and action. But in these ways the physical educator may stay informed and keep in touch with authoritative views regarding desirable practice.

3. As curriculum planners work to develop and conduct the program of physical education, they should be guided by professionally sound, written, overall program plans. Many departments lack continuity and direction in their program efforts because they fail to develop written statements of philosophy, policies and procedures to guide staff action; or fail to follow written courses of study when prepared.

One might question who should prepare these written statements which provide the blueprint for staff efforts. Should it be the school administrator, the physical education administrator, or the total staff? The administrative officer of the school plays an important role in establishing general policies; however, it is the responsibility of the physical education administrator to develop the program within the framework of general policies for the school. Following modern administrative practice he will see that the staff shares in the planning of everything that affects them. As problems occur and decisions must be made they should be fully discussed at staff meetings. These duly recorded decisions then become the policy statements which govern procedure.

It is surprising how few secondary school physical education departments have staff meetings or written policy statements or documented courses of study. Many pitfalls and serious problems may be avoided by departments if a basic philosophy to which all within the department may subscribe is developed. Adhering to this philosophy, the staff may then select the policies, rules and procedures needed to carry on its program of physical education.

4. Today's curriculum builders know that they achieve more effective results by making provision for students to share in planning and carrying out plans. There is a wealth of psychological findings to favor group planning. In addition to providing important democratic experiences for students, it also creates a more dynamic setting for learning. Everyone reacts more favorably when he feels his wishes are given serious consideration.

Many teachers misunderstand the role of the instructor when students are given a voice in program development. Later discussion will indicate the role of an instructor as an organizer and the merits of a student leader's core. It is enough to point out here that the teacher does not and should not relinquish his position in the teaching-learning process.

5. One of the cardinal principles of curriculum building is that departmental planners seek to provide for progression in learning motor activities. This can only be accomplished when students are scheduled into physical education classes according to their grade level, or on the basis of tested competency and maturity.

It is true that school administrators sometimes schedule students in physical education classes rather arbitrarily with the unfortunate resulting practice of mixing grade levels in classes. This can only result in constant repetition of experiences and lack of progression. This sort of repetition tends to make the physical education class merely a recreational experience. Academic people point to this fact perhaps more than any other in criticizing physical education. They would not condone a similar mixing of students in their own subject matter field. Would we respect the science department if the same content and the same experiments were given students semester after semester? It is doubtful if other teachers can support physical education as an equal learning experience to other fields when they see class after class playing touch football or kickball every fall, basketball all winter, and softball all spring, as the instructor sits or stands on the sideline or remains too frequently in his office while the fiasco continues.

Many departments of physical education have won friends on the faculty by reorganizing their programs so that instruction rather than pure recreation characterizes class procedure. When physical education is organized to permit progression of learning experiences, repeating activities only when learning is geared to higher levels of difficulty and competency, few would question the educational contribution the program makes to the total curriculum. The stature of physical education would increase to recognized significance if physical educators would follow the lead of those who are conducting their programs so that real learning takes place.

6. In curriculum building qualified leaders recognize that the task of instruction is more complex than simply teaching the skills involved in successful activity participation. They visualize their responsibilities to include the teaching of those learnings associated with motor activity.

Much more goes on in the mind of the learner than the details related to the learning of the game. Consider, for example, the student who sets out to learn tennis. There are a number of things connected with tennis which, if learned, would enhance the value of the total learning experience, such as the rules and courtesies of the game. Many people play tennis but have never learned to abide by the rules or to observe the standards of behavior expected in the sport. Should not this kind of thing be taught in the physical education class? And what about the student learning something about the quality and construction of rackets, balls and shoes? Should the student be taught to see the place of tennis in the world of recreation; as an after school sport; as a future game suitable for husband and wife or the family or club? Should he not learn something of the history of tennis? Are these learnings associated with learning tennis important enough to be brought into lesson planning and taught along with the skills and fundamentals of the activity?

Oberteuffer[4] sets forth the following five categories wherein important learning falls: consumer interests; appreciations of sport and dance; social behaviors and development; relationships to health; and, contemporary status.

The modern physical educator believes that these associated learnings must be planned just as explicitly as plans for teaching the game's fundamentals. He or she visualizes that the problem of physical education is to produce the physically educated person, one who not only becomes a participant for life, but also an intelligent spectator. Thus the physical education class period must include knowledge, behavior, and understanding.

Selected References

Brownell, Clifford Lee and E. Patricia Hagman, *Physical Education—Foundations and Principles,* New York: McGraw-Hill Book Company, 1951, Chapter 9.

California State Department of Education, *Teachers Guide to Physical*

4 Delbert Oberteuffer, *Physical Education* (New York: Harper & Brothers, 1956), pp. 307-311.

Education for Girls in High School, Sacramento, 1957, Chapter 1, pp. 1-5.

Cowell, Charles C. and Helen W. Hazelton, *Curriculum Designs in Physical Education,* Englewood Cliffs, N. J.: Prentice-Hall, Inc., 1955, Chapters 4 and 9.

Davis, Elwood C. and Earl L. Wallis, *Toward Better Teaching in Physical Education,* Englewood Cliffs, N. J.: Prentice-Hall, Inc., 1961, Chapter 9.

Irwin, Leslie W., *The Curriculum in Health and Physical Education,* St. Louis: C. V. Mosby Company, 1951, Chapter 4.

Knapp, Clyde and E. Patricia Hagman, *Teaching Methods for Physical Education,* New York: McGraw-Hill Book Company, 1953, Chapter 5.

Kozman, Hilda C., *et al., Methods in Physical Education,* Philadelphia: W. B. Saunders Company, 1958, Chapter 8.

Means, Louis E., *Physical Education Activities, Sports and Games,* Dubuque: Wm. C. Brown Company, 1952, revised 1963.

Nixon, John E. and Florence S. Frederickson, *An Introduction to Physical Education,* Philadelphia: W. B. Saunders Company, 1959, Chapter 10.

Shaw, John H., editor, *Selected Team Sports for Men,* Philadelphia: W. B. Saunders Company, 1952, Chapter 1.

Shepard, Natalie M., *Foundations and Principles of Physical Education,* New York: The Ronald Press Company, 1960, Chapter 11.

Vannier, Maryhelen and Hollis F. Fait, *Teaching Physical Education in Secondary Schools,* Philadelphia: W. B. Saunders Company, 1957, Chapters 9 and 10.

Vernier, Elmon L., *Current Administrative Problems,* Washington, D. C.: AAHPER, 1960, Part II.

Organization of
the Program of
Physical
Education

Wood Glover and City Schools of Burbank, California

Despite the fact that lip-service has been paid increasingly to the dictum, "a sound mind in a sound body," ever since the Graeco-Roman world, there is still a lack of balance among those who write of education.

Thomas Woody

9

The degree of success experienced by any program of physical education in school or college depends largely upon the quality of its administration. Administration does not exist for itself; it is the instrument which creates and directs the program. This mechanism is designed to guide the program so that it may achieve its goals. Administration, then, is superstructure. The administrator's function may be compared, in one sense, to that of the director of a play. Both work behind the scenes to set the stage for action. The principal characters in the physical education production are students and teachers, while in the play, actors and actresses share the limelight. Thus, neither the physical education administrator nor the

111

director of the play are in evidence while the show is on, and yet, both are directly responsible for the quality of the performance.

The administrator who considers his own importance to the extent that the actual teaching situation and the student become insignificant is in the same category as the scholar who, concerned only with research, is assigned to teach a freshman class in his area of specialty. Neither one can do a satisfactory job for the student or the program.

The head of the physical education department must discharge a number of clearly defined functions. He is an agent of the principal with delegated powers authorizing him to act for the school in all matters pertaining to the organization and conduct of departmental affairs. His primary function is to act for the department he represents, keeping clearly in mind that he is a representative of both the administrative and instructional functions of the school. In addition, he has a professional obligation to uphold, demanding that the department carry out everything for which the profession stands.

The modern program of physical education is an outgrowth of sound educational philosophy. Moreover, it is in agreement with the general philosophy of its own school. It is an integral part of the total curriculum and, as such, all the efforts of the administrator are directed toward making the program serve the purposes of the school as a whole.

The Physical Education Administrator

The type of person best qualified to direct a program of physical education is one who possesses the character and personality which enable him or her to get along with many different types of persons. His duties bring him in contact with many, both within the profession and the community. He must be skilled in personal relations because he is the department's representative to the public. Successful administration cannot be expected of one who specializes in any one area of the broad field of physical education; rather, a rich background of preparation and experience in many phases of the total program is indicated.

The role of department head in relationship to staff may be defined in terms of providing the inspirational leadership necessary to develop a successful program for all students. This is done by example and concept. Stature is demanded enabling one to guide the staff in ways that affect required changes in department procedure compatible with the best educational thinking of the period. Scott points out that changes in fundamental concepts and practices occur slowly in education, and that friction between colleagues is a common result. He further states:[1]

> The ability to bring about the desired changes without seriously disturbing harmonious relationships is often a difficult task where problems of interscholastic and intercollegiate athletics are concerned. To accomplish this purpose involves not only the personal, social and professional acumen of the administrator but also a nice balancing of power, responsibility, diplomacy, judgment, courage, timing, and technical skill plus never-ending vigilance and willingness to work. Because changes occur slowly and are difficult to achieve, the head of the department of physical education should be a person of great faith and indomitable spirit, for the educational defeats will more than likely far outnumber the victories for the department which he represents.

Perhaps the most difficult problem facing today's administrator is to develop harmony among staff personnel. Physical education is a broad field, involving several major divisions. As the program has developed over the years, administrative procedure has tended to augment conditions contributing to the separation of areas within the total program. It is not unusual for a high school program to feature a Director of Athletics, Director of Intramurals, Head of Boy's Physical Education, and Head of Girl's Physical Education. In some programs staff members work only in one of the areas mentioned. It is not at all surprising that interests clash and tensions develop under these conditions.

The astute administrator is only too well aware of the damage caused by internal cleavages. He knows that administrators, faculty, students, and community are quick to spot staff tension. For

---

1 Harry A. Scott, *Competitive Sports in Schools and Colleges* (New York: Harper & Brothers, 1951), pp. 271-272.

this reason, he works hard to weld the staff, with its diversified interests, into a harmonious, cooperating group.

Characteristics of the Good Program of Physical Education

There are numerous ways to organize a department. Among the important factors which help to explain the difference between the mediocre and highly successful departments are: the philosophy motivating the staff; the number of persons involved; the extent and kind of facilities and equipment; the quality and number of indoor and outdoor teaching stations; the number and kinds of students to be served; and environmental conditions. In addition, the specific structure of a physical education department is constantly undergoing modification in response to increased enrollment, community demands, and the constantly changing plans of the staff designed to meet new needs. Nevertheless, sufficient similarity in basic structure may be detected to suggest at least three important characteristics which are integral qualities of most well organized and successful programs. These are democratic administration, a unified department, and programs structured to meet the needs, interests and abilities of the greater number of students in the school. These elements should be taken into consideration by the administrator as he approaches his task, regardless of the specific factors involved in the local situation.

DEMOCRATIC ADMINISTRATION

It is difficult to express in words the full meaning of democratic administration, as many people have discovered in recent attempts to communicate their ideas on the subject. Most administrators give some lip service to democratic ideals as they apply to administration, but the movement seems to be progressing rather slowly in actual practice. The chief difficulty seems to be in clearly understanding how to administer democratically. Ideas widely accepted often fall short of application because in practice their full meaning is not clearly understood by those who advocate them.

Many physical education programs do exist which are skillfully organized. In these, the astute observer can detect administrators, instructors, and students working together cooperatively in a democratic atmosphere, serving the best interests of all concerned. A cooperative effort of the entire staff in planning the budget, in scheduling classes, in determining policy, and in designing the program leads to greater returns than if the administrator makes these decisions alone. There is little doubt as to the merits of democratic group action as applied to curriculum building, planning of new facilities, supervisory functions, and instructional practices.

The basic principle of democratic administration may be stated simply as follows: each individual has a right to be a participant in decisions that will affect him. Everyone concerned with policies affecting them should have some voice in the development of such policies. In this connection, it is well to point out that the ability of the staff to participate in making decisions depends largely upon the degree of readiness of its members to carry out responsibilities predicated upon such policies. This is one of the limiting factors in democratic administration. There are teachers who resent being asked to serve on committees; some would rather the administrator made all decisions. Due regard for their personalities would make it easy for such *unready* persons to avoid participation with their *ready* colleagues.

The chief disadvantage of cooperative planning is that the process is slower. It often takes time for a staff to smooth out differences of opinion and emerge with a common point of view. And yet, it is the only way to develop shared understandings and unified action toward common goals.

There is confusion in the minds of some administrators and teachers as to where group opinion stops and specific responsibilities begin. This usually stems from the failure to recognize that after the staff has had an opportunity to influence policy it is the task of the administrator to delegate responsibility and commensurate authority to specific people to carry out policy decided upon in general staff meetings. Unfortunately, it is at this point that administrative function becomes most difficult. A staff, organized for democratic action, responds nobly; however, once the stimulating work of planning is finished and program implementation is under way, the daily performance of those assigned functions becomes routine and often lacks the challenge and interest to engender continual best efforts. Thus, operation of the policy begins to become ineffective and the administrator is taxed to the limit in seeking ways to encourage staff members to put forth maximal efforts in continuing to carry out their responsibilities. Both the administrator and the total staff must expect some short-range difficulties or temporary failures in order to obtain long-range success. It is their combined challenge to minimize these short-run failures, and to turn what appear to be temporary difficulties into a planned program of strength and solidarity.

In many situations the administrator may establish the procedure for democratic operation and then through pressure reduce the voice of subordinates to that of an echo of his own point of view. As yet nothing has been devised to make administration democratic in spirit. Here is the real test of democratic administration. By no means is it implied here that the administrator is to play an insignificant role in shaping policy. Rather, through aggressive leadership considerable influence must be exerted in policy making. A department may be said to be administered democratically in direct proportion to the extent to which the democratic basic principles comes into play in the making of every policy decision from hour to hour and from day to day. In accordance with the democratic principle, the administrator must not ask the question at every point, *What is my authority?* but, rather, *In what way may I broaden the participation among those who stand to be affected by this decision?*

UNIFIED PROGRAM

Practical daily experience of administration clearly demonstrates that coordination between the several phases of physical education lead to superior over-all results. In a happy, closely knit staff, ideas are continually being generated and the program moves ahead under full steam. When new approaches to program implementation or expansion are contemplated it is sometimes fitting that the staff and administrator indulge in idea sessions where every possible idea is given full expression. From these exchanges the valuable and workable plans will emerge in full agreement. All must add strength to the cohesive unit of organized action. The staff, composed of the administrator, supervisors, coaches, men and women instructors, custodians and students must also be unified. The following discussion suggests several factors which contribute to this unification.

One Over-all Department Head

The physical education program is more likely to function smoothly and effectively when one member of the staff serves as the head of the entire program. This administrator should not be appointed on a rotating basis, with only temporary responsibility. He or she should have complete portfolio of responsibility from above. The unified program may be accomplished with more than one head, although it becomes much more difficult to achieve. Departmentalization is the foe of unified administration because, under such an arrangement, conditions are established which tend to frustrate attempts to gain the close cooperation, economy, and effectiveness required by a unified program. Large departments following a policy of having a director for each major area have a tendency to become overly independent, each possibly developing divergent philosophies, goals, staff, facilities, and equipment. In such cases, where instructors are employed as specialists in one phase of the program, it almost invariably follows that they are led to feel a loyalty only to their area and not to the program as a whole. The practice followed by some school administrators of employing teachers of academic subjects, combined with some physical education responsibilities, is especially insidious. When this occurs staff members are simply not given sufficient opportunity to work with those in other aspects of the program. One would hardly expect such a staff to develop the perspective that leads to coordinated effort. Unity of action becomes exceedingly difficult in this situation. The result may be, and often is, useless duplication, serious omissions, undue emphasis, and conflicts in teaching.

The improvement of instruction and the growth of individual staff members cannot take place unless there is a great amount of group action. Cooperative effort is the keynote to a successful department. The conclusion is inescapable. The many activities, interests, skills, and contributions of the entire staff need to be pooled and coordinated. This is the important task of the administrator. He must give impetus to desirable departmental activities by providing inspired and dedicated leadership along democratic lines.

Staff efforts beyond specific assignments are carried forward because of real satisfactions gained by staff members from the activity and its recognized dividend to youth. They must feel that their work is an important and indispensable unit in the total program. Staff members lose interest without personal satisfactions in accomplishment. An example of poor management which may damage staff morale may be observed in the way staff meetings are conducted. If the staff meetings are regularly scheduled and often only concerned with routine matters, staff members are apt to feel they are wasting time. They may lose a desire to participate in the discussion of more important department problems when they arise. It is good procedure for the administrator to call general staff meetings only when problems involving the entire staff arise. Meetings should be scheduled almost daily if necessary until troublesome current problems have been handled satisfactorily. It is often desirable for the administrator to combine a social setting with staff discussion on important matters. This may be done away from the school environment.

Written Statement of Philosophy

The good administrator knows that a clear-cut statement of the philosophy, general purposes, and policies of the department helps the individual staff member make his maximum contribution to the program. As pointed out in Chapter 8, for best results these written statements will be developed by all. This is sound administrative procedure, resulting in a positive rather than a negative attitude on the part of the staff. Teachers who feel secure in program direction, and who shared in the charting of the course, usually respond by evidencing satisfaction on the job.

Each new staff member should be given a booklet or folder of departmental policies and pertinent facts which enable him to fit more quickly into the program. This is an essential procedure which is too often neglected. Failure to provide a new staff member with these materials usually results in confusion, leaves doubt as to his role in the total scheme of things, and retards effective action. He may hesitate to turn to others to seek answers to questions because of a fear that his peers may suspect lack of ability or intelligence. The new teacher needs to know, in general, what is expected of him—what he should be trying to accomplish in classes. He wants to know how others have taught before him. He seeks answers to questions concerning proper procedure in the use of equipment, class procedures, office routine, the degree of emphasis to be placed on various aspects of instruction, and many other problems. The skillful administrator anticipates these problems and invites questions and discussion. He facilitates smooth adjustment by providing written materials which help bridge the gap. He does not leave execution of policy matters to chance and trial and error.

The Multi-skilled Staff

The modern administrator seeks teachers who are qualified in several areas of the program, and familiar with all of them. The well-rounded staff, with members who possess various skills in many sports and activities, permits the administrator to better allocate teaching and leadership assignments. The practical significance of this is obvious. A staff member who can teach in several phases of the program is not only more valuable to the department than a specialist, but he is more apt to see all phases of the program in focus. The teacher who will be involved in leadership for co-educational classes, school recreation, intramurals and some sport in the interscholastic program is less likely to place all his interest and emphasis on one area of the program. In departments where rotation of teaching assignments is not practiced there is a real danger that teachers may lose the ability to appreciate their relationship and responsibility to the program as a whole. On the one hand the instructor is apt to develop a balanced outlook leading to cooperation with all others in the department, while on the other, the instructor is encouraged to develop a warped outlook, leading to independent action.

NEEDS AND INTERESTS OF STUDENTS

The administrator has a major responsibility in shaping departmental action so that his program is integrated into the blood stream of the educative process at that school. He recognizes that his department is not alone in helping students meet their needs and develop desirable interests. Each subject area and department has its special function, its unique contribution. Some of these desired outcomes overlap or are shared by other departments. Best total results accrue when harmonious interaction exists between departments, each recognizing its relationship to the whole, and each wishing with demonstrated eagerness to work with other departments rather than to work in virtual isolation. We are living in a society in which cooperative action as a means of achieving goals is increasingly becoming the normal pattern of operation. The physical educator is on sound ground when he develops the spirit of cooperation with educators in other areas in helping students cope with their varied needs and in helping them broaden their interests.

Unfortunately, a number of factors growing out of the nature of the physical education program create an atmosphere which leads some within the profession to feel that their program has more to offer than other academic subjects. This attitude is reflected in many ways by these individuals. Perhaps none is more detrimental to interdepartmental accord than the attitude that after-school responsibilities associated with physical education are more important than faculty affairs. Therefore, general faculty functions and committee work are to be avoided whenever possible. This attitude creates distrust and antagonism on the part of the classroom teacher toward physical education. It is possible to create a better understanding of the role of after-school leadership and still cooperate to a considerable degree with faculty interaction. The thoughtful physical educator will find many ways to demonstrate his desire to become a good faculty team member, and will avoid any behavior which will stultify his position as a member of the educational team.

Any administrator who desires his program to make a real contribution to the majority of students must be very well aware of student needs and interests which may be met through the program he directs. Failure to understand behavior and its results is tantamount to admitting that the physical education program is designed merely to teach students skill in activities, develop muscle, or to provide them purely with recreational outlets. Vital as these objectives are, it would be most difficult to defend physical education as an important experience for all students if these are the sole benefits and values. The central emphasis cannot be on sheer performance or on skill in the narrow sense alone. The student's physical education experience must be organized to foster attitudes which contribute to a sense of well-being and to useful citizenship. In this process each student will become equipped with personal values, increased knowledge, basic lifetime skills, and habits of health and exercise much needed in today's world.

Personality needs must be met adequately. The competent administrator understands these things and consistently plans the program with his staff to meet these needs. Salient evidence of program planning designed to enable students to meet their needs and develop valuable interests through physical activity might be noted as follows: (1) the program involving as broad a variety of activities as possible; (2) students being given every opportunity to succeed; (3) class size being based upon the number of students an instructor can *teach* effectively; and, (4) developing a sound record and marking system.

Variety of Activities

The program in both elementary and secondary schools is organized in such a way as to provide each student with a variety of experiences through physical activity. Sound program planning reflects an awareness that individuals differ widely in their interests in these activities. The program therefore should offer as much variety as is practical. Diversified courses should be presented in ways which enable students to acquire skill in several activities that capture interest, thereby providing ample opportunity to become physically fit beyond the normal demands of living. A general description of program organization to facilitate this will be found in Chapter 11.

Opportunity to Succeed

A real attempt is made to make each student's experiences a positive factor in his scholastic career. The problem of organizing the program so that students encounter success in physical education is a major concern of the administrator and the teacher. Departments which have come to grips with this problem have discovered that the key to its solution lies in the proper organization of physical education classes.

The wider the range of student abilities and background of skills the more difficult it becomes for the teacher to provide maximum learning for each student. Highly skilled students are usually held back when the learning pace is geared to other students with meager backgrounds or who learn less rapidly. The student with limited skills is also a problem. He may become discouraged as others show more rapid progress. If this situation is allowed to continue this type of student might become cynical toward physical education. This problem must be avoided and steps taken to alleviate it or values inherent from continuing participation in pleasurable activities may be lost forever.

Teachers forced to instruct classes in which there are no provisions for skill or achievement segregation are aware that neither the highly skilled nor the less skilled are given a proper opportunity to progress normally. It is not always easy to obtain official permission to organize classes in a more nearly homogeneous manner. School administrators sometimes resist this attempt in physical education, but insist upon it for many academic areas. This is often the fault of the physical education department because of its lack of instruction and progression emphasis. In most cases this situation can be gradually corrected with serious attention paid to better instruction, planned progression in courses of study that are documented in writing and executed in practice, and through persistent discussion. Two solutions are suggested to improve the quality of instruction. First, students must be assigned to physical education classes according to their year in school. Second, in teaching most activities students should be grouped with others of similar skills or achievement levels as disclosed through testing, or grouped within a class into skill levels.

Class Size

The number of students in a physical education class should be limited to the number the teacher can work with effectively. In a recreational setting one leader can handle literally hundreds of participants. In the instructional setting this is impossible and undesirable. Experience indicates that generally about thirty students is the maximum number an instructor can handle and guarantee the close contact and instructional rapport necessary to secure real instruction and individual guidance. Some activities demand smaller units such as handball, golf, gymnastics, and tennis. The same is true in adapted or corrective classes where individualized programs are stressed. Surely the time has arrived when a good physical education instructor can be given a small unit for intimate instruction when it is considered that one instructor in driver education works with only three or four at one time. Much depends upon the guidance emphasis of the school. If the ratio of counselors to students is high there is no better place to achieve close personal guidance and a discovery of student needs than that which could evolve from a sound and controlled physical education class situation.

The good teacher guides as he teaches. He keeps individual students in mind while he teaches. By knowing the abilities and backgrounds of his students and understanding them as individuals the teacher is in an excellent position to make group interaction serve the needs of each student as well as contribute to class goals.

Record System

The competent administrator seeks to create a record system designed to be readily usable in furthering each student's best development through physical education. Keeping functional records is a means to understanding the individual in order to help him understand himself. The following criteria may be used in setting up a record system:

1. The record should include information on major aspects of the individual's development as observed or measured by testing in the physical education program.
2. The record should show a progressive pattern in past years; should indicate present developmental status; and should indicate possible levels of attainment.
3. The record should be in a form useful for counseling.
4. The ideal record is unified. It is more than a collection of unrelated bits of information.
5. The time spent on keeping records should be in balance to the time devoted to their use.

The permanent record form should include, if available, past experiences that are likely to influence the student's present and future progress in physical education. Specific provision should be made to include results of medical examinations, test results in aquatics, results of all fitness and sports skills tests, brief history of physical education experiences, grades each semester in physical education, and instructors' comments on progress made from time to time. Permanent record forms should be kept in what is known as visible files, where the student's name is always visible. This procedure saves much time when a specific record is needed.

It is recognized that records kept by the physical education department constitute only a portion of the data collected and utilized by the school as a whole. Accordingly, physical education records ought to be available to the guidance department and others who might need this information. Conferences with parents are always more meaningful and objective when such records are available for instantaneous use. Records in other departments should also be available to the physical education department as needed.

Each staff member contributes to the data on the student's record form. It is sound procedure to assign responsibility for keeping records up to date to one staff member. His chief task is to supervise the work of recording information and to periodically summarize comments and recommendations made by instructors. It is sound procedure to assign a section of the student body to each staff member for counseling purposes. Periodic opportunities for individual guidance and discussion on progress could be provided. The individual record could become a valuable instrument for this purpose.

Few departments carry their record keeping and use to this degree, thereby explaining why the files are seldom used. If records are to be kept at all they should be effective enough to encourage use for the good of the student and improvement of the program.

Administrative Organization of the Program

The ideal program should be planned and organized in such a way as to provide every student with a wide variety of both instructional and recreational experiences each semester. This is true at both the elementary and secondary school level. To accomplish this goal the program must have its required instructional base, with many activities progressively planned. Instruction is incomplete and lacks real meaning unless many opportunities are provided for voluntary participation in activities which supplement and complement the instructional offering. Here great variety of organizational structure is necessary in order to attract most students frequently. Some cannot remain after school and must work at home or on jobs. Others can stay after school through the week but cannot participate on Saturdays and holidays. Some cannot participate at night or during the noon hour. Some do not have the skills or physical equipment to represent the school on varsity teams. All must be served. This requires careful planning, maximum use of all possible facilities, complete staff teamwork.

utilization of nonschool facilities and short-term nonschool leadership under certain conditions. The chart below represents the cohesive relationship of each segment of the total program depicted in pyramid form. It is obvious that no pyramid has strength, or will endure, without a broad and strong base, here exemplified by the instructional program.

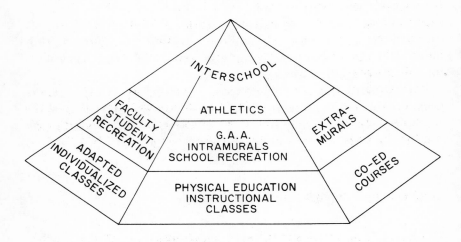

The diversified instructional program for all students within each class day occupies the base of the pyramid. Here are the regular physical education classes for boys and girls, co-educational classes, and individual classes for the atypical. It is here that all students in the school are exposed to expert instruction in all activities. It forms the base because it becomes the heart and soul of the total program just as the strength of any structure is measured in terms of its foundation.

Emerging from the class program, hence occupying the central and next important portion of the pyramid, is the broad program of intramurals and school recreation. Because of intimate contacts between instructor and student the intramural program gets greatest organization impetus from the instructional atmosphere, but should take place in addition to it. Fully developed, the intramural program provides the impetus and direction to its offspring, the extramural program. Here students with sharpened skills may find further expression and opportunity by participating with students of other schools on an informal and lightly structured basis. Faculty and students should both have opportunities for participation on campus, both separately and together. Faculty groups might also participate with similar groups from other schools when the varsity teams meet in some sports.

At the top of the pyramid, involving the more highly skilled students, rests the interschool athletic program. It should be an outgrowth and subsidiary to the other larger phases of the good program which make up the pyramid. If it dominates the structure, sound focus on values and outcomes is destroyed or obscured. The elementary school program would eliminate this phase and have intramurals as the apex of student opportunity, enriched with occasional extramural experiences.

In the modern secondary school physical education program all levels of the pyramid are essential. Each should be in proper proportion to the other. Only in that way do pyramids endure through the ages. Proper administrative planning and continual direction is vital if the entire structure is to be solidly built and constantly maintained without erosion. Good administration works unceasingly to strengthen each level of the program, fully cognizant that the success of the department and the program depends upon the full and proportionate development of each area. No one segment of the pyramid structure can be built with second class materials or workmanship. The mortar must be of equal quality throughout. The same skilled attention must be given from the moment the first segments are laid until the apex is completed.

Selected References

Brownell, Clifford Lee and E. Patricia Hagman, *Physical Education—Foundations and Principles,* New York: McGraw-Hill Book Company, 1951, Chapters 12 and 13.

Bucher, Charles A., *Administration of School Health and Physical Education Programs,* St. Louis: C. V. Mosby Company, 1958, Chapters 1, 2, and 3.

Gabrielsen, Alexander M. and Caswell M. Miles, *Sports and Recreation Facilities,* Englewood Cliffs, N. J.: Prentice-Hall, Inc., 1958.

Gaffney, Matthew P., "If I Were a Dictator," *JOHPER* (February, 1961), pp. 23-25.

————, "What are the Implications of Excellence in Physical Education?" *JOHPER* (October, 1961), Part 2, p. 95.

Irwin, Leslie W., *The Curriculum in Health and Physical Education,* St. Louis: C. V. Mosby Company, 1951, Chapters 14 and 18.

Oberteuffer, Delbert, *Physical Education,* New York: Harper & Brothers, 1956, Chapter 10.

Shepard, Natalie M., *Foundations and Principles of Physical Education,* New York: The Ronald Press Company, 1960, Chapter 13.

Vernier, Elmon L., *Current Administration Problems,* Washington, D. C.: AAHPER, 1960, p. 197.

Williams, Jesse Feiring, *The Principles of Physical Education,* Philadelphia: W. B. Saunders Company, 1959, Chapter 12.

Yukic, Thomas S., "Put It in Writing," *JOHPER* (May/June, 1961), pp. 37 and 64.

The Relationship of Physical Education to Health Education and Recreation

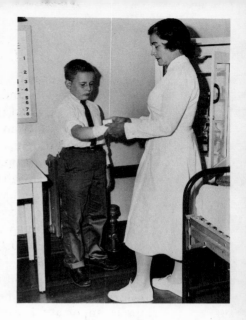

To get his wealth, he spent
   his health,
And then with might and
   main
He turned around and spent
   his wealth
To get his health again.

Author unknown

10

It is appropriate at this point to give some attention to the closely related fields of health education and recreation. Both are linked closely with physical education because of certain common denominators. These common ties outnumber the differences which cause some to feel they are separate and distinct. This statement does not minimize the fact that the need for specifically-prepared health educators is increasing.

The closeness of this relationship is borne out by the fact that our major national professional organization is the American Association for Health, Physical Education and Recreation. Many

129

college and university departments carry a title involving all three areas. Most directors and supervisors of city and county programs carry responsibility and title in all three areas.

Some graduates from physical education departments teach health education; many find that they have responsibilities in some phase of recreation. About eighty-five per cent of all secondary school classes in health education are taught by physical educators. Presumably they have had more professional preparation for this task than other teachers. Similarly, preparation in physical education is still the background for most of the nation's leading recreation administrators. It is an acceptable prerequisite for most recreation positions.

This chapter will point out something of the nature and significance of these related fields. Early recognition of these relationships is important because you may later become a specialist in one of them, or become a supervisor or director of two or more of these areas. Understanding them is valuable. Preparing for them is wise.

RELATIONSHIP TO HEALTH EDUCATION

Health has earned the right to its place as one of the cardinal principles of education. Health and physical education are not synonymous. Catching forward passes for touchdowns has little relationship to dental caries. The capacity to be in a position to score these touchdowns may have an intimate relationship to fitness and a state of well-being.

Health and physical education share a fundamental interest; namely, the preservation of health and the development of the integrated personality. Physical education uses motor expression—movement—as its media to educate the whole person, while health education deals with the acquisition of knowledge about living healthfully and directs attention upon immediate participation in healthful practice.

The definition of health which has received wide approval since its creation by the World Health Organization may help you understand its scope:

Health is a state of complete physical, mental and social well-being, and not merely the absence of disease or infirmity.

Thus one immediately sees the breadth and meaning of health which goes much beyond the physical. Those who see therein the reason for its complete separation from physical education must remember that physical education also is rich in its nonphysical outcomes—all contributing to the good life. Certainly health is an objective worth seeking—a goal that challenges our best efforts. Few real successes in life will be possible without a sustaining quality of health and fitness which is becoming more elusive in a changing society that places a premium on ease and tends to eliminate the need for physical activity.

School Health Education

It is unfortunate that many school districts continue to neglect health education as a necessary and integral part of the curriculum, and essential to the happiness and success of individuals, families and communities. Several reasons exist for this neglect. School authorities sometimes neglect health education because of the number and variety of nonschool agencies concerned with the problem. Education persists in regarding the accumulation of knowledge as a primary function. Health education favors knowledge as a basis for the development of worthy attitudes and habits, but true health education places greater emphasis on what the individual does with acquired scientific concepts rather than using the mind as a storehouse for information.

Parents are recognizing the school as the rightful place for dealing with many complex health problems—without usurping home prerogatives. An increasing number of school authorities are adopting more realistic policies and procedures favoring health education. Public health and voluntary health agencies employ specialists who cooperate with school personnel. In 1960 both the American Medical Association and the American Dental Association passed significant resolutions reaffirming their support of health education and physical education—as integral and basic parts of the school curriculum.

Like Caesar's Gaul, the complete health education program is divided into three parts: health services; healthful school living; and, health and safety instruction.

Health Services

Briefly, health services through health guidance and protection include things done *to* the student to improve his health such as periodic health examinations, immunization, and correction of remediable defects.

Chapter 11 points out the vital part the health services play in establishing and maintaining a sound physical education program. Note is made there of the inadequacy of the majority of school health services to provide the services required by the diversified program of physical education. Physical educators should bend every effort to assist the health services to expand personnel and facilities in order to fulfill its responsibilities in connection with the program of physical education.

Some of the important ways in which the health services should cooperate with the physical education department are as follows:

1. Provide an adequate, qualified staff to render services when needed.
2. Make the health records available to the physical education staff when needed for guidance purposes.
3. Conduct the medical examination at the beginning of the school year.
4. Participate in the development of a sound policy relating to temporary excuses from participation in the physical education program.
5. Participate in the development of a system of classifying students who must follow a restricted program of physical education.
6. Handle the area of school health problems, many of which are discovered in physical education classes.
7. Provide medical supervision at all athletic events involving contact. For practices and intramural participation administer the procedure to follow for contacting available physicians.

8. Advise the physical education staff as to proper first aid procedures.
9. Supervise the hygenic conditions of the physical education facilities.

The physical education department has responsibilities to the health services. It can cooperate best as follows:

1. Utilize the facilities of the health services.
2. Provide clerical and other assistance in conducting the medical examination.
3. Publicize the functions of the health services by acquainting students with the services offered and, when detected, send ill students to the health services.
4. Maintain the cleanliness of the physical plant.
5. Maintain safety standards in equipment and supplies, as well as keep hazards from all teaching station areas.
6. Establish the training room as a sub station of the health service.
7. Supplement the health services by taking every advantage in classes to reinforce their purposes.

Healthful and Safe School Living

This includes the things done *for* the student such as providing a sanitary and safe school environment, observe health principles in the curriculum and in teaching practices, establish sound health and emergency protection, and develop a favorable total school atmosphere.

The physical education program has an important role to play in establishing the level of health standards for the total school population. On the one hand, a meager program of activities, poorly administered and taught breeds discipline problems and is a constant potential source of injury and accident. On the other hand, a dynamic program, well administered and conducted has a great deal to contribute to a vigorous, healthy student body. In addition to the benefits derived from the wholesome exercise gained through participation in the program, school administrators are fully cognizant of the impact a good physical education program has in shaping a healthy emotional atmosphere in the school population.

Health and Safety Instruction

The aim of health instruction is to teach youth to live healthfully and happily. To achieve this aim youth needs a planned program of educational experiences with orderly arrangement for each grade cycle. Thus it becomes possible to acquire the knowledge, attitudes, habits, and skills necessary to maintain and develop his own health and to accept responsibility for protecting the health of family and community.

Three patterns of health instruction have evolved in school health education: direct teaching—health is the subject; the program of correlation—health is brought into other subjects; and, the program of integration—learning experiences are organized around a central objective.

The nature of physical education is such that there are countless opportunities for the teacher to correlate physical activity with health information. It is difficult to conceive of a physical education class without the student having some experience bearing upon his health.

Other Implications

Total health education utilizes the combined experiences of all three of these areas to produce a health-educated person. This is not possible unless all three receive ample emphasis. The periodic health examination, or the examination which precedes participation in physical education classes or varsity athletics represents an excellent laboratory experience for developing wholesome attitudes and understandings.

Health and safety instruction in the elementary school grades is usually accomplished through the efforts of teachers in all subject areas. This kind of learning continues throughout secondary school years through planned experiences in industrial arts, home economics, agricultural education, social studies, the biological sciences, and physical education. Special instructional courses are, or should be, provided in secondary schools.

It is advisable to select the one person best qualified to serve as health and safety coordinator. It is equally desirable to establish a health and safety coordinating council. Thus the contributions to health education from all sources can be identified, overlapping eliminated, and special courses designed to cover all facets of health instruction effectively.

Preparation of the Health Educator

Physical education teachers are expected to be better prepared to teach health and safety than other teachers. This is due to the close natural relationships which exist. For this reason physical educators should prepare, as much as possible, for these responsibilities. Whether or not they teach specific health courses, they should recognize their role and be ready to cooperate effectively. They will always be very much concerned with the health and physical fitness of all students. Each day's contacts will leave an impact on health attitudes, knowledges, and concepts that affect health status.

There is a trend toward the use of a health education specialist for direct teaching. Some school districts require a minimum of a health education minor—others demand the major and place a premium on further graduate work. Certain competencies are needed for this specialized field, with more background required in the biological sciences and in health education per se.

Many institutions require a teaching minor in addition to the physical education major because the job opportunities in many states require the physical educator to teach some academic courses. Selection of biological, physical, and social sciences also assists in providing better background for teaching health courses and understanding the broad field of health.

Although there may be immediate need for persons with minimum preparation, such persons cannot substitute for qualified health educators. They should plan to secure the additional preparation necessary at the earliest possible time.

Programs to help prospective teachers achieve competencies in health education are somewhat dependent on variations in curricular patterns and departmental structures in colleges and universities. The preparation of the health educator demands a balance of the sciences directly related to health.

Areas which are *essential prerequisites* to the health education minor program are:[1]

> *Biological and physical sciences*—for example: human biology anatomy, physiology, bacteriology, and chemistry.
>
> *Social sciences*—for example: psychology and sociology. It is possible that some of the background in physical, biological, and social sciences . . . might be achieved in part at least by other than traditional course organization. Special procedures may be developed by interdepartmental planning. The program should include health and health education courses with prominent emphasis on the *health area.*
>
> *The health area* includes—personal health and community health, vital statistics, epidemiology, nutrition, mental health, first aid, consumer education in health, care of the sick and injured, health problems of school children, rehabilitation, home and family health, environmental sanitation, accident prevention, and occupational health.
>
> *The health education area* includes—methods and materials, school health services, healthful school living, safety education, and organization, and administration of school health programs.

General Considerations

> The health education minor should include appropriate course work, laboratory, and community field experiences in health education.
>
> There is no substitute for actual participation in field experiences. Until field experiences can be included, directed observations may serve as a temporary measure.

[1] Health Education Conference Report, Washington, D. C.: AAHPER, 1955, p. 6.

The content of a particular program cannot be determined by considering course titles alone. The value of any offering depends upon the way it is organized and conducted as well as the effectiveness of the teacher and his methods. These suggestions must be adapted to the needs of the individual institution.

Evolving a program of experiences effective for developing the recommended abilities and arranging these into specific course requirements must be the responsibility of each teacher education institution in collaboration with the various certification agencies.

A variety of teaching methods should be used in order to illustrate the methods which students would be expected to use in their own classes.

Student teaching experiences should be provided in the health education minor program as well as for major teaching fields.

As a part of the total professional preparation, students should be assisted in integrating health knowledge in a wide area through problem solving experiences such as in a seminar.

College instructors of courses in the health education area of the minor program should be individuals who have specialized in health education.

General Observations

It would be well for you to seek the counsel of biology as the science of organic life. It will aid in your efforts toward a better life for yourself, your future family, and for your students. Health is a positive quality, implying harmony of function, vigor, and a quiet joy. The healthy man has a wholeness or oneness of physical life while the unhealthy man is always distracted. And though the healthy man may be torn by temptations and puzzled by the unsolved problems of life, he has not often to fight a battle on two fronts, for health implies some degree of unity. The unhealthy man, on the other hand, has always to face bodily discord as well as ethical and intellectual difficulties. He is not at peace with his own body.

It is difficult to conceive of an effective health education program which is far removed from physical education. The very basis of health is the vitality, organic power, ability to resist fatigue and sustain effort which comes through participation in sports and physical activities under wholesome circumstances.

On the other hand, there are components of health and physical fitness other than physical activity alone. Proper nutrition, needed medical and dental care, sufficient sleep and rest, and the avoidance of excesses are very important.

An editorial in the American Medical Association News makes the following sound observation:[2]

> The ability to pass a physical achievement test does not automatically qualify a person as "physically fit." For example, it is quite possible for a youth to be unimmunized, with carious teeth, or chronic otitis, or even active TB, and make a good score on a so-called physical fitness test.

Thus the total elements surrounding the combined fields of health and physical education combine to demand unified concern.

Young children need seldom be conscious of health as such. They experience it through a variety of experiences such as the morning parental or school inspection, the physical education class, the rest period, the school lunch, and many other contacts with others.

Generalizations or inferences about health that grow from experience must be properly channelled, sifted, and their soundness identified. Physical education is replete with these generalizations about health. Alert teachers will see to it that youth develop and apply these generalizations in order to solve their health problems. In this process comes the mastery of interrelationships. Cowell expresses this concept succinctly:[3]

> Teaching for understanding is a difficult art and the chief distinguishing mark of a good teacher. Meaningful knowledge is applicable knowledge. . . . Physical education has been too long on activity and too short on understandings. If the learnings we produce are to be functional and transferable, they must be based, not on isolated facts, but on cause-and-effect relationships—understandings. Education for health is not a pursuit in splendid isolation! We seek not to teach the facts and principles but to give

2 "Youth Fitness," editorial viewpoint, *A.M.A. News*, February 20, 1961, Volume 4, Number 5.

3 Charles C. Cowell, *Scientific Foundations of Physical Education* (New York: Harper & Brothers, 1953), pp. 217-218.

them "arms and legs"—to see them result in human action. What people do with a fact depends less on the validity of a fact than on how they feel about it.

Career Opportunities in Health Education

Health education will continue to deserve and demand better prepared leaders. School districts will employ increasing numbers of health educators. You may wish to explore all possibilities with your faculty adviser. You may wish to prepare for a position with non-school health agencies. These are increasing at local, state and national levels. National organizations concerned with tuberculosis, the heart, cancer, infantile paralysis, and others are adding health education specialists to their staffs. Insurance companies are doing likewise. Some of these positions are attractive.

Public health beckons an increasing number of trained operatives. In many cases public health agencies and school districts have close working relationships. Colleges and universities are in need of better trained health education specialists with graduate preparation. Health educators with doctorates are in increasing demand to teach health as part of general education to undergraduates, and to prepare health education teachers in graduate courses. A shortage exists in this area. Larger city school districts and county systems are seeking the services of qualified specialists as supervisors, coordinators and directors.

Even as a physical educator you should be prepared to teach health education with competence. A growing national fitness emphasis will cause youth and adults to look to you for professional advice—for the answers to questions you should know. You will continually find yourself faced with questions about personal health and matters related to sex. Will you evade the issues, guess at the answers, or strive through preparation to meet these challenges in a positive and helpful way?

RELATIONSHIP TO RECREATION

Recreation has become one of man's basic needs. It was always so, but rapid changes in modern society have caused dramatic realizations about the relationships of leisure to creative and adjusted living. The character of recreation is changing rapidly. A generation ago it was comparatively easy to get away from urban congestion and enjoy the great outdoors. One could skate on sidewalks and streets and ride bicycles almost anywhere. The need for unorganized leisure pursuits persists. However, they are becoming more elusive.

Recreation as a public service is growing and achieving deserved jurisdictional attention. It is important here to: (1) briefly show the close relationships which exist with physical education; and, (2) point out the opportunities for professional leadership which may attract you in future years.

Education for Leisure

The schools must prepare youth for a leisure which increases with each decade. Skills must be taught. Attitudes and habits must be acquired. This can only be done through planned instruction and by providing opportunities for the practice of skills taught. Thus the schools have several important responsibilities in this regard.

Most learning can be related to what happens in recreation. Reading is one of the greatest recreative arts. Science, conservation education, geography, and other subject areas could stimulate recreational habits and hobbies. Indeed, learning is incomplete at the class period's end. Play and recreation, if oriented to education for living, provide the laboratory opportunities needed to complement and supplement formal instruction. This is particularly true of music, art, dramatics, and physical education. These are areas replete with skills that demand opportunities for expression. A lifetime of creative and challenging leisure receives incubation in school and community programs of recreation. The closer these experiences are related to class learnings the more lasting the impact.

Scope of Recreation

The preceding comments should have suggested that recreation is extremely broad in scope. Indeed, work to many is real recreation. But all people need changes in routine to avoid monotony, to provide new challenges, and to widen their sphere of activity. A wise balance throughout life involving cultural, social, and physical recreation is desirable. Whether one continues through life completely satisfied with the creative arts as their only recreative outlet or if one seeks to combine strenuous physical recreation with other forms is a personal matter. The latter might be more conducive to long and healthful living. Thus physical recreation will always be a safety valve—an emotional and physical outlet. Which is more valuable as life becomes more complex?

Recreation today is concerned with the provision of appropriate facilities for both organized and unorganized recreation. It is concerned with quiet and active activities. It must have trained operatives who know more about "skills in working with people" than they must know about "skills in activities."

Folk dance class at the University of Utah.

Physical Recreation

One of the most important parts of a sound recreation program is physical recreation. The physical educator, because of his special preparation, is not necessarily equipped or prepared to become a specialist in all phases of recreation. He or she should be particularly adept at leadership in physical recreation. By the same token the expert in social recreation may be very inadequate in conducting physical recreation.

Thus you will find that good preparation for physical education plus broad experiences places you in a natural position for recreation leadership and administration. The addition of a few courses in recreation leadership would round out desirable professional preparation. Most job specifications for a recreation administrator today list professional preparation in physical education as acceptable and desirable.

Administrative Patterns for Providing Recreation Services

1. The public schools are more and more assuming their rightful responsibility in:
   a. giving greater attention to instruction in skills which have lifetime leisure utility.
   b. providing increased recreation experiences for all students and the faculty in a variety of ways.
   c. assuming jurisdictional administration over school-community recreation for all children, youth and adults of the area.
   d. providing continuous use of all school facilities for recreation purposes at all possible times.
   e. joining with other governing bodies in financing and administering the total recreation program for the area.

It is obvious that the physical educator, a responsible employee of the school district, can move rapidly into a leadership role in recreation. This may provide increased salary, summer employment, and more important administrative responsibility.

2. Municipal government is rapidly assuming a more active role in providing recreation services. Many cities now budget for this department as carefully as for sewage disposal, street cleaning, police and fire protection, and other services.

No city recreation department can operate effectively isolated from public schools. It needs their facilities, the background of skills taught, and the specialized leadership possessed by some teachers. City recreation departments should concentrate on the major tasks which they can do more easily than the public schools such as the acquisition, development, and operation of parks, golf courses, marinas, and large regional facilities often outside the immediate area.

3. County government in recent years has become more active in recreation. Most counties have concentrated on providing major recreation areas, camp sites, trails, regional parks, marinas, and assistance to local agencies operating recreation programs.
4. One of the most effective practices has been the partnership efforts of a school district with city and/or county government in utilizing the resources of each for joint effort. This should result in more economical and effective planning and operation and avoid overlapping, duplication, and jurisdictional disputes. Some of the nation's best programs are operated in this manner.
5. State and federal governments have a real stake and obligation in recreation. Their major task has been to acquire and develop regional areas for public use and to provide consultive service to local agencies.

It is not difficult from this brief outline of recreational administration to see the opportunities that will be open to you as an experienced practitioner in the field. As a school leader your opportunities multiply as school districts become more active in providing recreation services through: (1) school recreation, (2) school centered recreation, (3) school connected recreation, (4) the community school, (5) the education centered community, and, (6) joint operation of recreation with other governing bodies.

Recreation as a Profession

Specialized courses in various phases of recreation leadership are needed today to meet four distinct areas of need:

1. All college students should have courses which better prepare them to utilize an expanding leisure more creatively and effectively. This is a part of general education—an integral phase of preparation for citizenship and adjusted living.
2. Teachers who may be called upon to assume recreation leadership responsibilities in addition to other educational assignments should prepare with at least a minor in recreation.
3. A complete professional preparation program is needed for those who expect to make recreation a career. This is the ma-

jor curriculum which may include some courses also found
in the physical education major plus other courses of specialized nature.

4. The terminal student who may never complete the college
   preparatory program but who will serve as a specialist in
   some skills phases of recreation department operation such as
   aquatics, dance, and sports. This would be the equivalent of
   a two-year or junior college program of preparation with
   emphasis in skill areas.

The growing need for leaders who have selected recreation as a
full-time career is a cause for concern. New communities each
year initiate recreation programs with a departmental organization, each demanding trained direction. College and universities
are unable at present, or in the foreseeable future, to supply sufficient numbers of candidates for these positions.

Tenure and salary levels are still somewhat more precarious
than for school district employees and teachers. The gap is rapidly
closing. A position under municipal auspices does not require
teacher certification. A position combining educational certification with recreational leadership responsibility gives double security for placement and future professional growth.

The physical educator who has taken all possible work to prepare for recreation leadership and who has gained experience
through summer employment and part-time school year assignments is ready to proceed vocationally in two or more ultimate
directions.

Study this matter carefully. Take every opportunity to gain practical experience in both directions. Time and opportunity will
dictate ultimate career definition.

Selected References

Health Education

Bucher, Charles A., *Administration of School Health and Physical
   Education Programs,* St. Louis: C. V. Mosby Company, 1950.
Fenton, Norman, *Mental Health in School Practice,* Stanford: Stan-
   ford University Press, 1950.

Florio, A. E. and G. T. Stafford, *Safety Education,* New York: Mc-Graw-Hill Book Co., 1956.

Fraley, Lester M., *et al., Physical Education and Healthful Living,* Englewood Cliffs: Prentice-Hall, Inc., 1954.

Healthful School Living, Report of Joint Committee on Health Problems, AMA and NEA, Washington, D. C., 1957.

Means, Richard K., *The History of Health Education,* Philadelphia: Lea & Febiger, 1963.

Moss, Bernice, "Health Teaching—A Physical Educator's Responsibility," *Journal of Health, Physical Education and Recreation* (Nov. 1954).

Oberteuffer, Delbert, *School Health Education,* New York: Harper & Brothers, 1960.

Turner, C. E., C. M. Sellery, and Sarah Louise Smith, *School Health and Health Education,* St. Louis: C. V. Mosby Company, 1957.

Recreation

Corbin, H. Daniel, *Recreation Leadership,* Englewood Cliffs, N. J.: Prentice-Hall, Inc., 1953.

Education for Leisure, Washington, D. C.: AAHPER, 1958.

Hutchinson, John L., *Principles of Recreation,* New York: The Ronald Press, 1949.

Jenny, John H., *Introduction to Recreation Education,* Philadelphia: W. B. Saunders Co., 1955.

Leisure and the School, Washington, D. C.: AAHPER, 1961.

Recruitment of Recreation Personnel, Washington, D. C.: AAHPER, 1958.

The Roles of Public Education in Recreation, Burlingame, California: CAPHER, 1960.

Part IV

THE PROGRAM OF
PHYSICAL EDUCATION

AAHPER

The Instructional Program of Physical Education

The one exclusive sign of a thorough knowledge is the power of teaching.

Aristotle

11 THE MEDICAL EXAMINATION

The problem of providing medical examinations for all students is one that has not been solved in a great number of schools. Rough estimates indicate that about seventy percent of high school graduates come from schools offering programs of physical education which have not provided the medical examination as a program prerequisite. A number of reasons contribute to this situation. Perhaps none is more significant than the fact that many school health service departments are unable to conduct the examination. Less than half of all high schools in the country employ the services of a physician. In these schools, and in others having more elaborate health services, the home physician is depended upon to perform this vital service. Many other schools simply ignore the problem.

When consideration is given to the fact that secondary school physical education, an area that demands vigorous physical exertion on the part of students, is a requirement in all but a few states, it is immediately evident that the administration of a thorough medical examination to all students is of signal importance. In fact, authorities in the field recognize that the medical examination *should initiate the program of physical education.*

Who is to blame for the failure of many schools to conduct regular medical examinations for all their students? Is it the school administration, the health services, or the physical education department? It is convenient for physical education personnel to say that it is the responsibility of others; however, the answer to the above question is more clearly revealed when one seeks to determine the area within the school most concerned with the problem. Obviously, the only area within the school which feels any urgency in the matter is the physical education department. None of the other departments, by nature of their content, have an imperative need to know the physical condition of their students. Only physical education content involves vigorous physical activity. The unique contribution of physical education to the school curriculum lies in the fact that physical activity is a vital part of its total program. Under these conditions it behooves this department to take the initiative in persuading the school health services to arrange an examination of all new students before the beginning of classes.

The physical education administrator should offer the services of his department to help in any way needed in administering the examination. The staff may assist by taking over clerical and other routine functions so that the work of the examining physicians may be reduced to the actual function of conducting the examination. In some instances the department must take leadership in securing physicians to do the job. It may even mean that the department must actually contact local physicians to solicit their cooperation in administering the examination. Although, whenever possible, the best procedure is to work through the school health services.

Once the examination is established, the physical education department must take steps to see that test results are used effectively in scheduling students to classes. This necessitates the development of some sort of scheme whereby the health services, on the basis of examination results, may classify students regarding possible limitations placed on their physical activity. Such a classification system enables the examining physician to evaluate each activity in the program from the standpoint of degree of vigor required.

There are a variety of classification forms in current use. The following may serve as an example. "A" may indicate no restrictions on physical activity; "B," minor restrictions with the limitation indicated on the card; "C," specific limitations indicated, requiring conference between the health services and the physical education instructor who works with the student; and, "D," a post-operative case or other temporary limitation prohibiting physical education for the time being.

Several forms must be developed to carry on the essential communication between the two departments. They should include the following information: degree of vigor required by each activity; readmission to classes after illness; and, a plan for reporting accidents.

Since the medical examination and the normal functions of the health services are so vital to the successful operation of the program, the astute physical education administrator explicitly encourages the development of good rapport between the two departments. He does this by informing the health service staff as to the objectives, content, and procedure utilized in conducting the physical education program. In addition, the department cooperates with the health services in the manner pointed out in Chapter 10. When physical education departments cooperate to this extent with the health services, reciprocal cooperation is more apt to be developed.

Testing: A Scheduling Device

A persistent problem confronting physical education departments since their inception is that of establishing a procedure that will make it possible to segregate the skilled students from the non-skilled. Such a plan is essential in order to organize the program so that progression in physical education activities occurs. As is pointed out elsewhere in this book no program can be effective unless a student is placed in a situation in which he has a chance to start at his own skill level and to proceed at his own best rate. Authorities agree that failure to group together students of similar skills when they are learning most motor activities is tantamount to creating a poor setting for learning.

Classification Tests

To avoid the stultifying practice of assigning students to activity classes without considering skill or achievement levels, many departments attempt to appraise the skills of new students through the use of performance tests. These are usually referred to as classification tests. In most cases standardized tests are used. National attention directed toward physical fitness has caused more and more departments to use physical fitness type tests to classify. The AAHPER National Fitness Test is internationally recognized and has proven to be sound. A few states have adopted their own test, as have a number of city wide programs. The valid physical fitness test is necessary in determining the kind and degree of strength, power, speed, and agility possessed by each student.

The general level of skill students possess in the basic fundamental movement patterns—running, jumping, climbing, striking, throwing, hanging, and carrying—may be best discovered by the use of standardized skill tests. A growing number of schools and colleges are using a physical fitness test along with a skill test to determine current skill levels. A few high school departments and a number of junior colleges and colleges have developed a locally developed test battery. These departments believe that more pertinent results may be obtained by developing a battery of test items representing the basic skills in the activities taught in their own programs. The advantage of the locally designed test lies in the fact that it may be directly geared to the program. However, construction of such a test takes time and requires considerable experimentation before it is ready to meet the requirements for validity, reliability, and objectivity. Once the department establishes the standard of proficiency it wishes all students to achieve, the locally designed test becomes a practical evaluating device.

Again, AAHPER has scientifically devised a National Sports Skills Test Program with national norms which has superseded local efforts. It provides, without undue loss of local staff time, a valid and reliable battery which should be used to motivate and to help identify individual weaknesses.

It should be pointed out that successful operation of the program of physical education is not dependent upon the use of classification tests alone. The use of some sort of classification test is perhaps more essential at the college level than at the high school level. The college student takes part in only a portion of the physical education program. For him it seems wise to attempt to discover his abilities in physical education activities or the lack thereof so that he may be counselled into activities he may pursue with profit. The high school student is exposed to the core program, therefore, the needed information as to his skills is available before he moves into the required elective program and its opportunities to center attention on a few activities. Nevertheless, knowing the general level of strength and coordination of the new student is of great help to a staff as it seeks to center its program efforts on the interests, needs, and abilities of its students. A sound basis for marking is also provided.

Achievement Tests

Classification tests are not reliable instruments for grouping students as the program enfolds. Achievement tests in the several activities which comprise the program serve this important function. There should be no confusion on this point. A classification test is a broad test designed to measure overall strength, agility, and coordination. It does not measure ability in a specific activity. There are two methods to do this: first, subjective evaluation of performance by the instructor and; second, an achievement test involving the fundamentals of the activity in question, such as the AAHPER test program.

Sport activities are complex, many of them involving several fundamental skills. Many people believe that expert evaluation of student performance in the total activity is the best way to quickly ascertain the variety of skill levels present in a physical education class. There is a great deal to say for this viewpoint when one considers that the best test of ability is in playing the game. Good standardized tests to be used in grouping students are recommended by most authorities because of the objectivity factor. Also, among other purposes, the achievement test serves to motivate student learning.

Sound organization of classes in physical education, whereby students are grouped according to the skill they possess in the activities to be taught, utilizes evaluation of performance and achievement tests. This procedure must be repeated each time a new activity is taught.

Scheduling

The manner in which students are scheduled into the classes has a great deal to do with the quality of physical education instruction. Effective organization of the program is possible only when students are assigned according to their year in school. That is, each grade level must be taught separate from other grade levels. Mixing of grades in one physical education class prevents the department from planning for progression in the activities that comprise its total program over the years. Class scheduling based entirely on tested achievement performance might supplant scheduling by grades.

The unfortunate practice, followed by many school administrations, of assigning students to physical education classes according to their free time establishes a condition which make it impossible for the staff to conduct an educationally sound program. The usual result of this kind of haphazard scheduling is for students to be exposed to the same activities a number of times. Diversification is impossible. Repetition of this sort is unjustified and outcomes are doubtful.

Considerable speculation in educational circles centers on the reasons why many administrators use physical education as a "dumping ground." On the one hand there are those who feel that administrators see the program as simply a play period that does not require prerequisites. Others argue that administrators recognize the potential value of physical education, but refuse to take the necessary steps to separate the classes because they have not observed programs that warrant the trouble required to change their scheduling procedures. It matters little why the practice prevails. The point is that as long as it does persist, programs of physical education which lack variety and which are essentially recreational in nature rather than instructional, will continue to plague the profession.

The Core Program

There are a number of satisfactory ways to organize a program of physical education. Nevertheless, a close study of successful ones reveals that all good programs offer the following: (1) a varied program of activities; (2) expert instruction in the physical education classes; and, (3) grouping of students in classes to permit progression in the activities which make up the program. These three qualities are among those which identify sound programs of physical education. Programs which do not measure up to these requirements must be considered substandard. The description of the core and the required elective form of organization of the program which follows is designed to create the kind of physical education which recognizes the above requirements.

As used here the core program refers to the program of physical education offered in the first two years of a four year high school or to the three years of junior high, and the first year of the three year senior high school. The general idea basic to this plan of organization is to introduce the student to all the activities to be included in the total program. Thus the student is exposed to a variety of activities, each experience merely long enough to provide a chance to discover whether or not it has appeal. Obviously, skillful organization and expert instruction is the key to success of this kind of program plan. The primary objective of the core is to provide the student with a digestible taste of a great number of activities so that he may, when given the opportunity in the last two years, be discriminatory in selecting activities he wishes to pursue further. It remains for the required elective and the intramural programs to provide the student with additional experiences in those activities which afford him the most pleasure and value.

Contrary to common practice, surprisingly few periods may suffice to awaken an interest on the part of the participant in most activities. To accomplish this purpose, and that is the primary task of the core, it is suggested that instruction be included in a greater variety of activities than are used in most physical education programs at the present time. To illustrate, in the two year core where classes meet daily, students will be exposed to from twenty-four to thirty-six different activities. This is in sharp contrast to the lack of breadth of offerings in many current programs. For instance, in a recent survey of fifty-five high schools in which physical education classes met daily, it was found that not more than eight activities represented the average number offered per program.

Since exposure to an activity in the core is brief, extreme care must be taken to captivate student interest. This means that the daily lesson plans must be carefully prepared so that real learnings evolve. The chief aim of instruction is to establish a learning climate which enables the student to improve skills and to enjoy the activity. Work in the unit is characterized by a balance of instruction in the fundamental skills of the activity with that of challenging participation in the total activity.

The Core in Operation

In describing the operation of the core program, consideration is given to the fact that local conditions weigh heavily in program construction. Description of the plan must necessarily be in terms broad enough to fit the circumstances involved in most secondary schools.

Before the new student begins active participation in the core the department needs to know two important facts. First, it should know the general physical condition of the student. For this reason the new student in the high school—freshman in the four year school and the tenth grader in the three year school—should receive a complete medical examination during the first week of school. Results of the examination are necessary before launching the student into vigorous activity. Second, the department should know the degree of motor fitness and general ability in physical pursuits the student brings to the program. The first week, then, is the proper time to administer physical fitness and skills tests. Armed with the above information the department is ready to start the core program.

Each activity taught in the core is allotted only a few periods, and poor instruction cannot be tolerated. Time is of the essence. Picture, if you will, a situation in which each activity is taught in a unit of not more than fifteen class periods. Sufficient learning must take place in that short period of time to enable the student to make up his mind as to whether or not the activity has appeal. To accomplish this purpose skillful organization of the class must exist.

We have already established the fact that homogeneity is an important factor in grouping students in physical education classes. Accordingly, the first day of a new unit an attempt should be made to identify the level of skill each student brings to the activity. This is the time to administer an achievement test, or for the instructor to evaluate student ability through analysis of performance in the total activity. Whichever technique is used the time devoted to the process should be kept to a minimum.

In small schools, involving one instructor per class period, the job may be accomplished in less than a period. In larger schools, where several instructors teach each hour, the problem is somewhat different. In most situations of this type intelligent use of facilities and space make it necessary for each instructor to handle a different activity. The following situation may serve to illustrate effective administration of tests in the large department: Three instructors are involved in teaching at the same hour. The first day of each unit the instructors combine their sections and administer all three skills tests to the combined classes. At the end of the unit the groups move to a different instructor. Each instructor teaches the same activity for three units of time. Since students have been tested in the three activities the first day there is no need to test during the second and third units. The same procedure is followed during the next block of three units. Thus, valuable additional time is available for instructional purposes.

Achievement test results are used to group students into squads according to their abilities. This sets the stage for effective learning. The good instructor may now develop his daily lesson plans to take full advantage of the small, segregated groups. Progress through the unit is marked by a wise balance of time devoted to drill and practice of fundamentals with groups working separately, and participation in the total activity with groups combined. Student leaders, functioning as teaching assistants have an important role to play in carrying on the unit.

This kind of organization gets results. The unit moves ahead rapidly. Students react well to the fast-moving action and look forward eagerly to the new experiences each unit brings. More significantly, students do have an opportunity to develop sufficient skill in each activity to accomplish the purpose of the core; namely, to become discriminatory in their ability to know the activities they want to pursue further.

The Required Elective Program

The required elective program is that portion of the program designed for the junior and senior classes. Here the students are given an opportunity to receive advanced instruction in those activities they had in the core program in which they were most interested. The idea is to allow students as much freedom as is feasible in selecting activities. Those offered in the required-elective area are carefully chosen by the staff, who keep student interest as a major criterion. To be sure, the carry-over value of an activity is a predominate factor operating in the selection of activities for this portion of the program.

The local character of the setting within which the program operates has a great deal to do with the kind of final program a physical education staff produces. The following important features of the required elective plan may be incorporated in the majority of current secondary school physical education programs:

1. Curriculum planners responsible for setting up the master schedule seek to provide a balance of activities so that each student receives advanced instruction in at least one from each of the areas of activities included in the total program. Most authorities agree that physical education achieves its purposes best when students acquire sufficient skill in several activities, of a carry-over nature, to lead them to be participants all of their lives. A program that permits students to specialize in one or two activities defeats this aim. At the same time, exposure to a great number of activities without enough time devoted to any of them to enable students to develop sufficient skill to bring them enjoyment also fails to achieve desirable results.

2. The time allotment for activities in the required elective program should be of longer duration than when they were taught in the core program. This second experience in an activity is designed to permit the student to achieve a rather high degree of skill in that activity. The number of periods a physical education class meets weekly and other local conditions bear upon the time that can be devoted to teaching each unit. It is recommended that from fifteen to twenty periods, depending upon the nature of the activity in question, be devoted to the unit in this portion of the program. This means that the student in the daily program receives advanced instruction in a minimum of fourteen to sixteen different activities during the two year period.

3. Students should be given an opportunity to choose activities. The degree to which election is possible is shaped by the department's ability to offer a variety of activities in each class period. In that connection it is apparent that the larger the school population the more instructors there are involved in the physical education department and; therefore, the more physical education sections there are available in each class period. It follows, then, that students are given more choice when several instructors are teaching at the same hour. We may again use the example of three instructors teaching different activities during the same class period to illustrate how student interest may be taken into account in sched-

uling. At the beginning of the year a schedule of activities to be taught may be distributed to the students in each class. The student, by a simple check system, rates each activity according to his preference. In making assignments the instructor gives student choice top priority.

Two other important factors must be taken into account. First, one must consider the student's ability in an activity as determined by his record in the core program. Since this upper division program is geared to those who have already developed a measure of skill, it is advisable to eliminate the very meagerly skilled student. Occasionally a student may select an activity in which he has demonstrated poor aptitude. When this occurs it usually is best to direct the student into one of the other two activities in which he has a better chance to keep up with the rest of the group. A second factor that limits the ability of the department to satisfy student choice involves the spread of interest shown by students in a particular class for the activities to be offered in a unit. Obviously, if most of the students choose the same activity, the instructors must, of course, use their judgment in order to equalize the number in each section.

PROGRAM ORGANIZATION IN HIGHER EDUCATION

Many of the finest programs of physical education are found in junior colleges, colleges, and universities. A number of factors combine to make this possible. None is more significant than the fact that collegiate departments of physical education usually are blessed with better and more varied context, better prepared instructors, and smaller classes.

Although there are differences between the programs at the two educational levels, there is much that they share in common. Both programs must be structured with the idea in mind that the student leaves the program for adult community living. This means that both levels seek the same program results. Much of the procedure used in the good college program can, with certain modifications, be used in many high schools. The task of the college department may be judged to be more difficult in certain ways than the situation facing the high school department. In most instances the high school department has four years within which to accomplish its objectives. The college department, with few exceptions, has, at best, four semesters to fulfill its program goals. Then, too, the majority of students who enter college have been exposed to inadequate programs of physical education in high school; therefore, many of them are still in the novice stage. Add to this the fact that the college physical education staff usually must start from scratch regarding knowledge of the physical abilities of the college student, and one begins to appreciate the enormity of the task of college physical education. The organizational plan described here is sound, clearly depicting a college program that recognizes the interests of the student and one which is structured to fit his abilities to perform.

In most collegiate institutions there is some sort of freshman or orientation week. From the standpoint of administration of the physical education program this is a crucial period which must be fully utilized if classes are to function from the opening day of regular classes.

The gymnasium should be open and the staff available to carry out the functions that enable the program to operate fully the opening week of the fall semester. The first part of the week should be utilized to give each student a medical examination; and the staff should provide whatever assistance the health services require to administer the examination. Scheduling of students for their examination requires the coordinated efforts of the physical education department working with the Dean of Students' office.

An opportune time may be found after completion of the medical examination to conduct students, in small groups, on a guided tour through the physical education facilities. This is an excellent time to acquaint new students with the many features associated with the outdoor and indoor playing areas. Staff members should be available to answer any questions that students may have after their tour. This is also the time to issue lockers and explain the locker and showering procedure. The students should then be given the water and land skills classification tests. This entire procedure, properly organized, may be completed in the first two or three days of the week. The remaining free time may be devoted to student advisory work.

The problem of scheduling time for each student to complete his examination, to have an opportunity to see the physical education plant in its entirety, to get his locker, to take his tests, and to receive advisement, requires precise timing and organization. The cooperation of the institution's administrative officers to provide time during the week for physical education activities is of paramount importance.

A glance at the week's activity in terms of sequence finds that the medical examination must be conducted first. Intelligent procedure suggests that subsequent events may be arranged for each student after he concludes his examination. A physical education representative might be the last person the student sees as he completes his examination. This staff member can assign the student a time to take the classification test and arrange a specific time for the student to join a group for a tour of the building. Moreover, this is the best time to issue the bulletin of information which describes the program of physical education. The bulletin should include a brief statement of the philosophy and objectives of the program; procedure necessary to use the facilities; description of policies relating to intramurals, sportclubs, managerial system, and rules governing participation in intercollegiate athletics. In this way a student may find out what physical education and physical recreation opportunities are open to him before he plans his program.

On the last day the alert staff will arrange a full program of recreational activities open to all new students. This is a splendid way to help the new student become acquainted with classmates and to let him know that the department is interested in him. The sooner a student gets the idea that the physical education department is composed of friendly people and that the program has much to offer, the more participation will take place. The informed staff will take full advantage of the opportunities extended to it by this pre-school week, thereby nurturing the good will of the student body from the start. A favorable attitude on the part of the student toward the physical education staff and its program is a determining factor in developing a well-rounded, successful program.

The Basic Required Course

This course is to be taken by the physically fit student who is meagerly skilled in physical education activities. The degree of skill possessed by each new student must be quickly and accurately determined through tests. Students who pass these tests will have demonstrated that they already possess the degree of skill the department desires all students to obtain at the end of their physical education requirement. These students are then placed in the required elective program where they have greater freedom to elect activities of their own choosing, but based upon competencies or weaknesses disclosed by the tests. Students who fail the aquatics skills test are required to take the beginning swimming course; students passing this test are considered to have met the swimming requirement. They may elect to take a more advanced course in swimming if they so desire. Students who fail to pass other skills areas are assigned to the basic required course where these weaknesses can be corrected.

The classification test is not an absolute essential. Many departments do a fine job of grouping students of similar abilities together by offering beginning, intermediate, and advanced classes in the several activities that constitute the program of physical education. Departments following this plan are most successful when they carry on an adequate counseling program whereby the student is guided into taking the courses most suitable to meet his interests and needs, and at the same time, within his capabilities to perform.

The primary concern of the instructor of the basic course must be *to teach skill as quickly and as effectively as possible.* Since only those students who are below average in physical skills are to be in this course, it follows that unless they can be taught a measureable amount of skill in a short time, all the other important values that can be gained through regular participation in physical activity are minimized. Competent physical educators know that when dealing with the novice results must come quickly or the student is apt to become discouraged; therefore, the best possible teaching must be carried out at this stage of the learning process.

At no other level of learning is the challenge as great nor the consequences for failure to get results more unfortunate. The college program is the last chance for the unskilled student to rectify the short-comings of his youth as they apply to performance in physical pursuits. Failure to make noticeable progress at this point usually causes the student to dislike physical activity the rest of his life. If participation in physical activities has value in the lives of adults, and medical evidence is plentiful, it behooves physical educators to lay their greatest stress on teaching skill to the meagerly skilled student.

Content of the Basic Course

Most authorities in the field of physical education agree, that regardless of the specific content which is selected for the basic course, emphasis must be placed on the fundamental skills of movement. It is at this point that sharp disagreement may be noted between professional physical educators. There seems to be two basic points of view as to how these fundamental skills are to be taught. One group believes that emphasis should be placed directly on instruction in the fundamental skills of activity. They would teach these skills in their unadulterated form, divorced from the game activity. Advocates of this view believe that specific instruction in the fundamental skills of movement for one semester will enable the college student to best overcome his major deficiencies; thereby, enabling him to profit more from his subsequent physical education experiences.

The opposing view suggests that college students will get very little out of a course that forces them to practice and drill the fundamental skills in isolation. These leaders believe that such a procedure, bereft of competition in the sport or activity, stifles interest and contributes to boredom on the part of the student. They believe that activities for this course should be selected from those included in the total physical education program; furthermore, that the activities chosen, as a composite, should include the majority of the fundamental skills involved in the activities offered in the total program. Emphasis in this case is placed directly upon the fundamental skills, but as they are found in sports and games. The bulk of class time would be spent on instruction and practice of the fundamentals, with sufficient time devoted to competition in the total activity to insure continued interest on the part of the learner. Advocates of this view suggest that psychologists agree that learning seems to go best when the learner is interested and challenged to learn.

Proponents of this view further point out that since the time element is a limiting factor for the college student—four semesters of physical education required in most institutions—it is unwise to spend one semester in attemping to do an instructional task that should be carried out in secondary school physical education. They reason that it is far better to provide expert instruction in the carry-over type of activity, stressing the fundamentals inherent within the activity.

City Schools of San Diego, California

Dance symposium at Kearny High School, San Diego, California.

Administration of the Basic Required Course

There is no one way to organize and administer the course that is better than all other methods. Various successful plans are in use today. One that perhaps has much to offer, and yet is not widely known follows:

1. Six activities form the basic content for the semester course, although in some instances four may be more suitable. Care must be exercised in selecting the activities so that in their entirety they include the fundamental skills found in most sport activity.

2. Each class should be limited to approximately ninety students, thirty in each of three groups. Three instructors are assigned to each class; each instructor to teach one activity per half semester. One of the instructors serves as the chief instructor in charge of the class. It is his responsibility to conduct meetings and to administer the class.

3. The objectives of the course depend upon local conditions, but of prime importance is the goal to help the student develop those skills which will enable him to gain satisfaction by participating in recreational activities of a physical nature.

4. The first day is devoted to administering an achievement test in the three activities to be offered the first half of the semester. The purpose of the tests is to determine the activities in which the student is below par in skill. The student is not required to take an activity in which he demonstrates proficiency. The idea behind the plan is simply that through testing a student may be placed in an activity in which he needs the most help. If the classification test is valid, most of the students assigned to the basic course are those who are meagerly skilled in motor pursuits. Occasionally the more generously skilled student is in the group. When this occurs he should be rescheduled into the regular program. It is a wise procedure to assign a fourth instructor to the same hour. He is to handle a regular physical education class. It is a simple process to reassign students to him.

5. Instruction in the class centers on the fundamentals inherent within the activity. When a student demonstrates that he has

attained satisfactory skill in an activity he is transferred to one of the other two activities. The shuttling of students from activity to activity is only possible under the kind of flexible organization described here. And, it is only this kind of organization that enables a department to shape its program to provide effectively for the meagerly skilled student. This works equally well for the men's and the women's program.

6. At mid-semester three different activities are started. The first day of the second half again is devoted to administering skills tests. Each student will receive instruction in at least two activities during the semester. The faster learning students may receive instruction in more than two activities. A variation of this plan, used successfully in several institutions, is to allocate three weeks per activity, thereby providing a brief experience for all students in the six activities. The advantage of this plan lies in the fact that the student receives an experience in a variety of activities, therefore giving him greater perception in choosing activity courses during the remaining three semesters of the requirement. Still another variety of the plan, one that perhaps is more effective than the others, involves teaching each activity approximately four and a half weeks. Thus, in a semester each student receives instruction in 4 activities, 2 each half semester. This plan, although not exposing the student to as many activities as the one mentioned above, does provide for enough time to permit real learning.

7. A student may complete the course and transfer to the required elective program by demonstrating satisfactory skill in all six activities. Whenever this occurs, the student is immediately transferred to the fourth instructor mentioned in 4, above. Administratively, if the student is transferred to an elective course during the semester, he will still be enrolled in the basic course. This prevents objections from the registrar's office.

8. In unusual cases, when in the judgment of the several instructors a student may gain greater benefits in other areas of the total program, skills in the various activities may be waived.

9. It seems appropriate to include a final, written examination at the end of the semester. Each student should be responsible for the material covering the activities in which he has participated during the semester.

10. The chief instructor will assign final grades after consulting the other instructors who have taught the various students during the semester.

This chapter has provided you with a brief introduction to the physical education method and some techniques for organization and administration. Later courses will help you to better understand how adaptations can be made in small and large schools, or when confronted with very limited facilities and staff.

Selected References

Bucher, Charles A., *Administration of School Health and Physical Education Programs,* St. Louis: C. V. Mosby Company, 1958, Chapters 15 and 16.

————, *Foundations of Physical Education,* St. Louis: C. V. Mosby Company, 1960, Chapter 9.

Teachers Guide to Physical Education for Girls in High School, Sacramento: California State Department of Education, 1957, Chapters 2 and 10.

Physical Fitness Through Physical Education for California Secondary School Boys, Sacramento: California State Department of Education, 1953; Chapter 2, pp. 31-34.

Cowell, Charles C. and Helen W. Hazelton, *Curriculum Designs in Physical Education,* Englewood Cliffs, N. J.: Prentice-Hall, Inc., 1955, Chapters 16 and 17.

Johnson, Granville B., *et al., Your Career in Physical Education,* New York: Harper & Brothers, 1957; Chapter 7.

Kozman, Hilda C., *et al., Methods in Physical Education,* Philadelphia: W. B. Saunders Company, 1958, Chapters 9-16.

Nixon, John E. and Florence S. Frederickson, *An Introduction to Physical Education,* Philadelphia: W. B. Saunders Company, 1959, Chapter 12.

Oberteuffer, Delbert, *Physical Education,* New York: Harper & Brothers, 1956, Chapters 8 and 9.

————, *School Health Education,* New York: Harper & Brothers, 1960, Chapter 17.

Williams, Jesse Feiring, *The Principles of Physical Education,* Philadelphia: W. B. Saunders Company, 1959, Chapter 9.

Individual
Physical
Education

A dwarf is small, even if he stands on a mountain; a colossus keeps his height, even if he stands in a well.

Seneca

12

The aim of school physical education is to involve 100 percent of the student body in the program. Participation falls considerably short of this goal in most schools. For one reason or another a number of students seek, and get, exemption from the program. Nixon[1] lists the following types of students who seek exemption from physical education:

(1) those suffering from physical defects or organic weakness; (2) those who have developed an antipathy toward normal play activities of youth; (3) those suffering from maladjustments of personality which mitigate against normal social relations with other persons; (4) those whose training in the fundamental skills has been so neglected that they are highly self-conscious about ex-

[1] John E. Nixon and Florence Stumpf Frederickson, *An Introduction To Physical Education* (Philadelphia: W. B. Saunders Co., 1959), p. 287.

169

posing their awkwardness before normally developed individuals; (5) those whose vocational duties involve great amounts of physical activity, . . . ; (6) those who elect certain school activities such as military training, driver training, girls drill team, and varsity athletics.

The physical education staff which seeks to involve the entire student body in its program must individualize its approach to meet the needs of students who fall within the above categories. Although students in well conducted physical education classes receive individualized attention there are a number of students who need more attention than they can be given in regular classes. For this reason specialized physical education is essential to make any program complete. Since the area is characterized by individualization of program, the term individual physical education seems to describe the area better than some of the other terms in current use.

Evaluation of physical education in most schools reveals that no phase of the entire program is more neglected and misused than the program for the atypical student. The picture is not overdrawn. The majority of departments simply do not attempt to develop programs to take care of handicapped students. To be sure, a number of departments do feature special programs for these students. A small percentage of these departments are doing a good job. However, many of them limit their efforts to postural work and remedial exercises. They therefore, fail to touch large numbers of students who need individual physical education. Furthermore, many departments administering remedial exercises lack proper medical supervision. Under such circumstances it is not surprising to discover that a number of students are assigned to the special program who cannot profit from remedial exercises. To make matters worse, there are always a few students who may receive serious damage from promiscuously administered exercises.

At this point one might well wonder what is best for a department to do regarding those students who could profit from properly administered remedial exercises. Should these students forfeit their physical education? If not, what other experiences should be provided for them? In seeking answers to questions like these a staff is guided by the fact that physical education is committed to a policy of providing a program for all students. Once this fact is established there is no question as to the departmental responsibility for finding a place for these students in the program. Unfortunately, acceptance of this view does not mean that it is a simple matter to involve the handicapped student properly. Far too many programs, as currently organized and conducted, are too narrow in scope and lack the program characteristics necessary to provide meaningful physical education for the physically handicapped student.

A department has definite responsibility to develop a program to accommodate the student who has a remedial defect which may be helped or corrected by physical activity. It must be emphasized that no attempt should be made to develop a remedial program for the structurally atypical student without the close cooperation of a health service department capable of assisting in the prescription of proper exercises and activities. Physical education departments which permit such programs to be carried on without the specific guidance of qualified medical authorities, even when they have staff members who have specialized in the area, might do more damage than good. Until such time comes when the above conditions are met, these departments would be on far safer ground if they confined their efforts to that of promoting a sound adaptive sports program. In such a program, by careful planning and close supervision, the physically handicapped student may pursue a program of activities within his capabilities, one that will develop his interests in physical activity and enable him to gain the same kinds of experiences provided the normal student.

Recognition that all students who need more instructor attention than they can get in regular physical education classes immediately suggests that a number of students, in addition to the physically handicapped, require individual physical education. Common sense suggests that many students who fall within the categories previously listed would profit by physical education individualized to meet their needs.

To assist the physical education staff in developing a sound individual physical education program, these guiding principles are pertinent: (1) students unable to participate in the normal program with profit, regardless of the reason, should be assigned to individual physical education; (2) the program for the student assigned to individual physical education is initiated by a conference between the student and special instructor and through guidance an honest attempt is made to establish the kind of physical education most suitable to the student's condition, capacity, and interest; (3) the activities thus taught should be as nearly like the regular program as is possible; and, (4) individual physical education classes should take place during the same periods as regular classes so that students may be transferred back and forth between the two programs according to their changing needs.

Program Essentials

Application of the above principles to current physical education programs suggests that many, in their present form, are not prepared to include many students who need individual physical education. Among the many features of a good program of physical education two distinguishing characteristics stand out as prerequisite to the establishment of individual physical education. They are: (1) a broad program of activities, arranged so that progression from beginning levels to higher levels of skill is possible; and, (2) adequate staff to develop individualized physical education.

A varied program, including a number of recreational type activities is of utmost importance in providing the kind of setting within which individual physical education may flourish. Not many atypical students will fit into a program involving a few activities, repeated over and over again, especially when most of the activities are of a team sport nature. A balanced and full program of physical education is likely to meet the interests, needs, and abilities of most handicapped students.

Work in the area of individual physical education necessarily involves considerable time with individual students. The teacher-pupil ratio must be small enough to provide this time. In large schools, with several instructors, it is appropriate to assign one to be in charge of this phase. This person should have special training to prepare him to develop and conduct the program; however, any well trained, interested staff member may do a good job. In smaller departments instructors may be assigned part of their teaching responsibilities for this purpose.

Scheduling

There are several channels through which a student may be selected to participate in individual physical education. They are: (1) students who fail the medical examination; (2) students returning to school after illness; and, (3) students originally assigned to regular physical education classes who have been sent to the program for a variety of reasons.

Perhaps the bulk of the students who will compose the program are discovered by the thorough medical examination all students should have when they enter the secondary school. All students discovered with handicapping defects which require modification of the kind and amount of activity should be assigned to the program. The instructor in charge should work very closely with the health services staff in planning the physical education experiences for these students. Since each student must be treated individually in terms of his specific defect, it follows that the physician's role is defined in terms of authorizing the degree and kind of activity in which the student may participate. It remains for individual conference between the student and instructor to establish mutually selected plans for the student's specific assignments in physical education within the limits established by the physician. In fact, this conference initiates the student's program of physical education.

The degree of success experienced with the physically handicapped student depends largely upon his degree of motivation to want to improve his condition. The instructor in charge should be skillful in counseling to be effective in guiding the student in formulating meaningful objectives. Care must be taken to help the student select realistic goals obtainable through hard work. Unrealistic goals lead to discouragement and the student is not as likely to carry out his corrective assignments. When this occurs, progress to normalcy becomes uncertain and the program fails to accomplish its purpose.

A second way students may be assigned to the program of individual physical education is through assignment by health services following their return to school after illness or operation. Many such students are not yet ready to carry on a full program; accordingly, they require individual assignment to physical education in keeping with their physical condition. It would be extremely unwise to permit students who have been out of school for any length of time to return directly to their regular physical education classes. For this reason, it is recommended that they be required to report first to the health service. The health service may, in turn, send those students requiring a temporarily modified program to the instructor in charge of individual physical education. Before these students may rejoin their regular classes they must be cleared by the health service.

The physical education department that utilizes this kind of flexible organization offers concrete evidence that it believes in individualizing its program to meet the needs of students. Another advantage of this kind of arrangement, not to be overlooked, is that it establishes a close working relationship between the individual physical education class and the regular class. The constant flow of normal students into individual physical education classes brings the atypical student into direct contact with physically normal students. This tends to create a setting within which the handicapped student participates with other students in a positive, healthy manner. At the very least it avoids labeling the individual physical education class as undesirably different, as other methods of organization sometimes do. For instance, whenever the handicapped student is completely segregated from the normal student in physical education there is always the danger that the program may actually reinforce the adverse conditions faced by the student in his out of school environment. The modern physical education program should be developed with care so that the handicapped student is encouraged to live in harmony within a world of physically normal people.

The third channel through which students find their way into the individual physical education program is by reassignment from regular physical education classes. The instructor of a regular class may transfer students to the individual physical class who fail to adapt themselves to the other students. A variety of reasons may lead to such transfers. For example, a student may become a disciplinary problem, and, if permitted to continue in his class may be a constant source of trouble, thereby disrupting the learning situation for the other students. Rather than permit the class to suffer it may be necessary to remove the trouble maker and attempt to determine why he does not adjust to the group. Since the person in charge of individual physical education is skilled in guidance, it is sensible to give him an opportunity to ferret out the difficulty. Another example of the kind of student who may profit from individual physical education is the sub-par student in skills. On occasion an instructor will find a student who is so poorly coordinated that participation in physical education classes with normally skilled students is a constant source of embarrassment. From the standpoint of ability to take part in physical education such a student is handicapped. It is obvious that this student needs an individualized physical education, structured to his sub-par performance level. Failure to treat the meagerly skilled student individually is tantamount to making physical education a setting for very negative results. The student's physical education becomes a continuation of frustrating experiences, adding to the chain of similar experiences he may be meeting throughout his day. At the very least, physical education is a great waste of time for him, not to mention the disrupting influence his presence may have on the learning atmosphere for the others in the class. At worse, physical education could reinforce the circumstances which are at work to cause serious personality damage.

INDIVIDUAL PHYSICAL EDUCATION IN OPERATION

The Conference

The student's entrance into the individual physical education program is initiated by a conference with the instructor who serves as coordinator. It is logical to assume that most of the students assigned to the program at the beginning of the school year are those with limiting defects detected by the medical examination. For these students the initial conference takes time, perhaps 15 minutes or more per student; accordingly, active participation in the program may be delayed several class meetings. Students reassigned from regular classes as the semester proceeds also enter the program via the conference. For many of these students the conference requires no more time than is necessary to assign them to a group already functioning. In other words, the initial conference for many students who are temporarily assigned to individual physical education may be brief, simply functioning as a reassignment vehicle.

The purpose of the initial conference is twofold: (1) to establish a program for the student in line with his abilities to participate; and, (2) to create a desire on the part of the student to participate in the program.

The degree of success achieved in the conference depends a great deal upon the personal qualities of the instructor. In all contacts with these students the instructor, functioning as a counselor, should be himself, but should not impose himself. He should be genuine and sincere. He is likely to fail if he attempts to play a role that is not natural to him. He must vary his approach according to the manner of the student to be counseled, but he should not assume a role foreign to his own nature. By being oneself the teacher functions as a relaxed counselor and is more likely to establish a friendly, pleasant atmosphere, so necessary if the conference is to accomplish its purpose.

Perhaps the most distinguishing characteristic of the successful counselor is that he genuinely likes his students, and takes an interest in them personally. Such a counselor will be respected and appreciated by his counselees. When problems develop they will be more apt to seek him out for assistance. When this occurs the guidance process is effective.

Securing satisfactory results at the initial conference, even under the best of circumstances, is not always possible. Much of the difficulty lies in the ability to communicate with the student. That is, the instructor is attempting to sell physical activity to the student who may not be interested in buying. As one might suspect, a goodly number of students who qualify for individual physical education possess limited skills in physical activity. These students are often reluctant to take part in a program calling for participation in activities they have avoided in the past. Success in launching many of these students into a meaningful program of physical education requires considerable skill and diplomacy on the part of the instructor in this initial conference. It is necessary on occasion to devote several conference periods before an interest may be discovered or developed. The adviser cannot take a passive role; an attempt should be made to find out what is interesting to the student, and use that to proceed. The counselor must be prepared to organize and create physical education interests within the student's potentiality and range.

To achieve these ends the instructor need not be overly alarmed at what is sometimes called imposition. Most handicapped students have had meager experiences in activities of a physical nature; accordingly, they do not know what kind of activities would be appealing. This does not mean that the adviser should force certain activities, but it does mean that he must often assume the lead in selecting a course sequence that is appealing and attractive to the student. Guided by the results the student made in the medical examination and the analysis of his present abilities in motor skills as determined by tests, the instructor, functioning as a counselor, is in a good position to launch the student's physical education program on a positive basis.

Class Organization

The idea that atypical students, with their great variety of needs, may be assigned together in a class which operates as a unit is far from the truth. Indeed, consideration of the vast differences existing among these students readily reveals the impossibility of such an arrangement. One would be hard pressed to visualize effective physical education flowing from a class situation involving a number of different types of physically handicapped students, such as normal students possessing meager skills in physical activity, students forced to follow a modified program for a time due to illness, problem students, and the wide array of disabilities of a physical nature. It would seem much more reasonable to picture the individual physical education class closely interrelated with the regular physical education class. The core program, described in Chapter 11, is ideally organized to absorb many students from individual physical education classes. All that is required to permit moving students into phases of the regular program is to have the individual physical education class scheduled at the same time as the core classes. To be sure, the instructional class program must be carefully planned to permit the flexibility necessary to transfer students to different sections. The core program concept of organization enables this process to be accomplished without disrupting the work of the several instructors involved.

It is reasonable to assume that in most instances a number of students assigned to an individual physical education class may, from time to time, participate successfully in core classes. When such situations occur it is a simple matter to transfer students from the individual physical education class to appropriate core sections. As soon as the unit is finished and a new unit is to begin these students are returned to their individual physical education class.

The following program organization may serve to illustrate the kind of flexible organization required to permit the sound interchange of students between the individual physical education class and the core classes.

The Setting: Four instructors teaching the same class hour; instructor A teaching a unit of volleyball, instructor B, golf, instructor C, badminton, and instructor D, the individual physical education class. Instructor D has 18 students, involving these defects: 6 postural deviates, 3 heart cases, 1 mild cerebral palsy, 2 crippled, 1 post-operative, 2 students recently returned to school from illness, 1 problem student, and 2 meagerly skilled students.

Procedure: Instructor D, knowing the abilities and limitations of his students, assigns 7 students to the core as follows: 3 postural deviates and the problem student are assigned to instructor A; 2 heart cases are sent to instructor B, and 1 meagerly skilled student is assigned to instructor C. Instructor D is left with 11 students. He organizes a unit of activity as follows: The remaining heart case, the post-operative student, and the 2 students temporarily assigned to him participate in shuffleboard. These students are limited to very mild activity. The remaining 7 students are taught a unit of archery.

At the conclusion of the unit the 18 students return to instructor D. The same procedure is followed as the classes move into a new unit. The basic philosophy operating here is that whenever a student in an individual physical education class may participate successfully in an activity with normal students he is transferred to that group. When the normal class moves to another activity, determined to be outside the capabilities of the student, he is returned to the individual physical education class.

Selected References

Bucher, Charles A., *Administration of School Health and Physical Education Programs*, St. Louis: C. V. Mosby Company, 1958, Chapter 17.

Daniels, Arthur S., *Adapted Physical Education*, New York: Harper & Brothers, 1954.

Fischer, J. A., "Evaluation of the Adapted Phase of the Basic Instruction Program," *64th Proceedings CPEA*, 1961, pp. 75-77.

Fischer, J. A., "Social and Psychological Adjustment Problems of the Handicapped," *61st Proceedings CPEA*, 1958, pp. 211-213.

Hooley, Agnes M., "We Can Serve the Student with Disabilities," *JOHPER* (March, 1959), pp. 45-47 and 62.

Irwin, Leslie W., *The Curriculum in Health and Physical Education*, St. Louis: C. V. Mosby Company, 1951, Chapters 14 and 15.

Newberg, Sam, "Adapting the Physical Education Program to the Atypical," *63rd Proceedings CPEA*, 1960, pp. 116-119.

Oberteuffer, Delbert, *School Health Education*, New York: Harper & Brothers, 1960, Chapters 11 and 14.

Scott, Thomas M., "Organization and Administration of Adapted Physical Education," *61st Proceedings CPEA*, 1958, pp. 211-213.

Stafford, George T., *Sports for the Handicapped*, Englewood Cliffs, N. J.: Prentice-Hall, Inc., 1947.

City Schools of Long Beach, California

Intramurals
and
School
Recreation

No student should be deprived of his or her opportunity for participation in a great variety of recreational experiences which may contribute more than we know to a long and happy and normal life.

Louis E. Means

13

Your opportunities and responsibilities for leadership in physical education extend far beyond the class instructional program. Indeed, instruction is incomplete and lacks full meaning unless students are provided with laboratory experiences in the great variety of activities and sports which make up the content of physical education.

The total program starts with a sound and carefully conceived curriculum of physical activities progressively arranged from grade to grade through which unique educational outcomes are possible. From this basic core of instruction the program structure is built to include sports and recreational opportunities for all boys and girls. If you believe in the value of sports participation here will be the chance to prove your foundation of faith; if sports are valuable for the varsity athlete they are just as good for the major portion of the student body. This is the great American dream of democracy in sports; rarely attained by most leaders to date. The broad intramural program, accentuated by extramural experiences with students of nearby schools, and appropriate inter-school sports for the highly skilled at the secondary school level, all provide the vehicle through which this objective can be accomplished. An omission of any of these ingredients provides only a partial program, and deprives students of experiences that should be available.

The school recreation program should be a flowering and an outgrowth of the instructional program, whether it be in reading, the arts, dramatics, music, creative expression, social or physical recreation. The physical educator need not be an expert in all forms of recreation but he or she should be well equipped to handle all matters pertaining to physical recreation. The physical educator has responsibilities for providing opportunities for physical recreation not only in the school but also in the community, for education does not stop at the school bell's ringing. It continues without interruption for each individual throughout his life. *Education for living* takes on real meaning, erasing old concepts of *education for making a living.*

Few other areas of education offer so many chances for imaginative leadership as does physical education. Here you are placed in a setting of appropriate facilities, given all or most of the youth of the area, and with equipment and training which should enable you to reach the hearts and desires of all students with a program that meets needs and interests. Working to accomplish these ends is your primary function.

Given proper skills instruction and some motivation and minimum attention, most youth will find ways to participate in various features of the intramural program—a voluntary adjunct to required instruction. Here the emphasis is placed on pleasurable activity. Ways are found to secure for each youth his or her level of skill. Situations are provided for many winning and losing experiences, and for a feeling of belonging and occasional leadership. Students who, because of limited skill, physical attributes, or outside work or home requirements, cannot become members of interscholastic squads and teams can find in the broad intramural program frequent opportunities for expression and enjoyment.

DEFINITION OF TERMS

A simple definition of terms used in this connection might help you to better understand your leadership role beyond class responsibility. Intramurals, as a purely American term, has come to mean the total program of voluntary sports and activities organized within a school for the students and faculty of that school. Various events might be planned for boys and girls, either separately or together. It might include all types of activities from the sedentary to the very active. Usually, it includes activities of a physical nature, although some programs have grown to include all the voluntary opportunities of a recreational nature on or off the school grounds. It may include organized and unorganized features; competitive or merely socio-recreational.

Extramurals, as distinguished from interschool athletics, is an extension of the intramural program which involves numbers of students and teams from one school in participation with similar groups from one or more other schools. Here the emphasis is still on mass participation, but the flavor of participation and some competition with others is added without the usual characteristics of coaching—long practice sessions, high skill development, lengthy schedules of games, and eligibility found in interscholastic athletics. Winning individuals or teams from the intramural program might be used, or other methods of mixing and selecting players could be utilized. Extramurals are considered to be an outgrowth of the school intramural program culminating in brief experiences of similar nature with other schools in one form or another. This might take the form of play days or sports days, or many other kinds of features.

School recreation is a much more recent term which includes all opportunities provided for students and faculty of a recreational nature, usually limited to the school population. This could be more inclusive than physical recreation, also involving reading, the arts and dramatics, music, and social recreation. Activities could be conducted on campus, or anywhere the school family could be accommodated on appropriate or needed facilities.

School connected recreation is a broader term suggesting that the school or school district may be the administering agency for the operation of school-community recreation, either solely or in cooperation with other governmental jurisdictions. In all of these situations the physical educator should play an important and central role. No recreation program can attain its optimal objectives without proper attention to physical recreation. Your professional preparation should include sufficient theory and practice to enable you to become a leader in this field. This means that your leadership should be manifested in instruction and in many forms of extra-class program development. This does not mean that you as an individual must teach classes all or most of each day and then personally direct many other programs to completely meet the needs of all students. You must remember that you are preparing for a career which has many facets and many leadership responsibilities. You may teach a limited number of classes and have responsibility in addition for other extraclass activities. You may become a department head, responsible for all phases of the total program. You must know enough about these total responsibilities in order to see that they are provided. You may pass through the entire leadership gamut yourself. Indeed, it would be well for you to have these experiences as early as possible.

HISTORICAL BACKGROUND OF INTRAMURALS

Early American physical education was a transplanted European heritage, heavily centered about formal method. Prior to the twentieth century youth had chores and duties at home which absorbed all nonschool daylight hours. There was little time for recreation and not as much need for activities which contributed directly toward the elements of physical fitness. Each generation has found itself in a more highly automized society, with shorter work week and more time for leisure. Late in the nineteenth century we began to borrow outright the British idea of sports. Formalized exercise and gymnastics found a rival for emphasis. It was then some time before a truly American concept of sports began to emerge. These evolutions clearly reflected the character and temper of the struggling new democratic nation.

There is ample evidence that boys participated in various sports in our early American schools in spite of hostile teachers and the Puritan philosophy of the sinfulness and foolishness of play. Students began to organize their own activities in the midst of faculty indifference. To be sure this early effort by students was haphazard and lacked direction. Actually, most student organized effort was confined to colleges, and younger youth had little opportunity of this nature. Sports clubs in colleges soon began to seek competition with similar groups in other institutions, and out of this movement came our system of interschool athletics, so highly organized today. Self-organization was gradually superseded by supervised and school administered programs. It did not take long for secondary schools, and finally elementary schools, to emulate the college pattern and to develop programs of intramural sports as part of the physical education program.

The period of student control was strongest between 1900 and 1914. College athletic departments soon found the growing "youngster" of intramurals in their family to be unwieldy and in need of better organization. Full fledged intramural departments began to take over active management on many campuses starting about 1914.

Two forces shaped the nature of intramurals in those early days. First, and foremost, was the varsity athletic influence which too often prostituted intramurals for the sake of discovery of more varsity material. Second, the influence of a few large city recreation departments began to broaden the concept of recreation in intramurals, and succeeded in leaving an impact upon mass participation rather than selectiveness.

During World Wars I and II temporary setbacks in progress were noted, followed by an acceleration of intramurals in the schools. Young men returning from the service brought back a desire to provide greater sports opportunity to youth which had been freshened by their military experience. Women leaders throughout the past half century have steadily developed a sound and functional philosophy of intramural programming, usually unhampered by the stress and demands of the interschool competitive program for boys. Most institutions of higher education are now giving more attention to the significance of intramurals in the total program, and requiring majors to take courses in this area of leadership, share in the management and officiating of such contests, and to learn of its values through intensified self-participation on campus.

Other factors have influenced the growth of intramurals in our schools. The depression period of the 1930's left a profound influence, bringing a new emphasis on recreation and the wise use of leisure time, and on sports which could be used throughout life. New governmental support and leadership brought program emphasis and new facilities for schools and many youth related agencies. Many war memorials also took the form of sports buildings and community centers. More recent trends to attract Americans to the great outdoors for healthful recreation as an antidote to crowded urban living and metropolitan congestion are producing splendid opportunities for youth and adults to do interesting things in the mountains, in the desert, at the waterfront, in the forests, and elsewhere. These outdoor education-recreation activities are rapidly becoming a part of the physical education program through instruction, intramurals and school recreation.

This latter development cannot be passed over lightly or too briefly. Never before in the history of this nation has the character of its people and their way of life been more quickly changed and reshaped. Recent urbanization of unprecedented dimension, the effects of industrial change, a shortening work week, and an almost universal desire to enjoy recreational activities, particularly in the outdoor environment, all exert influence on better programs of skill instruction and school recreation. Old patterns of physical education curriculum content need to be revised in light of these developments. Certainly school recreation must reflect them. Modern education must prepare citizens for increased and creative leisure, regardless of the degree of emphasis on the intellect, the sciences and technology, and basic academic ideology. Intramurals and school recreation can move forward to meet this challenge with a feeling of confidence and service not possible a few years ago. No longer should intramurals be used for the identification of future varsity material for the coach. They are an integral part of the educational scheme and must receive increasing attention.

PHILOSOPHY AND OBJECTIVES OF INTRAMURALS

It would be well to take a brief but specific look at some of the reasons why intramurals are important, and a necessary part of the responsibilities of the physical educator. Authorities differ somewhat on the exact objectives, but the similarity of underlying philosophies predominate all. Intramurals are important, and an indispensable part of the total physical education program because:

1. They help tremendously in developing physical and mental health and efficiency;

2. They provide the laboratory for the practice of recreational skills learned in the instructional setting;

3. They prepare the individual for a lifetime of recreational competency by providing many in-school experiences of similar nature;

4. They help students to grow socially, to develop greater group cooperation, and to assist in creating lasting friendships;

5. They provide additional opportunities to acquire bodily coordination and prowess, and the perpetuation of skills that can be valuable throughout life;

6. They help identify outstanding performers who might find further expression for their skills and interests in the interschool sports program;

7. They provide a needed incentive for continuing participation which might otherwise be lacking;

8. They provide opportunities for youth to *belong,* to want to be recognized, to multiply the chances for many successes and some disappointments in a desirable setting, and to find new opportunities for recognition.

It can be seen from the above that one of your great challenges as a physical educator lies in the field of intramurals and school physical recreation. You must prepare for this leadership role. A theoretical knowledge that these things are important is not enough. You should get as much experience as possible as a participant *on campus* and as a leader in the program. You must also include in your professional preparation all possible information about methods of organization and administration of such a program. You should visit and study the programs in operation in schools of your area to see how well they exploit the program. You will discover that some have not yet fully developed a program—and you can easily recognize your opportunity for on the job leadership when the time arrives after graduation.

SCOPE AND POTENTIAL

Individual imagination and ingenuity are the only limitations to broad planning and operation of intramurals. This is true even with limited facilities and staff. Your challenge will be to try to reach every boy and girl as often as possible with a variety of sports and activities. This cannot be done with anything less than enthusiasm and real effort. Affording this phase of physical education second or third class citizenship will achieve little. A good program can be developed regardless of teaching or coaching assignments you may have.

The secret for successful operation lies in your ability to plan for the use of every possible facility at every hour the plant is not in use for class instruction. This will mean planning to balance the use of facilities for intramural and interschool activities. It will mean the use of facilities when varsity teams are away, on week ends, at night, on holidays, during noon hours, during activity periods, and at odd times. It will mean the use of nonschool facilities for some events such as commercially operated bowling alleys, golf courses, shooting ranges, regional and mountain areas, riding stables, and the like.

Can you operate this type of program alone? The answer is obvious. The secret of your success will depend upon the way you gradually build a staff within and without the faculty; the way you involve local citizens who have special skills and could assist; the way you budget your time; and the devotion you have to your broad leadership role and responsibilities. It will be easy to make excuses for an inadequate program based upon problems relating to bus transportation of students, lack of sufficient noon hour time, limitations of the physical plant, lack of staff, your own apparent overload of schedule, lack of funds, and many others. All or some of these problems do plague program development, but the enterprising leader will find ways to solve each one satisfactorily. Why not talk with local school leaders to see how they solved these problems? In doing this you may in your own mind see solutions to some of their problems they have failed to solve, or have tried to avoid.

The good program will include many opportunities for participation in the team sports, and in individual and dual sports. It will not necessarily be bound by traditional sports seasons or local sports preferences. Such a program will include coeducational activities, student-faculty mixed events, organized and unorganized features, outing activities, student administered program segments, and some opportunities for extramural sports.

The schools have most of the capital outlay facilities for recreation in most communities; they have most of the community's youth a good part of the time; and they will have you and others who have professional preparation and vision. Complete utilization of these resources will depend upon several conditions. Maximum efficiency and economy will not prevail at the community level unless careful thought is given to this problem. It has been satisfactorily solved in many places by leaders with courage and vision. Other communities hope they will have this kind of leadership in the years ahead. You will undoubtedly be a part of community thinking and planning on matters related to recreation. You and the schools should play an important role.

PRACTICAL PROBLEMS OF OPERATION AND ADMINISTRATION

It may be that the scope and outline of such a program as described herein causes some confusion in your thinking. You may wonder if a broad program is feasible or practical. You may doubt whether it could be carried out successfully. Rest assured that it can and should be done.

A school, a city, a state, or a nation is not built in a day. Such is the case with the development of a broad and sound physical education program. One must set immediate and long range goals. Each month, each semester, and each year should see certain planned accomplishments toward the desired objective. This is true with the steps that may be necessary to secure adequate facilities. It is true as you move ahead to build a faculty and student staff capable of handling this diversity of activities. It is true as you start out from scratch with your first intramural events, gradually adding and planning for the future. Remember, increased facilities and staff are rarely provided until you have actually demonstrated their need through a program in action which makes existing staff and facilities clearly inadequate.

Also, remember this point. It is doubtful whether a school administrator, a school board, a group of parents, or the citizens and tax payers of any community really exist that would not welcome this type of program and gradually assume a support relationship after adequate demonstration has taken place. Hundreds of actual examples of this truism could be cited.

As your program grows, you will involve faculty members who have certain skills and recreational interests of their own. You will build a student staff of leaders who are eager to assist under proper conditions. You will utilize every possible bit of facilities. Your mass of students, now aware that you care for their welfare,

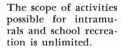

The scope of activities possible for intramurals and school recreation is unlimited.

become your most ardent supporters, thereby gathering parental support as you move ahead. This is an area of great leadership opportunity for you. Indeed, your future professional growth and advancement may be closely tied to the way you approach your opportunities through well planned and directed class instruction and the extra class program of physical recreation and athletics.

THE EXTRAMURAL PROGRAM

Extramural athletics might be defined simply as the expansion of the intramural concept between schools without the complex problems that necessarily characterize interscholastic sport. Herein exists a splendid medium for greater expansion of competitive values to large sections of the student body not usually proficient enough to make the varsity teams. It also permits inclusion of many sports and activities not usually found in the varsity program such as archery, bowling, volleyball, badminton, softball, shooting, table tennis, and others. Boys lacking in size and maturity of the athlete may achieve some of the values we claim for outside competition. Extramurals offer one of the finest mediums for the objective of democracy in sports.

Extramurals are most practical where schools are clustered close together and travel is at a minimum. Long schedules are eliminated. Extramurals offer an excellent experience for junior high school youth; and indeed at all grade levels. Cities having two or more junior high schools would do well to expand their intramurals into a workable extramural program. Extramurals should never replace the broader intramural program, but should provide a final enrichment opportunity following many of the intramural events.

The problem of awards and team uniforms need not embarrass the extramural program. These games are played solely for the fun and enjoyment of the participants, with no undue premium placed on victory. Great loyalties can be developed through such a program, since students have ample proof that the director and his staff are vitally interested in all the students and not just the varsity star. These events can be staged without great preparation, without admission charge, and attended by favorable public opinion. No coaching time is required.

Extramurals are not suggested as a substitute for a broad and comprehensive varsity program in secondary schools and colleges. This should always stand at the peak of the competitive pyramid.

A CHALLENGE TO LEADERSHIP

You have now seen some of the possibilities for leadership beyond the teaching of classes. Once again you must decide whether the profession fits your interests and provides sufficient challenge.

That intramurals and school recreation have become an integral part of the education scheme can no longer be doubted. Some educators, many of them former athletic coaches, go so far as to suggest that interschool athletics be greatly curbed or eliminated, and that intramurals be substituted to enable all students to receive equal attention. The modern program should include able administration of both phases of activity. The intramural program should activate and attract the entire student body and faculty. Interschool athletics should form the peak of skill and specialization, crystalizing school spirit wisely, but with neither intramural or interschool sports dominating the other in any way. Both should be accorded the best of staff time and attention; both should have ample budgets to sustain adequate design. Both should be accorded first class citizenship. The central emphasis of the future may well be a program for the maximum welfare of the entire student body and the education family.

This can be your great opportunity for a career rich in service. Leadership for such a program will be very rewarding. You will help administer a program which has real appeal because it lacks exclusiveness; it is true democracy in action. As you conduct and enlarge such a program you will be amazed to find that your interschool teams become stronger, your material more abundant, student and faculty morale and support more sustained and enthusiastic. If you also coach, and the formula for winning seems temporarily lost, the degree of effectiveness of your total program will sustain you and carry over any temporary periods of uncertainty.

You will not have made the mistake of "putting all of your eggs in one basket." You will have been wise enough to build a program with educational significance which meets the test of time and critical evaluation.

Your authors firmly believe that every effort you make toward this kind of program development will yield rich dividends in personal happiness and satisfaction, job security and respect, and will help pave the way to professional growth and advancement.

Selected References

Allen, Catherine, "Creativity in Recreation," *JOHPER* (May/June, 1961), pp. 18-20.

AMA Committee on Aging, "Education of Children and Youth for the New Era of Aging," *JOHPER* (March, 1962), pp. 24-26 and 76.

Bucher, Charles A., *Administration of School Health and Physical Education Programs,* St. Louis: C. V. Mosby Company, 1958, Chapters 18, 20, and 21.

Teachers Guide to Physical Education for Girls in High School, Sacramento: California State Department of Education, 1957, Chapter 11.

Physical Fitness Through Physical Education for California Secondary School Boys, Sacramento: California State Department of Education, 1953, Chapter 3, pp. 23-31.

Cowell, Charles C. and Helen W. Hazelton, *Curriculum Designs in Physical Education,* Englewood Cliffs, N. J.: Prentice-Hall, Inc., 1955, Chapter 19.

Hutchinson, John L., *et al., Leisure and the Schools,* Washington, D. C.: AAHPER, 1961.

Irwin, Leslie W., *The Curriculum in Health and Physical Education,* St. Louis: C. V. Mosby Company, 1951, Chapters 12 and 13.

Kozman, Hilda C., *et al., Methods in Physical Education,* Philadelphia: W. B. Saunders Company, 1958, Chapters 16 and 17.

Means, Louis E., *Intramurals: Their Organization and Administration,* Englewood Cliffs, Prentice-Hall, Inc., 1963.

Merkley, John and Ted E. Gorden, "A Successful Summer Junior High School Playground Program," *JOHPER* (February, 1961), p. 22.

Morland, Richard B., "On Building an Intramural Point System," *63rd Proceedings CPEA*, 1960, pp. 139-143.

Mueller, Pat and Elmer Mitchell, *Intramural Sports*, New York: The Ronald Press Co., 1960.

Scott, Harry A., *Competitive Sports in Schools and Colleges*, New York: Harper & Brothers, 1951, Chapter 11.

Vendien, Lynn, "Are You Teaching Leisure-Time Skills?" *JOHPER* (November, 1960), pp. 40-42 and 78.

Vannier, Maryhelen and Hollis F. Fait, *Teaching Physical Education in Secondary Schools*, Philadelphia: W. B. Saunders Company, 1957, Chapters 18, 20, 21, and 22.

Coach Healey at New York University.
Courtesy of David Merkowitz

Interscholastic
Athletics

The first need is a nationwide understanding of the necessity for clean, wholesome recreation that comes from participation in athletics. A youthful participant need not be an expert or a champion. Thus, there is need to provide the facilities and a program. Participation by youth will follow.

J. Edgar Hoover

14

The previous chapter discussed your leadership opportunities in meeting the needs and interests of all boys and girls in the "sports for all" program of intramurals and extramurals. Every normal youth hungers for opportunities to participate and compete with his or her peers in sports—unless an early environment has denied the proper acquisition of minimum skills. We come now to the program of athletics between schools, the apex of skills development. It is hoped by this time that you have seen the total program in focus and recognize the part interscholastic athletics should play in school life and as a motivation for youth.

There are people who feel that interschool sports are unnecessary and even harmful. Others feel that other parts of the program are but stepping stones to the interschool competition. Neither point of view is tenable in itself. Athletics can be a very important part of the secondary school program, or they can be a bad influence on individual and group development. Athletics are neither good nor bad just because they are athletics. They are good or bad depending on the leadership which conducts them and the atmosphere which surrounds them.

We shall consider interschool athletics as an integral part of the educational experience of youth, because we assume that you will approach your responsibilities in this phase of the program with intelligence and understanding.

Relationship Between Physical Education and Athletics

Interschool athletics are a part of a sound physical education program. They are not a substitute for physical education, and should never be organized and administered so as to limit or curtail the other phases of the program. Emphasis placed on athletics should never be allowed to monopolize the scheduling of staff or facilities. Athletics provide the laboratory where learned skills can be tested and utilized. Here youth must learn to sublimate the self to the good of the group, to sacrifice personal desire for a cause bigger than self. Here we have the crucible in which character and lifelong habits are heated and forged. These things are all true of physical education class experiences, but the drive toward team perfection creates emotional and physical stresses that transcend the usual class activities.

One must be most careful on the job to keep a balanced perspective, to avoid placing undue emphasis which could wreck a balanced program. The temptation is sometimes strong. The press, over-zealous parents, school alumni, businessmen, and others may bring forces to bear which challenge your best efforts. When this condition is present you can retain perspective and program balance by always keeping one fact clearly in mind. Consistently strong interschool teams will be much easier to attain and maintain if a broad and comprehensive program of class instruction, and many intramural sports are provided as a basic and constant opportunity for all students. Here is the point where many young men make a tragic mistake. Poor varsity teams rarely if ever emerge from a totally good program. This fact has been documented in many communities. When the formula for winning is temporarily lost many coaches wake up to the truism of the above statement, often too late.

Before discussing this kind of sports program in greater detail we should pause to see whether interschool athletics are similar at all age-grade levels or whether you as a school-community leader may have some decisions to make which are not always completely understood by less informed citizens.

Competition for Younger Children

The urge for team play and cooperative competition does not manifest itself until about age nine or ten. The kinds of physical activity for younger children should be based on the nature and needs of their age level. Obviously, real athletic competition at these younger ages should be limited and carefully controlled. Lasting contributions of highly organized sports are greater if delayed until more appropriate years.

Developmental needs must be met. Self-testing activities are very important to youngsters. Athletic competition should be introduced gradually and not by a sudden careful imitation of adult athletic patterns. Adult sports should not be "cut down to size." No miniature imitations of "big time" sports are necessary. Body-contact sports should be avoided. Many skills and learnings from simple to complex should be stressed.

Attempts to protect children should not cause leaders to deny them the kinds of playing experiences which are needed for physical, emotional and social growth. Some well-planned activities in basic movement types of sports should be organized. Often these take the form of play days and sports days. Travel is minimized. Expensive team uniforms are unnecessary. Long schedules do not fit the shorter interest span of young boys and girls. Trained and sensible leadership will see to it that young boys and girls get a program designed to fit their capabilities and meet their needs, and prepare them for later intensified athletic experiences.

Junior High School Athletics

As far back as the time of Aristotle the question of whether interschool athletic competition should be sponsored for junior high school youth has been argued. In some states, such as Texas, a very intensive program exists today. In other states the program is rapidly gaining proponents when circumscribed by certain limitations such as in New York. In other states, intensive competition between schools is very limited, such as in California.

All professional physical educators have a stake in the issue of whether athletics are suitable for the junior high school student. There is no philosophical debate as to the merits of competition. The competitive experience has been judged good in our society. We accept as good the competitive aspects associated with painting a picture, weaving a hooked rug, or writing a novel. We endorse as wholesome the competition which takes place at our county fairs, school-age science exhibits, Miss America contests, and in offering scholarships to our institutions of higher education. The dispute lies in how soon, how much, and what kind.

Many authorities have argued, without very much reliable research on which to base their claims, that youth at this age is not ready physically, emotionally and structurally to be placed in a program with all the pressure elements of high school and college athletics. Research, although advancing, is still meager, but it continues to minimize the physical and emotional damage that might result. Perhaps the proper answer lies elsewhere.

Before taking concrete steps in this direction any staff at the junior high school level should ask themselves: "What are we trying to do in the physical education program for junior high school students? What are the factors involved?" Answers to these questions reveal the role competitive athletics ought to play in the program. Professional physical educators seek to extend the opportunity for physical education experiences to all girls and boys. They visualize a program that is structured to meet needs, awaken interests, and, one that is suitable for the age level and sex of the junior high school youngster. Programming at this level is characterized by exposing youth to a wide variety of physical pursuits. There is no defense for specialization here.

Experience over the years suggests that junior high school athletics, on an extensive basis, often prevents the development of the total program for all students because of these factors:

1. Whenever interschool athletics is developed it costs money. When money is limited, as it often is, it becomes difficult to maintain the broad program for the many in the face of the development of the interschool program for the few.

2. It takes time to develop athletic teams. The question is: Do youngsters have the time and energy to participate on the team and still take part in the varied program of instruction?

3. Athletics monopolize space, facilities and equipment. It is not fair to all students to reserve the bulk of the physical education program for the few.

4. It takes a great deal of staff time and energy to develop teams. Is the staff adequate in size to divert the amount of time necessary to develop athletics and still meet the requirements for all students?

5. The question of purity of motives must be answered. Do we favor athletic participation to glorify ourselves or is the welfare of the participant the overriding consideration? There is no short, crisp answer to this question. There are too many factors that enter the picture.

This is the "golden age." Junior high school youngsters offer little resistance to almost anything we offer. They have not yet reached the age of discrimination. They will go wherever we lead them. Their very susceptibility places a great responsibility on physical educators. Their welfare is in our hands.

We must examine our motives closely before endorsing interschool athletics at this level. Wise leadership will avoid undesirable directions of the program by keeping the interests of the participants the controlling influence as it develops athletic activity exemplifying educational experiences of the highest calibre.

When all factors are given careful consideration it is justifiable to conclude that junior high schools should never place program emphasis on competitive sports at the expense of a previously developed instructional and intramural program. When all the ingredients of a sound and diversified program have been provided, there is no valid reason why a sensible, modified interschool program cannot be activated and maintained.

The High School Program

Interschool athletics has its greatest flowering at the high school level. Maturity levels have been reached which permit intensification of training and more sports specialization than that recommended in the years of broad sampling in junior high school.

High school football demands the best equipment and above all, highly trained and educationally sound coaches.

Your challenge as a director or coach is to provide competitive experiences for as many students as possible. This means providing many sports, no squad cutting, intelligent scheduling, as many teams with schedules as possible, and wise athletic administration.

Program Scope

The extent of opportunity will depend somewhat on the size of the school and its location. High schools in clusters fairly close together can provide competitive activities for both girls and boys in almost any sport. This could include such sports as archery, volleyball, golf, tennis, bowling, softball, badminton, soccer, skeet and skish among others not commonly used today. All sports do not demand the same intensive coaching, costly equipment, and travel expense as do football, basketball, baseball and track.

Some sports are particularly adapted to the involvement of all sizes and types of boys such as wrestling, swimming, water polo, cross country and gymnastics. Here the small boy is just as important to team success as those with greater size and maturity.

Leadership for the Program

It is obvious that a normal sized physical education staff cannot handle all sports in a broad program. Several teachers of academic subjects may become involved in the leadership of athletics to supplement the efforts of the physical education staff. Teachers who give part-time leadership to coaching are usually better teachers and counsellors for their experiences. They succeed in getting closer to students and often become more effective teachers. At the same time their own health and physical fitness is better preserved and strengthened.

The practice of bringing faculty from other subject areas into the athletic program as assistant coaches is not only necessary but may result in finer relations between physical education and the several areas within the curriculum. It should be emphasized, however, that the head coaching positions should be held by qualified physical educators who are assigned full time to the physical education area. There are fundamental reasons why this should be so, as you should now fully understand without detailed discussion.

Every precaution should be taken to safeguard the health and safety of all participants. This will require close cooperation with local medical authorities to insure adequate pre-practice examinations, prevention and care of athletic injuries, availability of physicians during all contests involving strenuous activity and constant appraisal of physical status.

Differences Between Programs for Boys and Girls

High school interscholastic sports for boys can include any or all sports except boxing. This is dependent on the size of the student body, the number of coaches who can give leadership, the kind of facilities, and to a degree the geographical location. Sports sponsored will also depend to a degree on the availability of other nearby schools willing to schedule contests in these sports.

Girls' programs have been much more limited or nonexistent in many areas. Leaders of girls' sports have rightly insisted on trained sports leadership by women. They have given greater support to the extramural type of participation. In a few states girls' athletic teams have received equal or even superior support to those for boys. It is doubtful whether this degree of pressure-packed competition is necessary or advisable for high school girls.

Women leaders, through the years, have reviewed and strongly supported their policies to permit and stimulate greater interschool participation on a controlled basis. This has been particularly true in tennis, golf, swimming, volleyball, archery and badminton. It is anticipated that future years will see more attention to competitive opportunities for girls in these and other sports. Women authorities have been careful, and rightly so, not to let the interschool phase of activity get out of focus with the basic program of physical education instruction and intramurals.

They have too often been allocated an unfair percentage of the total budget and facilities, a condition that must be avoided. In reacting to the excesses they have observed in boys' athletic programs they have tended to favor sports days, shorter seasons and more sports, and invitational events. They have tried to let extramurals and interschool events emerge as a natural outgrowth of class instruction and intramurals. Extreme care has been exercised to avoid exploitation; accordingly, scheduling to determine champions, publicity of events and gate receipts have been kept to a very minimum. Women physical educators have insisted on the use of general school district funds to finance their total program, thereby guaranteeing a closer tie to the total educational program. The Division for Girls' and Women's Sports of the American Association for Health, Physical Education and Recreation is the central controlling force in the nation on policies and procedures for girls' sport activities.

Concerns and Issues

1. Can we make athletics an educational enterprise?

Everyone involved in physical education would like to see the field strengthened. The way we administer and conduct athletics holds us back. Through our intramural discord we have contributed to the difficulty in developing educational stature for athletics. We have let ourselves be distorted by administrative clap traps, such as eligibility rules, separate administration, overemphasis on winning, glorification of the champion, salary, tenure and rank.

The academic tradition works strongly to prevent physical education, including athletics, from becoming an integral part of education. There still is that deep seated belief in the minds of many that the only things of real value in the school are found between the hard covers of a book. Physical education people, as previously pointed out, must work in cooperation with those informed educators who are seeking to dispel the myth of 'mind-body' separation. People in education must be convinced that physical education, like other fields, contains more than just knowledge.

As we look objectively at American education we see that the *status quo* has been disturbed. Evolution is occurring at a fast rate. Physical education—athletics—is destined to play an ever stronger role in the school. We have a lot to do before athletics can become educationally important. We need to eliminate the clap traps, create real harmony between our divisions and accentuate the values that can flow from athletic participation. The key to the problem is personnel. The direction school athletic programs take in the decades ahead depends on the young people moving into the field. If they have perspective, reinforced by sound school administrative supervision, athletics will achieve its educational niche and make a major contribution to the work of the school.

2. What is the role of the coach?

We are a profession split three ways: boys' physical education, girls' physical education, and athletics. This is our Achilles' heel. We are the only segment in education so divided. At the collegiate level we even have our professional organizations open to one sex only. These sharp cleavages cloud the issues and render us incapable of penetrating to the heart of our problems together.

There is no need here to trace the complex series of situations and circumstances that lead to the decisions which have created the three faces we present to our publics. It does matter what we are doing to break down the barriers so that we may fashion harmony within our ranks.

Better programming, involving a wider range of recreational type activities, is the answer to developing greater harmony between the teachers of the boys' and girls' areas of physical education. The problem of absorbing interscholastic athletics as an integral part of the physical education program appears to be more difficult to solve.

From the beginning we have fought a losing battle to wed physical education and athletics. Witness the fact that we still say physical education and athletics. "I am a coach," and "I am a teacher of physical education" are heard at every hand. The point is, if we have not accepted the sameness of the two aspects of our field, how can we expect others to see us as one area?

The physical education faculty of teacher education departments in institutions of higher education have a great responsibility to provide undergraduate majors with the kinds of experiences that will eliminate this dichotomy in their thinking. One of our most pressing problems today is to educate school administrators to recognize their responsibility in carrying out supervisory functions as they apply to interscholastic athletics. If they can be helped to seek qualified physical educators to administer and conduct the athletic program, the danger of unsavory practices creeping into the program would be eliminated.

Good high school athletic administration has been successful in many communities in developing a sound community attitude toward the total program. Some coaches, obsessed with the ego drive to excel and to establish coaching reputations, have aided and caused outside influences to lose sight of the true purposes of competitive athletics. Communicating with all concerned constitutes one of the continual challenges to you as you work in the field of athletics. Your every effort should be applied to the development of a broad, comprehensive program that will reach every student, leave its favorable impact in every home, and become a model for inspection and emulation by others.

College and university athletics have not always provided an admirable pattern which high schools could emulate with success. State high school athletic associations have been a stabilizing influence on good athletic administration. The hypocrisy and lack of integrity exhibited by too many institutions of higher learning must be carefully avoided by high school leaders. The program must reinforce the educational values of interscholastic sport or it has no place in the educational scheme.

Likewise, professional sports have not always set a pleasing model for high school athletics or leaders. Commercialization, sponsorship of tobacco and alcohol products, antics of some coaches, and observable personal living habits of athletes all have had some influence upon the results one seeks for youth through athletic opportunity.

The fact of the matter is, a good coach, directing a program which gives opportunity for all, can be one of the most powerful and influential forces for the building of good citizenship in any community. Set your goals high. Strive hard to fulfill them. Your personal reward will be worth every effort. As you move on through the years you will grow to appreciate the impact for good you are having on the fine youngsters who participate in athletics. You will know that they have been strengthened through your leadership, often with deeper and more permanent contributions than even the home or the church may have made in their lives.

3. Should the coach teach in the instructional program of physical education and/or in other subject areas?

The current trend in school administration of placing the coach in the classroom has spread over the country. This practice simply reinforces the cleavage existing between instructional physical education and interscholastic athletics. Unification of program cannot be achieved with non-qualified, part-time people serving as leaders of a major segment of the program. We are partly to blame for this practice. School administrators simply have reacted to the program that has been developed. Regardless of who is to blame, professional physical educators deplore the procedure because of the damage that results to the total program.

We have previously discussed the harm that is associated with this practice. There is another aspect of the situation not yet made clear. By placing the coach in the classroom rather than in the instructional physical education program the administration is admitting that the coach is not capable of handling the physical education of girls and boys. Does this make sense? Do we really believe that the coach does not need to know anything about the forces and factors that shape the individual? What is the job of the coach in secondary schools? Is he a teacher of a sport activity or of people?

The modern architect wants to know something about the person for whom he is building a house. This desire on the part of the architect to become acquainted with the personality of his customer represents progress in architecture. Would it not represent healthy progress in the area of physical education if coaches would be required to learn all they can about growth and development of the child?

We must admit that the people in agriculture know more about pigs, or the growth problems of a grape than some coaches know about the individual. If coaches knew more about the nature of the child they could have a great impact on social living.

Physical education leaders are well aware of the advantages of involving the coach in the instructional program of physical education. Abundant evidence suggests that the part-time person—the specialist—stultifies efforts to upgrade the quality of school physical education. There is no serious debate as to the kind of pre-professional experiences needed by those who are to serve in the area of competitive sports. They must have successfully completed at least a major in the area of physical education during their undergraduate program. Anything less represents inadequate preparation for teaching in any phase of school physical education.

4. Is amateurism dead?

The future holds nothing for amateurism in its present form. An amateur athlete, according to the dictionary, is one who has never competed for money. Sport is a marketable enterprise in the United States. People will pay money to watch athletic contests. This was clear early in our culture. It has developed to a high point today. The youngster on the playground may receive a prize of considerable monetary value for winning a race, a set of golf clubs for winning a city amateur golf tournament, and the school boy may receive $100,000 for signing a professional baseball contract.

Actually, according to the original definition of an amateur brought to this country from England, there are very few amateurs in the United States. Certainly not the girl or boy who is furnished meals, transportation and equipment to participate on school athletic teams. This English concept of amateurism, which sprang out of a class society, was brought to this country with our first sport participation and we have been attempting to live up to it ever since. The problem we have been facing for some time is one of re-defining amateurism to meet the conditions which exist in our culture. Obviously, the task is a difficult one. As we cope with the dying concept of true amateurism we must be realistic in terms of our way of life in the United States. We can make a start by agreeing on at least these four points:

A. There is nothing immoral in selling one's skills. The professional athlete is held in high esteem. In our socio-economic structure we accept this view. If we go to great lengths to offer scholarships in science, music and mathematics, we are ridiculous not to do so in athletics.

B. The American public will pay for what it wants. It will pay for a lug of apples, a new car, or to see Roger Maris hit home

runs. The "gate" is here to stay. Scott[1] suggests the only answer to
the problem of the school retaining control over interscholastic
and intercollegiate athletics: "Since the control of an educational
function and the source of the funds for its support tend to be
quite closely related, the source of funds for the conduct of the
program of competitive sports should be the same as the source of
funds for the support of all other educational enterprises. . . ."

C. The immorality involved in athletics is in the hypocrisy
operating which says one thing while doing another. This applies
to the "pay under the table" associated with some collegiate institutions as well as unethical leadership that makes a sham out of
rules and regulations. The heart of our dilemma is morality, not
economics.

D. We must establish new rules that are reasonable. And we
must live by them. Violation of rules should result in individual
punishment, not group punishment. A tradition in jurisprudence
is that man must stand the punishment of his own crimes.

5. Can we learn from the Russians?

Whether a justified contemplation or not, the policies and directions taken by Russia as a world rival bear scrutiny. Either by
wisdom, by accident, or by careful study of American mistakes, the
Russian government has given complete support to a program
they feel can in time outstrip all nations in athletic ability—and in
fitness and stamina of youth.

Their efforts have been placed completely behind a program of
mass participation, which involves daily instructional physical
education with heavy emphasis on vigorous activities, intramural
and interschool sports, and support for sports clubs that extends
beyond school years. They are dedicated to the concept that with
several years of this complete mobilization of all youth in sports
the skilled stars are bound to emerge—and in greater abundance
than in all other nations. When coupled with a constant effort to
sharpen coaching skills and playing techniques a formidable program results.

To a great extent this has been the American concept, at least
in theory. Too often our zeal for temporary expediency has pro-

1 Scott, Harry A., *Competitive Sports in Schools and Colleges* (New York: Harper
& Brothers, 1951), pp. 220-221.

duced an aristocracy of sports rather than a democratic program of sports opportunities for all. Our right of free choice and self-determination is the big difference with Soviet procedures. It can continue to be the driving force which makes a nation great and self-sustained, but only if every leader in the nation strives to help make it work. You share in this great challenge in the years ahead.

Selected References

Ainsworth, Dorothy (Editor), *Individual Sports for Women,* Philadelphia: W. B. Saunders Company, 1955.

Bucher, Charles A., *Administration of School Health and Physical Education Programs,* St. Louis: C. V. Mosby Company, 1958, Chapter 19.

Conant, James B., "Athletics—The Poison Ivy in Our Schools," *Look Magazine* (January 17, 1961), pp. 56-61.

Cowell, Charles C. and Helen W. Hazelton, *Curriculum Designs in Physical Education,* Englewood Cliffs, N. J.: Prentice-Hall, Inc., 1955, Chapter 20.

Cozens, Frederick and Florence Stumpf, *Sports in American Life,* Chicago: University of Chicago Press, 1953.

Fait, Hollis F., "Should the Junior High School Sponsor Interscholastic Athletic Competition?" *JOHPER* (February, 1961), pp. 20-22.

Forsythe, Charles E., *The Administration of High School Athletics,* Englewood Cliffs, N. J.: Prentice-Hall, Inc., 1954, Chapter 10.

Hughes, William L., "The Place of Athletics in the School Physical Education Program," *JOHPER* (December, 1950), pp. 23-27.

Lawther, John D., *Psychology of Coaching,* Englewood Cliffs, N. J.: Prentice-Hall, Inc., 1951.

McGee, Rosemary, "Comparison of Attitudes Toward Intensive Competition for High School Girls," *The Research Quarterly* (March, 1956), p. 60.

Means, Louis E., "Extramural Athletics," *JOHPER* (January, 1949), pp. 23 and 52-54.

Meyer, Margaret H. and Marguerite M. Schwartz, *Team Sports for Girls and Women,* Philadelphia: W. B. Saunders Company, 1957.

Miller, Donna Mae and Katherine L. Ley, *Individual and Team Sports for Women,* Englewood Cliffs, N. J.: Prentice-Hall, Inc., 1955.

Nixon, John E. and Florence S. Frederickson, *An Introduction to Physical Education,* Philadelphia: W. B. Saunders Company, 1959, Chapter 16.

Paterson, Ann, *Team Sports for Girls,* New York: The Ronald Press, 1958.

Phillips, Marjorie, *et al.,* "Sports Activity for Girls," *JOHPER* (December, 1959), pp. 23-26 and 54.

School Athletics, Educational Policies Commission, Washington, D. C.: National Education Association, 1954.

Scott, Harry A., *Competitive Sports in Schools and Colleges,* New York: Harper & Brothers, 1951, Chapters 4, 5, 6, 8, 9, 10 and 12.

Shepard, Natalie M., *Foundations and Principles of Physical Education,* New York: The Ronald Press Company, 1960, Chapter 8.

"Standards in Sports for Girls and Women," Washington, D. C.: *DGWS, AAHPER-NEA,* 1960 (Rev. Ed.), p. 57.

Turner, Marshall, "Emphasizing Educational Athletics," *64th Proceedings CPEA,* 1961, pp. 11-16.

Vannier, Maryhelen and Hollis F. Fait, *Teaching Physical Education in Secondary Schools,* Philadelphia: W. B. Saunders Company, 1957, Chapter 19.

Part V

CONDUCTING THE PROGRAM OF PHYSICAL EDUCATION

Successful
Teaching in
Physical Education

Ambition is not a vice of little
people.

Montaigne

15

The student preparing to teach
physical education has a right
to wonder whether his potential career will be enjoyable.
Throughout this book significant information is presented
regarding the steps the professional student may take to plan
for a successful career. Suffi-
cient information is included to provide a general understanding
of the demands placed upon the teacher of physical education.

A realistic appraisal of the setting within which the teacher
works reveals that many elements combine to determine whether
the individual is destined to enjoy the years spent in his professional career. To be sure, the situation in which one finds himself
contains elements which contribute to the degree of satisfaction

one experiences on the job. For instance, the manner in which the school is administered, the type of community within which the school is located, the caliber of the physical education program, and many other factors combine to create either an attractive or unattractive environment in which to work. It is obvious, as one evaluates the factors bearing on the matter, that the degree of pleasure the physical educator receives from his work is measured largely by his effectiveness as a teacher and leader.

The Criterion

What constitutes successful teaching in physical education? The answer lies squarely on the quality of results the teacher secures in the teaching-learning process. Good results are those that achieve the objectives which have been established. Thus, the ultimate worth of teaching lies in the degree to which the student is helped to reach these objectives.

Learning is a dynamic phenomenon involving change in the learner. The learner may or may not make progress. Whatever occurs can be identified, both in kind and in degree. For example, the golfer may display competence in the practice cage, yet fail miserably on the golf course. The baseball player may hit line drives nearly every turn at bat in batting practice, yet strike out ignominiously in a game situation. The tennis hopeful may experience considerable success in stroking the ball again and again against a wall, but on the court find it impossible to duplicate his practice form. These participants have not had their skills directed toward a rewarding end result. Under the pressure of the game situation they were not able to perform satisfactorily. They possess *spurious learnings*.

Individuals who learn to play golf, baseball, and tennis well enough to seek participation in these activities outside of class have achieved *authentic* results. That is, they have learned enough to make them wish to seek more participation. It is apparent from this view that the fundamental responsibility of the teacher is to organize learning for lasting, usable results. This is the criterion to use in measuring the worthwhileness of the results achieved by the teacher. When authentic results are gained it can be said that teaching is successful.

Application of this criterion to the total program of physical education suggests that some of the best results are obtained by participants in interscholastic athletics. The good coach gets results; other factors being equal, his teams win their share of victories. In addition, his players learn, through working together in practice sessions and game competition, the other values sought by the program—physical fitness, respect for others, sportsmanship, democratic qualities, and positive outlook on life.

This does not mean that the coach is a better teacher than those involved in other areas of the program. He may get better results because of the greater interest he carries into the planning and instructional responsibilities associated with coaching. However, an examination of the characteristics of good organization for learning would disclose that much of the credit for success in athletics stems from the nearly ideal learning conditions operative in most coaching situations. Players are on the team because they already possess some skill in the sport. Participation is voluntary; and, the motivation arising from publicity and spectator interest associated with varsity athletics makes them highly appealing to participants. In addition, the coach usually works with better equipment and usually deals with smaller groups. Consideration of these factors enables one to understand that conditions are operating in the interscholastic athletic program which make it less difficult for the coach to get good results than is sometimes true for the instructor of the physical education class.

Consider for a moment the setting within which the teacher in the instructional program works. He may be forced to teach under conditions far from ideal. Among the hazards he may face, not normally faced by the coach, are these: a mixture of grade levels in each section; the novice in the same class with the highly skilled student; required participation; often excessively large numbers of students in each class; inadequate facilities, equipment, and space for the number of students; and, the possibility that he must follow a rigid schedule which may ignore the readiness of his students to move ahead in the learning process.

No one familiar with the practical problems associated with school physical education will deny that the above conditions exist; and yet this does not satisfactorily explain poor results. Many teachers, even under the worst possible conditions, do a commendable job of instruction. To be sure, better results could be obtained by the good teacher if obstacles were removed. The important thing to keep in mind is that failure to obtain good results is usually disastrous, whatever the reason, and whoever may be responsible. When a student does not learn to play at least a fair game of tennis while in class he may give up the game in disgust; the student in the golf unit who cannot learn to hit the ball with some degree of success is apt to avoid the golf course the rest of his life.

Physical educators must recognize these truisms, for if all concerned were more urgently aware that it is their job to get good results, just as it is the job of the newspaper reporter to get news items, poor learning conditions would not be tolerated. One teacher standing alone can not completely eliminate the many hazards which frustrate attempts to get good results. He can do the best with what he has. Furthermore, he can inspire his immediate colleagues to join forces with him to work to upgrade program quality. Perhaps of even greater significance is the fact that he and his associates can join forces with other professional workers and, through concerted efforts, remove many of the hazards which contribute to a poor setting for learning.

The Role of the Teacher

Good teaching is richly rewarding; poor teaching is frustrating. The good teacher is one who gets the job done; consequently, students enjoy his classes as they gain authentic results. Someone once said that the satisfied teacher is one who produces alive, alert, stimulated students. The poor teacher fails to motivate students; accordingly, his students are usually difficult to manage. On the one hand, teaching is stimulating and enjoyable. On the other, teaching becomes a chore and the school day is laden with unpleasant problems associated with conducting classes.

Many teachers fail to teach effectively because they do not fully understand the role of the teacher in the learning process. There are many outstanding teachers of physical education. Many others share the viewpoints and qualities indicated within the following types:

1. The *dish it out* teacher who feels that his chief responsibility lies in simply presenting the activity to the student. This teacher has little compassion for students. Lesson plans do not reflect serious efforts to encourage students to put forth the energy to learn.

2. The *fearful* teacher who feels that the most important thing is discipline. Preoccupation with the problems of maintaining order curtails the amount of class time devoted to participation. This teacher is usually found in the program featuring large classes. He has lost sight of the fundamental responsibilities associated with instruction.

3. The *confused* teacher who operates in terms of expediency because he lacks convictions or understanding as to the role of physical education. Teachers who believe that theory is impractical are in this category.

4. The *mechanics* teacher who stresses minutiae. He becomes bogged down in handling the details of class management. Routine matters become the important consideration. His attitude toward the class is, "The task must be done." With grade book in hand he communicates the idea that his greatest concern is to cover the material.

5. The *let 'em have fun* teacher who does not believe there is much value in the physical education class other than that of giving the student an opportunity to work up a sweat and have a good time. The specialist often displays this viewpoint. The coach of the varsity sport or the dance enthusiast often feels that teaching other activities in a required class is of secondary importance as compared to his or her special interest.

There are many ways to state the functions, obligations, and responsibilities of the teacher as he functions in the teaching-learning process. The following factors appear highly significant in studying the role of the teacher.

1. Teachers are the key to the quality of education. Administrators and supervisors achieve their goals only as they succeed in assisting teachers in doing their job in the best possible way. Good teachers share one important quality; that is, they are able to inspire the learner to want to learn. The good teacher arouses the

student's curiosity and stimulates him to act. The manner in which superior teachers go about the task of producing eager students varies in terms of their own personality traits. It is clear, however, that inspired teaching can be done only by the teacher who is himself inspired. The teacher for whom both the activity and the students are routine will never stimulate anyone.

2. The effective teacher is versatile. To qualify as one who is prepared to carry out the functions associated with work in the program, the teacher needs to have a broad understanding of the nature of the learner; possess a depth of understanding of the contribution physical education makes to the larger area of education; be reasonably skilled in a variety of activities, and know how to teach them; and recognize the complexity of the teaching-learning process.

3. Organization of the learning situation in physical education is a complicated task, including many facets. The more important factors that bear on the problem are these: (1) the *students,* with regard to their range of present skills, capacity to learn, methods employed by each in going about the task of learning, and the attitude they have toward the total learning situation; (2) the *activities* selected, considering the quantity and quality of facilities, equipment, and space available; (3) the *plan* utilized in organizing and conducting the class; (4) the *methods* used by the teacher in carrying out his plans; and (5) the *evaluation* techniques used to chart student progress.

It is the teacher's task to organize these various elements into an intelligible unity. If he is a skillful teacher the bulk of his energies are spent in administering the whole process. In a broad sense, the task of the teacher is similar to that of the school administrator. The administrator deals with the entire school curriculum and staff, the teacher with his students. The basis of good administration is to make it possible for other people to function. Accordingly, the administrator sets the stage for learning by establishing the conditions which enable teachers in the school to work effectively. So it is with the teacher. His efforts center on the five elements involved in the physical education learning situation. His main concern is to coordinate these elements into a smooth pattern so that students may achieve good results.

Actually, then, the teacher's relationship to the class is as a good organizer. In this capacity he directs or guides, depending upon the situation of the moment. As an effective organizer he will not center all authority in his own hands, and yet, he is the directing force in the entire operation. His prime function is to enable the group to get things done. He fulfills his task by doing all that he can to keep student activity moving at a maximum rate of speed toward class and program objectives.

The Nature of Learning

What is the essential difference between an effective organization for learning and an ineffective one? The answer to this problem goes to the very heart of the whole process of teaching. Psychological research discloses that learning is well-organized when it is richly meaningful to the learner. The more meaningful the learning the better it goes. To help clarify what is meant by meaningful learning consider the relative degree of meaning in these two illustrations:

In the first case a class of some fifty students was in the midst of a unit of volleyball. On the particular day in question class action reflected a minimum amount of planning and instruction by the teacher. The period began in a haphazard fashion. A few students started a casual game of volleyball, others used several volleyballs to shoot baskets, while the remaining members of the class stood along the sidelines doing very little. Horseplay and ineffectual participation in volleyball and basket shooting occupied the first minutes of the period.

The instructor, who also was the basketball coach, arrived on the scene several minutes after the bell had rung. He immediately blew his whistle sharply, demanding the attention of his listless students. After lining them up for roll call he appointed six boys to choose sides for three games of volleyball. When this was done and the games were in progress, the instructor returned to a corner of the gymnasium and engaged in conversation with several of the boys on his basketball team. The remainder of the period was spent in haphazard play, marked by arguments and poor play.

The second and contrasting situation pertains to a class of the same number of students, also engaged in a volleyball unit. Class action here was structured to encourage the students to take much of the responsibility for what occurred. The class was divided into six squads, each with a student leader. The first ten minutes was devoted to a drill to practice the pass from the back court to the front line, followed by the set up to the "spiker." The instructor used one squad to demonstrate the proper procedure and technique in executing the fundamentals involved.

Following the demonstration each squad, under the direction of its leader, worked on the drill. The remainder of the period was spent in competitive participation in the total game. Things went along very well without the need for persons to act as officials. Each player had been prepared to call infractions of rules on himself. During the play the three courts were the arena for hotly contested, well-organized play.

The instructor was the organizer of the total situation. During the drills he moved from squad to squad, offering individual help where needed. While the games were underway his major task was to see that all activity proceeded smoothly. He did this by offering encouragement and individual instruction where needed.

These two illustrations provide a striking contrast. In the first instance the learning situation was characterized by the lack of instruction and supervision one normally associates with the so-called "bat and ball" type program. It is incredible that, with the possible exception of a few, the students could derive any real learning from this kind of organization. In the second illustration the organization centered upon dynamic learning situations, with a maximum of student control. These examples of class organization point up a fundamental principle of instruction. The basis of all successful teaching, whether in the required class, the intramural or G.A.A. program, or on the athletic field, is to create situations as rich as possible in meaning for those who are to learn. In the first class, described above, there was relatively meaningless activity while in the second class there was evidence of relatively meaningful learning.

The Role of Motivation

Essential agreement among modern psychologists with regard to the nature of learning may be summarized as follows: Learning of all kinds is a process which begins with a compelling problem in the mind of the learner, and proceeds toward its solution by the apprehension, clarification, and application of meaning. This implies that purpose must be present, that the learner must have a goal in mind. Motivation, then, is an essential condition of learning.

Analysis of the role motivation plays in learning reveals three fundamental purposes it serves in the learning process. First, it stimulates the individual to *act*. One learns best when he is interested. Outside pressure to learn, such as grades, desire to graduate, parental wishes, and so forth may be effective to motivate the learner to put forth effort to learn. However, these external forces will carry the learner just so far. The quality of results are determined in relationship to the strength of purpose in the mind of the learner. Second, interest and motives serve as *selectors* of action. The learner reacts favorably toward those things he is interested in, tending to reject those learnings which have no appeal. Third, motivation alone is not enough to establish a good learning climate. The learner's *action* must converge upon well-defined, obtainable goals.

By further probing into the impact motivation has on the learning process one can detect two kinds of motivation operating in educational endeavor. They are *extrinsic* motivation, wherein learning occurs due to operating factors which are external to the act itself, and *intrinsic* motivation, wherein learning carries its own reward. In most instances both kinds of motivation are involved whenever a number of students are brought together in a class situation.

Experienced teachers are fully aware that at the beginning of a course some students are in class simply because they are required to be there. For these students extrinsic motivation may be at work in its lowest form. The skillful teacher seeks to make course content understandable and challenging. He develops lesson plans to encourage the student to grasp potential values. He uses a great variety of teaching tools and techniques to accomplish the desired transformation of student viewpoint from negative to positive. Extrinsic motivation usually begins to function on a higher plane for most students when exposed to good teaching. As the work of the course proceeds, some of these disinterested students may become stimulated to the point that they come to class eager for what is to take place. At this point extrinsic motivation blends with intrinsic motivation and learning goes on at a faster pace.

A major problem of instruction is solved when teaching is good enough to cause the learner to develop a genuine desire to want to learn. Experienced teachers know that there is no substitute for real effort on the part of the learner if good results are to be obtained. The good teacher seeks to bring students from the extrinsic motivation level to the intrinsic level. It behooves all teachers to understand this about their role in the teaching-learning process. Learning goes best when the learner wants to learn. It is the teacher's prime responsibility to bring about this kind of a positive attitude on the part of the learner.

The problem of motivating students in physical education is of the same nature as that faced by all other teachers. To be sure, the informal atmosphere associated with participation in pleasurable activities may make the task of stimulating students somewhat easier for the teacher of physical education. However, this does not mean that the physical educator works only with students who are intrinsically motivated. The facts suggest that conditions usually present in most high school programs create a much different picture.

The most significant factor in the physical education situation involves the quality of experiences students have had previously in activities. Students who have had good experiences usually enter the program with a strong desire to participate and with an eagerness to improve their skills. Many others who have had a history of poor experiences in sport activities may enter the program as reluctant participants. A few students may even be violently antagonistic toward physical education. It is logical to assume, therefore, that the physical educator is likely to find students in each class who possess a wide variety of attitudes toward the program.

The superior teacher seeks to establish conditions which enable interested students to learn at a maximum rate and, at the same time, to encourage uninitiated students to develop a positive attitude toward participation. The point is clear. Every teacher of physical education has as his or her most important responsibility the task of teaching so well that students become dynamically challenged to learn. Those teachers who enjoy success emphasize in their planning the creation of a setting within which all students are given a chance to achieve the feelings that come with successful accomplishment. Success enhances motivation. Instruction has its best chance to be effective when the learner becomes motivated. Real learning occurs when the learner is trying to learn. This is the reason good teachers work hard to create interest, make activities appealing, and practice and drills challenging.

Selected References

Brownell, Clifford Lee and E. Patricia Hagman, *Physical Education—Foundations and Principles,* New York: McGraw-Hill Book Company, 1951, Chapters 10 and 11.

Bucher, Charles A., *Foundations of Physical Education,* St. Louis: C. V. Mosby Company, 1960, Chapter 15.

Teachers Guide to Physical Education for Girls in High School, Sacramento: California State Department of Education, 1957, Chapter 1, pp. 6-11.

Cowell, Charles C. and Helen W. Hazelton, *Curriculum Designs in Physical Education,* Englewood Cliffs, N. J.: Prentice-Hall, Inc., 1955, Chapter 2.

Davis, Elwood C. and Earl L. Wallis, *Toward Better Teaching in Physical Education,* Englewood Cliffs, N. J.: Prentice-Hall, Inc., 1961, Chapters 4, 5, and 6.

Knapp, Clyde and E. Patricia Hagman, *Teaching Methods for Physical Education,* New York: McGraw-Hill Book Company, 1953, Chapters 1 and 2.

Kozman, Hilda C., *et al., Methods in Physical Education,* Philadelphia: W. B. Saunders Company, 1958, Chapter 3.

Oberteuffer, Delbert, *Physical Education,* New York: Harper & Brothers, 1956, Chapter 7.

Van Dalen, Deobold B. and Marcella M. Van Dalen, *The Health, Physical Education and Recreation Teacher,* Englewood Cliffs, N. J.: Prentice-Hall, Inc., 1956, Chapter 11.

Vannier, Maryhelen and Hollis F. Fait, *Teaching Physical Education in Secondary Schools,* Philadelphia: W. B. Saunders Company, 1957, Chapter 3.

Williams, Jesse Feiring, *The Principles of Physical Education,* Philadelphia: W. B. Saunders Company, 1959, Chapter 10.

Principles Guiding Program Development in Physical Education

Expedients are for the hour, principles for the ages.

Henry Ward Beecher

16

What must any instructor do if his students are to achieve lasting, usable, and meaningful results? This question very well may be phrased to apply to the department of physical education as a whole. One might ask, "Is there any magical set method that somehow will do the job?" "Is there any *one* technique of teaching that will always work?" Obviously, there is no one way to teach that will be effective for all teachers, nor is there any approach to the learning process that is best in all situations. No single way has as yet been devised as best in organizing the program of physical education. To probe into the heart of these questions one must turn to what is known about the psychology of learning and apply that knowledge to the practical teaching situation. In the following set of six principles Mursell has found an extremely satisfactory bridge between the psychological knowledge about the conditions by which authentic learnings take place and the teaching situation:

The learner's mind must work in the right kind of *context* if he is to learn well. He must set up the right kind of *focus*. The right kind of *social* relationships will help him enormously. To some extent he must work in his own *individual* way. Each particular job of learning must be a part of a *sequence* of developing power and insight. The right kind of *evaluation* is essential, for the learner needs to know it too.[1]

Application of these principles to physical education serves two important purposes. First, any teacher, coach, supervisor, or administrator may use these principles to evaluate any phase of learning. All of them operate simultaneously in the teaching process. When learning goes well the principles are working at a high level; when learning slows down, things have occurred to destroy the harmonious operation of the principles. Since they function interdependently in the learning process it is understandable that when one principle bogs down the impact is felt by the other principles. The result invariably is substandard learning. Full knowledge of these principles enables the teacher to identify the cause or causes of the slow down, thereby permitting him to take steps to correct whatever is impeding the learning. Therefore, as the instructor plans and conducts his class or practice sessions, he may evaluate efforts in terms of the ways in which the principles reveal themselves during the group action. In other words, he may measure his effectiveness in view of the level at which the principles are working. They give him the clues as to how to reorganize the situation to bring about a better learning climate.

Second, these principles may be used by any administrator or staff to evaluate the effectiveness of the entire program. One of the most serious errors has been that of failure to do a good job of teaching in the instructional program. If the program is to remain as an important part of education the quality of the entire program must be improved. The logical starting place to upgrade quality is in the physical education class. School administrators and faculty tend to make judgments in terms of their past experiences as students in physical education, what they see of the current program in their school, as well as what the student body feels

---

[1] James L. Mursell, *Successful Teaching: Its Psychological Principles* (New York: McGraw-Hill Book Co., Inc., 1946), p. viii.

about it. The best way to sell the program in a school is to provide a dynamic program that gets good results. In order to help you understand what constitutes good teaching and good organization of the learning situation a critical examination in the light of these six principles is desirable.

The Principle of Context

Meaningful learning must go on in a dynamic, concrete setting. Context means the actual materials which one uses in the learning situation. Physical education context includes the facilities, equipment, and space utilized by the department. It is true that the social setting contributes much, but that is not what is meant by the learning context.

In analyzing the task of instruction as it applies to the use of context in the learning process, two fundamental questions immediately arise. What is the essential difference between an effective and an ineffective context? In what ways is the principle of context specifically related to the organization of learning? The specific nature of the questions becomes clear as one studies the distinguishing characteristics of a good setting for learning.

1. A good context for learning must be one in which the learner dynamically and strongly interacts.

The experienced teacher is well aware of the tremendous influence context has on program results. The quality and quantity of context is vitally important. Well-equipped gymnasiums and ample well-groomed outdoor teaching stations characterize good context. And yet, there is more to the principle of context than this. The manner in which students react to the activities taught more clearly reveals the effectiveness of the principle. Excellent tennis or handball courts are of little real value if students dislike tennis and handball classes. In evaluating a teaching-learning situation in terms of this principle the primary consideration is the attitude of the participants as they use the context. If they do so with a will, interaction is of the highest order.

Vigorous interaction depends upon good organization and

quality instruction. It is more apt to be forthcoming when context is of good quality, but good context does not guarantee dynamic interaction. A poorly organized activity class may lead students to participate in a mechanical, disinterested fashion, even when facilities and equipment are of the very best. This is low grade interaction. Conversely, a well-organized, skillfully taught class may use meager context and produce enthusiastic students who learn easily. Context is good only in terms of its use. It is not enough to merely evaluate the context in isolation. One must observe students as they use the context to make an accurate appraisal of this principle. Context which appears excellent when examined alone may prove to be inadequate when used by excessively large numbers of participants.

2. A good context is concrete.

A physical education program which draws its activities from the normal leisure time pursuits of youth and adults is highly appealing because it deals with important, concrete experiences. It is best if these meaningful activities are taught in their natural setting. Good learning demands a dynamic, concrete setting.

The basic elements of skiing may be taught in sawdust or straw, and the fundamentals of golf may be learned on the school playfield. But the full benefits of instruction in skiing or golf are best achieved when the participants are given an opportunity to use the ski slope or the golf course. This means that every effort must be made to find a way to include some instruction and participation in the natural setting, even though that setting is off the school grounds. Obviously, this is not always possible to do for some activities included in the core. It is often possible to arrange for a field trip to the site when these activities are taught at the required-elective level. The intramural program should be organized to accomplish this end. Scuba diving may be taught in the swimming pool and excursions to large bodies of water may be planned in connection with intramurals or recreational aspects of the program. Many departments regularly utilize off-school facilities in this way. Furthermore, it is possible to take advantage of the expert instruction of the specialist associated with the site to demonstrate and to help organize the instructional aspects of the activity.

Things are happening on the American scene that are highly significant to physical education context. In recent years increasing leisure and higher incomes have led to a great upsurge in recreational participation by an increasing number of people. Money spent in leisure time pursuits is helping to bolster our national economy. Recent estimates[2] of the amount of money spent annually in the business of leisure places the figure at about $40 billion a year, more than all federal personal income tax receipts. A few years ago *Life Magazine* correspondents all over the country were asked to find out what people were doing with their spare time and money. These researchers found that boating, fishing, swimming, skin diving, water skiing, bowling, softball, horseshoes, archery, and golf headed the list.

Facts such as these regarding the leisure time pursuits of people cannot be ignored by physical educators. Examination of present programs reveals that most departments include few of these activities. There should be no question as to whether these activities belong in the program. The profession of physical education for many years has recognized that one of its prime objectives is to teach young people the skills involved in activities they can use for the rest of their lives. We must heed the conditions of the times and take a good look at our programs. The time has come to discard traditional notions about content. We must find ways to "break the log jam"; activities that abound in our sporting and recreational worlds must be taught in our programs. If it is boating and fishing, we must offer them to our students.

3. The concrete and dynamically compelling experiences should be *copious*.

A limited context will not service the wide variety of interests and needs represented in a total student body of a school. No matter how vital a few activities are, they simply will not appeal to all students. A good total program must include a wide range of activities. The more indoor and outdoor space and the more varied the equipment and facilities available the more chance there is to capture the interests and, therefore, meet the needs of larger numbers of students.

2 Robert Coughlan, "A $40 Billion Bill Just for Fun," *Life Magazine*, Dec. 28, 1959, p. 70.

The Impact Context Has on Physical Education

Learning cannot take place without context. Every teacher applies context in his work, sometimes inexpertly, sometimes with keen and imaginative insight. The difference between effective and ineffective context is one of degree. A small gymnasium, poorly lighted and maintained, with meager, second-rate equipment, featuring a small, poorly marked outdoor area constitutes poor context. The modern gymnasium, with its multiple teaching stations and spacious, well-marked and well cared for outdoor facilities represents good context. The real key to good context is staff ability to stimulate dynamic interaction between the student and the context. Therefore, in the final analysis, the degree to which the students use the context determines whether the principle is operating on a high plane to enhance learning or on a low plane to stifle learning.

Expanding Available Context

As physical educators seek to improve their programs, inevitably they must broaden the scope of their offerings. The following points may be helpful in guiding a staff as it seeks to enrich its program:

1. Departmental planning should make maximal use of the available context. It is a rare department that offers as wide a variety of suitable activities as is possible under existing circumstances. A beginning step to broaden program content would be to take stock of the present schedule of activities and determine wherein additional activities might be added. Once plans are developed, extreme care should be exercised to coordinate the boys' and girls' programs so that existing context is used effectively each hour of the day. Pre-planning of this nature, involving the entire department, serves the additional purpose of developing a finer relationship between the men and women in the department. Often times the lack of mutual planning creates situations that

lead to friction, as well as to conditions where facilities are not used.

In seeking ways to add variety to their instructional programs, many have found that activities not included at present could be offered if the staff felt inclined, or were capable of teaching them. A number of departments have solved this problem by soliciting the help of skilled persons outside their own staff. In one school an enthusiastic archer, a member of the social science department, lent his efforts to the development of a unit of archery. He did such a splendid job of introducing archery to the student body that it became one of the most popular activities in the program. In a short time an archery club was formed. Members were limited at the outset to students; however, by popular demand faculty members and adults from the community were permitted to join. Club activities included the construction of bows and arrows from raw materials available at nominal prices, target archery, field archery, and instruction in the art of hunting game. Here is an excellent example of the exciting results that can accrue when a concrete activity is taught by an enthusiastic expert. Other schools have recently formed ski, scuba diving, square dance, and skating clubs with satisfying results.

School physical education staffs all over the country are seeking and finding ways to include leisure time pursuits in their offerings. For instance, the introduction of fishing in the program of one school started a chain of events that revolutionized the department's entire program. In this particular case the head of the department was able to engage the aid of one of the highly skilled fishermen from the commuity to help initiate fishing in the program. The response to this activity was immediate and startling. This man was able to bring the sport of fishing to the gymnasium. His knowledge and enthusiasm created a tremendous desire on the part of the students to use their new found talents. Excursion trips to nearby streams were made available. Everyone wanted to get into the units on fishing. As in the case of the archery unit, the entire community became involved. The result was an almost fantastic reversal of opinion by faculty and administration toward physical education. The staff was quick to take advantage of the good will thus generated and easily secured administrative blessing to offer other activities associated with the out-of-doors.

Within a short time a unit on firearms was in full swing. The local police department provided instruction and the necessary weapons. This was quickly followed by a unit on camp lore, supervised by the local representative of the state forestry department.

Once a staff puts its collective efforts at work to broaden the program, it finds that the only limiting factors are its own ingenuity and the time limitation. If physical-recreational activities are important to include in today's physical education programs, and it is here contended that they are, then it behooves all departments to seek the assistance of an expert to help prepare and direct these instructional units.

2. Following the initial appraisal of present activities and completion of plans to include additional ones that may be taught with the present context, the next step is to study the community to determine the possibilities of using off-school facilities. Many departments are now using roller and ice skating rinks, bowling alleys, riding stables, golf courses, fishing areas, rifle ranges, and swimming pools to enrich their context. To be sure, obstacles lie in this procedure; nevertheless, in many instances carefully structured plans can work wonders.

The use of facilities away from the school grounds may be brought into the program in at least these ways: (1) The entire unit may be taught in the off-school area. This is possible when the facility is located near the school. (2) Portions of the unit might be conducted at the off-school site. Special arrangements may be made to take the class to the area once a week or several times at the end of the unit. (3) The area may be utilized in the intramural or recreational portions of the program. (4) The area may be used as a portion of the interscholastic athletic program.

In addition to enriching context the use of community facilities serves the purpose of bringing the community into closer touch with the school physical education program. Opportunities are available for public understanding of the total program whenever students participate in full view of the public.

Another reason for using community facilities as part of the instructional program is that students are encouraged to develop interests in the kinds of activities available to them once they leave school. Activities such as these are concrete.

3. From the very beginning of departmental efforts to upgrade the quality of its program, steps should be taken to develop long range plans for the procurement of additional facilities and a more adequate operating budget.

Original construction of major facilities for physical education rarely serve the needs for a full program. Even in recent construction this statement holds true. In most cases sufficient capital outlay facilities must be provided in stages with increments added as rapidly as possible. Original plans are often poorly conceived. In too many cases the program specialist is left out of the pre-planning. Architectural errors are apt to be made which curtail the functional program. Older structures are substandard due to population growth and altered requirements in construction due to a changing program of physical education.

It is apparent, therefore, that all physical education departments should be constantly at work on plans to secure additional context. It is their task to persuade the school administrator that such requests are educationally sound and justifiable. Decisions to allocate funds for new construction rests in the hands of the local school board. The superintendent is the one to present program needs of this kind to his board for action.

The school administrator is more apt to react favorably when he is given facts to justify expenditures. The physical education staff must produce these facts. There are three steps to the kind of fact gathering process that are necessary. First, the staff must know what constitutes a full program. It must turn to authoritative sources to determine such things as recommended number of indoor and outdoor teaching stations required to develop the full program. Second, the staff must complete an accurate survey of the extent of its present context. Third, these facts about the present situation must be organized into a well documented report and presented personally to the superintendent for implementation.

The Principle of Focalization

Focalization is one of the most important aspects in the art of learning. Its relationship to the other five principles may be likened to the relationship of the spokes to the hub of a wheel. Destroy the hub and the spokes collapse; impair focus and the principles lose their effectiveness.

The word focus is usually associated with picture taking. An improperly focused camera takes blurred, distorted pictures. Proper manipulation of the lens brings the camera into focus and enables it to take clear, sharp pictures. The same thing occurs in learning motor skills. In the beginning stages of learning the novice produces jerky, awkward movements. Good instruction stimulates the learner to put forth the effort necessary to learn fundamentals involved in the total action pattern. As learning proceeds movements become less inept, and, in time, become graceful and smooth.

Focalization has to do with establishing the conditions which encourage the learner to put forth effort to learn. The discussion

Monte Rariden, The Citadel

Attaining nationally recognized standards of performance or setting new records provide great challenge to students.

of motivation in the last chapter is pertinent to this principle. One may readily see the important role focalization plays during the teaching-learning process by examining its distinguishing characteristics.

1. The learning situation must be organized so that it is a challenge to understanding.

A boy may learn to swim faster if his goal is to make the swimming team; the handball player may be spurred to new heights if he plays with others whose skills are superior. The boy, interested in a girl who happens to be a good tennis player, will likely learn to play tennis more effectively than if he lacked this potent motivator.

Experienced teachers recognize the importance of constantly challenging the learner. The coach devotes hours to planning practice sessions which are designed to stimulate his players to put forth maximal efforts. He knows that what takes place on the practice field must make sense to the players. The successful coach avoids the futility of bored, half-speed performance. So does the competent teacher of the instructional program. He plans daily lessons so that all that goes on is structured to produce interested, responsive participants. He recognizes the powerful impact keen competition has on learning; accordingly, drills and work on fundamentals are developed with this in mind.

2. Focalization *unifies* the job of learning by coordinating the specific phases of the total action so that the participant will see the desired response pattern as a whole.

There is a theory that to learn an act of skill one must first learn each part. This theory is based on the notion that to master the whole one must master the parts, that if one learns to do singly all the elemental acts in a complex function, putting the parts together will be relatively simple. Psychological evidence has long since destroyed this myth; and yet, many teachers organize lesson plans on the "part, part, part, whole" basis. The Gestaltists' view of "whole, part, whole" seems to be much more appropriate. Gates expresses the modern concept of learning a complex act as follows:

Learning to do the parts singly is by no means learning to do the whole. The greatest difficulties are often encountered in putting the elements together. Moreover the elements are often already sufficiently developed without the preliminary practice; if not, they are usually more economically perfected in practicing the whole. Those which do not develop sufficiently while practicing the whole may well be handled singly later, but not until it becomes necessary. We should not begin with elaborate formal exercise of the elements or make them a large part of the course of training but should utilize them as strictly preventive measures where difficulty is beginning to appear or as remedial measures where a particular defect or deficiency is apparent. When thus singled out for specific treatment, a particular aspect of a total performance has a significance and character it could not have as an isolated segment practiced without respect to its membership relations. In the case of very complex tasks, it may be necessary to break the total performance into functional units, practicing each of these sections as a whole. Special attention then has to be given to the integration of the "sub-wholes" into a working pattern.[3]

This concept has great meaning to those who teach sport activity. The skilled golfer is well aware of the disastrous results which occur when any one phase of the golf swing is improperly executed. He knows that a change in any part causes a radical change in the act as a whole. In the golf swing, as in any other act of skill, the significant characteristic is organization. Once the complete pattern is established, the specific movements tend to fit together in proper relation. The golfer is keenly aware of the organization of his swing by the feel of the swing. If the swing feels right he knows the ball was well hit, if it feels wrong, he knows before he looks that he has missed the shot.

The job of learning any skill, including motor skills, is not one of orderly progress. A good focus provides the learner with a clue to follow as he seeks to master the act. Having a good focus and a goal in mind the learner can tell when he is succeeding in his efforts to master the act; but even if he seems to make no progress for a time, he is constantly aware of the relationship of all his attempts toward the desired pattern as a whole.

Many of the difficulties in teaching complex skills stem from the fact that activities are often taught in an artificial environment,

[3] Arthur I. Gates, *et al.*, *Educational Psychology* (New York: The Macmillan Company, 1948), pp. 347-348.

rather than in the setting in which it eventually will be used. When one considers the broad variety of sport activities that should exist in the program, it is obvious that many activities will be taught without the benefit of the natural environment. When this is so it must be recognized as a limiting factor in learning. Teaching golf in a gymnasium, using cotton or plastic balls or using the cage, will serve satisfactorily to enable the learner to get a general idea of the golf swing. The actual game of golf, however, introduces new conditions. The golfer must adapt his strokes to the distance from the hole, the contour of the ground where the ball lies, the condition of the turf, the amount of wind, and to a number of other changing conditions of the game. In order for the principle of focalization to work at a high level it is necessary, therefore, that wherever possible the activity should be carried out in its natural setting.

There is considerable evidence to explain the commonly observed fact that the student who is well coordinated and skilled in several sports will more readily acquire new skills. A well coordinated individual is one who is competent in the fundamental skills of running, jumping, throwing, striking, carrying, and climbing. In physical education the fundamental skills are diverted into sport skills through adequate instruction. Since sport skills merely represent new wholes portraying different combinations of the fundamental skills, it follows that individuals who possess dexterity in these basics need only to reorganize previous learnings.

3. Focalization is a part of *interest*.

In learning sport skills, or anything else, there is a magic formula operating to produce successful results. The formula is:

$$INTEREST \rightarrow EFFORT \rightarrow SKILL$$

Teachers recognize, although they often fail to grasp its full significance, that interest is a potent factor in motivation; and that if understanding is present, the activity will be interesting. Focalization, operating at a high level, functions to sustain interest during the learning stages. This suggests that the first step the instructor must take is to work hard to capture the interest of the learner. As long as interest is present the learner will try to learn. And, it is only during the trying stages that authentic learning takes place.

Time and again good focus is disrupted by the instructor, often because of preoccupation with the details involved in class management. Consider the organization of a beginning unit in tennis as an illustration of how the teacher may ignore the principle of focus:

A number of students are on the courts some minutes before the class is scheduled to begin. Exciting singles and doubles play holds the center of the stage. What happens when the class officially commences? The instructor arrives on the scene, blows his whistle as the signal for the students to gather around him for roll call. Then, with no attempt to build upon the participation of the past few minutes the students are assigned to small groups on the several courts for drill on the forehand stroke. Gone is the enthusiasm that existed before class; in its place often comes resentment when a group is forced to stop abruptly what it was doing in order to do something else. Needless to say, listless play characterized the period.

This illustration demonstrates his instructor's oblivion to the possibilities inherent in the situation on the courts upon his arrival. The group may have needed to practice the forehand stroke; however, to ignore a good learning atmosphere and harshly move into one that is much less satisfying is not intelligent procedure.

To demonstrate the relationships existing between focalization and context, one need merely refer to the distinguishing characteristics of each principle. For instance: Take any good activity and teach it in its natural environment (concrete), organize it well (challenge), and the result is bound to be stimulated, eager participants (interaction). As learning proceeds, and students respond vigorously (interest), it follows that motivation remains high as they seek to master the fundamentals involved in the activity (unification). It is recognized, of course, that all students will not enjoy every activity included in the program; accordingly, as many as possible are included (varied).

The Principle of Socialization

Effective learning depends to an important extent upon the social setting in which it takes place. There is something that the group contributes to a learning situation that cannot be found any other way. A great deal of value stems from social exchange in the learning situation. Just as in the first two principles of learning, this principle is based upon psychological findings. It is also in keeping with common sense and common experience. It is not a separate technique, but goes along with good context and focus. The full impact on learning exerted by socialization reveals itself as one studies its distinguishing characteristics.

1. The amount of learning that goes on which can be attributed to the presence of the group is called *social facilitation* or the *social increment*.

The learner will do most things better when he does them in a group of individuals similarly occupied. The improvement in his work, due to the presence of the group, is known as social facilitation or the social increment. It seems to be greatest when all members of the group are aware of what the others are doing. As a skillful organizer the instructor will work to unleash the powerful influences on learning contained within the group potential. If he is successful, a positive group spirit will become the controlling influence in the learning situation.

The most crucial period in the learning process occurs at the outset of a course or at the beginning of a unit. A new group is often composed of a few students who are resentful, suspicious, bored, and even strongly antagonistic to the work of the course. This is especially true of required classes. The negativism radiating from such a social atmosphere blocks learning.

Experienced teachers know that the attitude of a group is a controlling factor in determining the amount of learning in progress. They know that their most pressing task with the new group is to develop a positive rapport among group members. Superior teachers seek to establish learning situations within which students are led to feel at ease.

In most instances little real learning goes on in solitude. The individual is gregarious, and learns best in a group rather than alone. Physical activities are seldom enjoyed in isolation. Although activities such as archery, hiking, horseshoes, golf, and swimming may be carried on by an individual, the feeling of associating with others who have the same interest gives impetus to a pursuit, adds meaning and justification, and raises its value. Even such pursuits as going to the movies, watching television, or working in the garden become more enjoyable when one shares the experiences with amiable company. The "socializing" influence of group action carries the values of participation far beyond immediate satisfaction.

2. Skillful use of *incentives* enhances the possibility of learning taking place.

Much has been made of the use of incentives in the learning process. Recent investigators in psychological research substantially agree on the following points, thereby suggesting the kind of personal and social relationships that should be maintained in a learning situation.

First, the learner benefits by gaining a clear idea of the impressions he is making on others. The learner should know how he compares with standards set for the class and in terms of how well he is doing compared to others in the group. He is apt to be more responsive if he recognizes his own progress. A sound grading plan, involving evaluative criteria that everyone can understand, helps the learner know how he stands in terms of the work of the course. He should have ready access to the grade book and the teachers' evaluation.

There are countless ways to use incentives effectively. Every teaching situation is rich in episodes that occur which are conducive to some form of incentive or another. For instance, as the work in a unit progresses the competent teacher keeps attention directed to the learners who are making the most progress. He does this in such ways as to stimulate others to put forth greater efforts to keep up with those who are doing well. The first nonswimmer to get his feet off the bottom and prone glide from the side of the pool, or the first to jump into deep water, stimulates his companions to put forth renewed efforts to overcome their timidity. Competition of this kind, used properly, acts as a potent incentive to learning.

Second, praise for success gets far better results than constant blame for failure. This does not mean that unwarranted praise is desirable; it means, rather, that learning goes best when a positive atmosphere dominates. Negativism is a deterrent to learning. The successful teacher knows the importance of being fair and objective as he strives to establish a positive atmosphere.

Third, the instructor should be cognizant of the importance of permeating the setting with a friendly spirit. The learner reacts best to what goes on when he feels at ease and enjoys the associations with his peers and when he respects and likes his teacher.

3. A group *democratically* organized and conducted has a better effect upon learning than one that uses either the autocratic or laissez-faire methods of organization.

There are essentially three ways to organize students in a class situation. First, the group may be autocratically organized and conducted. This type of organization characterizes the so-called formal programs of physical education and some of the more progressive ones as well, especially in their prescribed portions. Here class activities proceed chiefly by directives from the instructor and action reflects submission on the part of the students. Student interests and needs are not taken into account. The atmosphere created by this method of conducting a class may have a serious psychological effect upon some students. A few may rebel and become stubborn disciplinary problems, others may meekly accept the unpleasant situation, while for others it may be a serious disintegrating experience. The least damaging influence of the autocratic organization is that it leads to less effective action and achievement. Certainly, the operation of the principle of socialization is at its lowest level.

Second, the class may be allowed to shift largely for itself. This laissez-faire organization, even though there may be an air of general amiability, offers little improvement over the autocratically controlled group in terms of the kind of learning possible. This kind of organization is seen in the so-called "bat and ball" programs, wherein students receive a doubtful recreational experience rather than an instructional one.

Third, this is the type of organization which skillfully utilizes the democratic group process. Recent ample research findings, especially in the field of industrial psychology, indicate that a group democratically organized and conducted has a markedly better effect upon the learning and achievement of its members than by either of the first two methods.

The program may be organized in such ways as to encourage the student to assume responsibility for carrying on activities of his own choosing in cooperation with others. Probably the best opportunities for giving the student rich experiences in the democratic group process are found in the recreational phases of the total program. The intramural coordinator has an important function in carrying out the recreational portions of the program, but in a less direct way than does the instructor of a class or the coach of an interscholastic team. His task is to help students who share an interest in an activity, plan and carry it through. And this is the essential characteristic of the democratically functioning group.

Although the instructor must play a more direct role in the class situation and in the interscholastic athletic program, it is both practical and essential that these phases be organized so that the principle of socialization is permitted to operate with merit.

The core, required-elective method of organization described in Chapter 11 beautifully illustrates democratic administration of the instructional program. The core program provides the learner with perspective by exposing him to a variety of activities. The required-elective program enables him to select activities which appeal to him and provide opportunities to develop a measure of skill in them. Through the media of the student leaders' core he has opportunities to share in the responsibilities and authority associated with conducting both levels of the instructional program.

Opportunities for democratic experiences and leadership also abound in interscholastic athletics. Success in any sport depends a lot upon team spirit, that elusive quality which is generated when the group operates as a closely knit, harmonious unit. A team needs its leaders. The football squad must have faith in its quarterback; the basketball team reaches its maximum potential when a "take charge guy" is on the team; and, in baseball, success is greatest when the team has a leader to hold it together.

An instructive instance of the operation of this principle at a high level is provided by the organization of the practice sessions of a varsity golf team.

The players are reasonably skilled in the art of playing golf. They know what good results are and can often detect the sources of errors when they are made. As one might suspect the class schedules of the members of the team vary to such an extent that it is impossible for the players to leave the campus for the course at the same time. This situation lends itself to a wide range of freedom in practice sessions. Consequently, unless the coach wants to meet them as a group, the players are scattered over the course in pairs, threesomes, and foursomes. To all outward appearances there is very little instruction going on. However, the critical observer will immediately recognize the dynamic learning situation ensuing. The players are constantly helping one another; when one gets a little "off" his game others will quickly spot the difficulty and point it out. After the round is over the boy having the difficulty may be found at the practice tee, where, under the watchful eye of a fellow player or his coach he will work to "iron out" his difficulty.

Golf is receiving its share of curriculum emphasis for both boys and girls and is an ideal sport for intramural, extramural, interschool and co-recreational programs.

In this case it is clear that the situation itself is taking charge; the group has assumed responsibility for its own doings and its own achievements. The high degree of cooperation obtained grew out of an ideal context and focus; and, it matters little whether the coach was completely aware of the advantages of this kind of organization. The situation created the manner in which the learning has to be organized. This is high level operation of the principle of socialization. Since this rarely occurs in most other phases of the program it is important that all teachers know how to establish comparable conditions.

The Principle of Individualization

Meaningful learning must proceed in terms of the learner's own purposes, aptitudes, abilities, and experimental procedures. This is what is meant by the principle of individualization.

The most significant distinguishing characteristic of this principle is that *individuals differ from one another in many respects.* This is a commonly accepted psychological proposition. The question that must be answered is: How does knowledge about individual differences bear upon the organization of learning in physical education? This fact has a great deal to do with sound administration and skillful organization of the instructional program. Among the more important ways that it has an impact on the program are the four discussed below.

1. Learning is and must be an individual matter. Each individual must do his own learning. Individuals differ in terms of any single characteristic or trait that may be singled out to be measured. This is the reason why programs should be diversified, and that a balance of activities from the several areas of activities should be sought. No matter how popular an activity may be, it will not appeal to all students.

2. The skill levels that students bring to the program must be determined at the outset. The common practice of placing the student in instructional classes solely on the basis of available free time forces the department to conduct its program with the principle of individualization working at a low level. The attempt to provide for progression in the program is made exceedingly difficult. Grouping students according to their grade in school permits the department to organize its instructional program so that this principle functions more effectively.

3. The instructor must recognize that guidance is an impor-

tant part of his responsibility. He must understand human nature, be cognizant of the problems of youth and know how they think to qualify as a first-rate teacher of competitive activities. With this background of knowledge the teacher is in a position to know each student so that he is able to cope with basic personality traits, including quirks. Since individuals differ from one another in special aptitudes and interests, and in methods of working, it is the task of the teacher to organize the learning situation with these differences accorded special attention. Ideal context can be ruined by poor teaching, just as a context that looks inadequate may be measurably vitalized by first-rate teaching.

The importance of adequate guidance in physical education is obvious when one attempts to meet the needs and interests of the student. In view of the principle of individualization it is suggested that the primary consideration in guidance is to discover the interests of the student and to attempt to organize his experiences so that these interests are nurtured. A declared interest, even though strong, is, in itself, no guarantee of superior ability. It does indicate that the student concerned probably will do better in that respect than in others.

There are few, if any, innate or natural interests. Awareness of the fact that interests are the product of the kinds of experiences the individual has had in his past makes it plain that one of the important functions of instruction is to awaken a curiosity in vigorous activity. The key question the physical educator must keep foremost in his thoughts is: How can he, through instruction, help the participant gain enough skill to want to participate? The degree of success in answering this question depends, to a considerable extent, upon a continuous guidance program and a flexible classification of students. The aim of guidance in physical education is to encourage the student to seek his own superior level. The instructor's function is to guide the developmental process.

4. Abundant psychological research indicates that most individuals fail to achieve anywhere near the potential ability they have in any field of endeavor. It is this fact that spurs the teacher along. He knows that no matter what skills, or lack of them, the participant brings to an activity it is possible to help him become more skilled.

The reason for this relatively low efficiency in relation to capacity stems from the inadequate experiences the student has had in early years. Many students lack skill in physical activities because they have had little or no instruction in fundamentals—the basis for the development of sport skills. This does not prevent students from developing interest and a measure of ability in certain activities; rather, it explains the serious errors in their established action patterns which contribute to ineffectual performance. Experienced teachers are vividly aware of the difficulty involved in helping students correct faulty performance. They know that the basic job of instruction is to help the meagerly skilled students achieve enough skill in several activities to bring satisfaction from participation.

Examples of high level operation of the principle of individualization are observed wherever one finds sound programs. Perhaps the following example may help the reader understand this principle more clearly:

A student had reached the sophomore year in college with a physical education record somewhat less than mediocre. He had faithfully attended his required classes, but refrained from participation in the extensive recreational program which was available. He was quiet and shy, and seemed emotionally immature for his age.

His physical education adviser became concerned about this student's poor adjustment. A check with the young man's major adviser disclosed two highly significant facts: (1) He was a brilliant student, earning a solid A average; and (2) he had very few friends; apparently he spent most of his time in academic matters. His physical education record card indicated that he had demonstrated almost no ability in motor coordination.

With the above information in hand the physical education adviser made an effort to "sound him out," hoping to discover something that he might be able to do that would bring him some measure of success. It appeared that this young man had no desire to participate in anything physical. His only interest was in theoretical knowledge, centering on the field of geology. In desperation, his adviser suggested that he might like to join one of the Saturday hiking groups. The adviser tried to make it appealing by pointing out that the group might very well appreciate help in recognizing features in the terrain through which they might hike.

The proposal proved successful beyond any expectation. The

student consented, somewhat reluctantly, to join a group immediately. In the familiar environment of his major interest he soon lost his reserve. With the first question regarding rock formations along the way he became absorbed in sharing his knowledge with his companions. The enthusiastic response from the group led him to become a regular member of the hiking club.

Here is a revealing case in which the value of a student's physical education experiences turned on finding the opportunity suited to him as an individual. The success of the physical educator in dealing with this unusual case depended on mutual discovery of this opportunity. This is operation of the principle of individualization at its very best.

The first-rate teacher of a motor skill does not teach an activity or a system. He teaches a learner. He does this by getting the learner stimulated to want to learn. He makes an expert analysis of the learner's performances as learning proceeds. With skill and dispatch he locates key points that need to be emphasized in the learner's thinking and in his actions. Opportunity is then given for the learner to obtain more practice and drill so that he may develop skill in his own way.

A rich context, sharp focus, and good socialization can be destroyed for the individual if he discovers that he is not making progress. The moment he becomes discouraged these principles function on a lower plane. On the other hand, skillful development of individualization will establish a meaningful focus, lead to enjoyment in associating with the group, and lead to satisfactory results even where the context is limited.

The Principle of Sequence

Up to this point the major portion of attention has been placed on the specific job of learning and its proper organization in terms of the principles of context, focalization, socialization, and individualization. This is the practical concern of every teacher, for if the separate acts of learning are not meaningful everything fails.

There is another consideration, implied throughout this chapter but not yet made explicit. The teacher must be concerned with the effectiveness of a series of learnings arranged in order of time or sequence. He is teaching not only fundamental skills but also sport skills; not only the proper stance and grip in golf, but also the game of golf. He must go even further in his thinking and planning, for he is not only teaching an activity, he is trying to bring about certain changes in his students. He is concerned with developing the individual as a total person. Obviously, then, the controlling orientation, both in the separate learnings and their sequence, must be the same. The implication is clear; the sequence of meaningful learnings must itself be meaningful, if authentic results are to be gained. This is what is meant by the principle of sequence.

An examination of some of the more important distinguishing features of meaningful sequence should help to document the importance of this principle in organizing the total program.

1. Acquiring skill is a *continuous* process; it is essentially the same at the beginning as at the end.

The individual usually does not suddenly acquire an entirely new skill. Any trait or ability possessed by the individual at any time, whether it is a technique of applying make-up or shaving, an attitude, a mental skill, or a motor skill, has had a past history of experiences in the development. The professional baseball player did not develop overnight; neither did the varsity athlete. If there is any sense to sequence of growth and development in learning, one can recognize the germ of ability in one's earlier years.

Many students reject sport activities because they have had unsatisfactory past experiences. A student may demonstrate his lack of adequate background in normal play pursuits by adopting the attitude that physical activities are somewhat beneath him, or that he simply does not like sports. Many unskilled individuals adopt a snobbish attitude and display distain toward anything which calls for the use of muscles.

Many environmental factors combine to keep young children from developing enjoyment and skill in a wide range of motor skills commensurate with their potentialities. Not only have they lacked instruction in many of the activities most youngsters enjoy, they have had little opportunity to participate in many of the physical-recreation activities commonly employed in the adult recreational world. This unfortunate situation does not satisfactorily serve to explain the large numbers of students who are not materially affected by the time spent in the physical education program. It should point out to physical educators the need for concerted, skillful action in arousing the interests of students toward recreational sports which will prove to be of real value now as well as in adulthood. It should also suggest to the teacher that he must keep uppermost in mind the unmistakable fact that the final test of growth of skill is in terms of the learner's ability to put learnings into operation in the game situation. The program must be the school's laboratory in which the young person is taught physical recreational skills that may fit into his specific life pattern.

In accepting this as a real function of the program one need not conclude that all students must be urged to seek skills in new activities. It suggests, however, that instruction for beginners in a wide variety of leisure time activities is a crucial task of the physical educator. Furthermore, since all students do not participate in the same activities, it follows that they should have ample opportunity, in one way or another, to obtain an appreciation for the more common sports in which they are not participants.

The first time an individual attempts to bowl, his results are meager in terms of results achieved by the experienced, skilled bowler. He may do the same things as the expert, but his uncoordinated movements cannot be compared favorably to the smooth, rhythmical action which characterizes the accomplished performer. Many people have bowled a time or two and then have given up the game in disgust because of poor results. This discouragement can be prevented if a competent instructor is available to help when difficulties are encountered. This kind of assistance is the important job of the teacher in relationship to this principle. The unguided learner seeks immediate progress. Most of the pitfalls in learning motor skills occur in the early stages of learning. Immediate returns are often meager; consequently, effective methods must be used by the instructor to help the learner achieve visible results as quickly as possible.

The teacher of physical education must be constantly aware that the learner needs to feel that he is making progress. He must be led to enjoy participation from the outset or the danger is real that he will turn away from the activity. The instructional program must be flexibly organized to permit the individual student to fit into a situation which will enable him to start where he is in terms of skill, and, under adequate guidance, move ahead at his own maximum rate.

2. Development of skill depends upon *purpose* present in the mind of the learner.

A student who does not want to learn will not get very far. Learning a sport skill is a complex process. It is not surprising that it takes place more surely when the participant really wants to learn. This point is made clear in the discussion of the principle of focalization; and, it is significant here. It is appropriate to point out again that the student will make the most progress if he is encouraged to try to learn. The close interrelationship existing between focalization and sequence is seen at this point. The real opportunities to teach come during the trying periods. Effort, part of focalization, is sustained only when purpose, part of sequence, remains firm.

3. Learning a skill is always a movement from *crudeness* to *discrimination*.

In the beginning stages of learning a motor skill it is a serious mistake to insist upon detail, accuracy, and precision. Superior teachers know that it is a mistake to attempt to teach too many specifics to the novice. They recognize that when details—exactness in execution of fundamentals—are demanded the learner becomes confused. The general idea—the process—must be grasped before complex detail. Basic skills are mastered only after the learner has had time to practice under skillful supervision. Premature attempts to force discrimination can inhibit the whole learning process. In short, the learner may lose sight of meaning in the face of a storm of detail.

Progressive change in performance characterizes achievement of skill. As learning proceeds it is not important that earlier learnings are retained; it is important that they should be assimilated. Correct responses are built in this way and errors are eliminated. Knowledge that progress is being made usually leads the learner to put forth more intensity of effort; self-confidence is aroused;

and there is renewed eagerness to improve as the learning becomes easier and more enjoyable. In the later stages of acquiring skill the pattern as a whole becomes clear and precision evolves. The act becomes smooth and graceful. A great deal of productive practice goes into the acquisition of skill. Once the learner is rewarded with the thrill of success he will need little urging to continue to practice. The deep satisfaction that accrues will usually lead him to seek every opportunity to participate in the activity for a long time to come.

The Principle in Operation

The principle of sequence works at low levels when classes are organized so that little relationship exists between one lesson plan and the next. Instruction which stresses work on fundamentals with little time devoted to participation in the entire activity, ignoring the fact that learning by the Gestaltist method serves to unify all action, demonstrates a lack of understanding of this principle. So do classes that consist of simply playing the game. At this point it should be easier to see the dynamic relationship existing between sequence and focalization.

Sequence operates more effectively when instruction involves planning to set the stage, introduces the activity, and attempts to keep the fragments together as learning proceeds. It is even better when the principle of individualization is seriously considered. That is, when students are brought into the planning and given as much control over what goes on as they can accept. Under these conditions daily experiences are taught in relationship to what went on before and with an eye to what lies ahead. Each daily lesson functions as an integral part of carrying on the long-time continuous sequence of learning. Daily lesson plans may be compared to specific episodes in a novel. Both are instrumental to the final goal; the one, enjoyment and skill in participation, the other, development of the plot. This is the kind of setting which enables all the principles to function at maximum levels.

Application of the principle of sequence to the total program suggests that physical education has not, as yet, gone very far toward the development of an integrated program. In departments which feature instruction for girls and boys in separate classes, meagerly developed intramural, G.A.A. and recreational experiences for all, and interscholastic athletics in a category all by itself this principle is operating at its lowest level. It works better when the staff meets together regularly to coordinate its diversified program. Under these circumstances the instructional program is more apt to be rich in activities chosen from the normal pursuits of people. Activities are organized so that students are grouped with others of similar skills and given opportunity to advance from their present level of skills to more advanced levels. The voluntary aspects of the program become the outgrowth and extension of the instructional program.

The Principle of Evaluation

Evaluation is part of the learning and teaching process. In no sense is it functionally separated. The better the learner and the teacher are able to evaluate their actions the better the learning is likely to proceed. From the very beginning of the learning process the participants should be helped to visualize correct action patterns. With a picture of the skilled performance in mind the learner is encouraged to constantly make a valid and discriminatory appraisal of all aspects of the total act. This, in its simplest form, is the principle of evaluation.

Evaluation is continuous; students are constantly making value judgments of their own actions, those of the teacher, and those of other students. The teacher also continually appraises the effects of his teaching in terms of student results. Evaluation must be taken into serious account. The program must be organized in such a way as to put students in positions where they are encouraged to analyze their own results. The students' evaluation of the progress being made becomes the central consideration in the whole process of evaluation.

The following example illustrates how this principle operates in the teaching-learning process, and may be helpful to the reader as he seeks to understand the meaning of evaluation.

An observer of a high school baseball team practice participated in an interesting episode involving evaluation. The coach, a former collegiate star, was watching batting practice when the observer arrived. The boy on the mound appeared very wild. Batters were forced to "hit the dirt" often. The coach believed that the best way to build up the confidence of his hitters was to give them plenty of practice in getting out of the way of the ball. He expressed this thought, as he turned to the observer and said, "If they can keep from being hit here with that wild left hander on the mound, they won't have anything to worry about during games."

After a few players had their turn at bat a boy came up to the plate who obviously was a poor hitter. The best he could do was to hit a few weak foul balls. The coach poured out a constant stream of advice, designed to improve the batter's courage. It seemed that the coach felt that the only thing wrong with the boy was that he was afraid he might be hit. The coach remarked to the observer, "Too bad Mike is yellow, he is a sweet fielding second baseman. All he needs is a little 'guts,' but he just can't stand fast ball pitching. Guess I will never be able to use him."

A little later on in the practice session the observer managed to get Mike aside and point out his major difficulty. His error was not in lack of courage; rather, he kept the bat on his shoulder until the ball was at the plate. The observer pointed out the necessity of being set to swing. He explained that the bat must be off the shoulder and ready to move forward as the batter strides into the ball. After a few swings at an imaginary ball with the new concept Mike seemed to get the idea. The next time at bat he surprised everyone concerned by hitting two balls to the outfield.

Here is an illustration of evaluation. In this instance, two of the individuals evaluated incorrectly and one did very well. Mike knew something was wrong but had no notion what it was. The coach was aware that the boy was getting poor results, but his analysis proved inaccurate. The observer evaluated correctly. He went to the center of the difficulty by appropriate evaluation and helped Mike understand the crucial feature of batting that was not previously clear.

Written and performance tests, measuring, marking, keeping records, and making reports are the more familiar instruments of evaluation and should be considered and treated as factors in the crucial task of bringing about more effective learning. Testing in physical education may serve the following functions: to classify students, to determine student progress, to inform parents, to motivate, to diagnose and guide, to determine teacher efficiency, and to provide material for research purposes. Tests should be used only when they are valuable in enhancing learning. Viewed in this light it is clear that testing and measuring are important factors in organizing meaningful learning situations.

Observation of current practice discloses at least four attitudes toward testing held by people in the field: first, the extreme view that testing will solve most of the problems in physical education; second, all testing is worthless; third, testing is too difficult and takes too much time; fourth, the rational view that tests are to be used as one means of improving instruction. A test is used only when it contributes to learning, and when it will supplement subjective evaluation on the part of both the teacher and the learner. Under the impetus of this concept it is possible to move ahead in the formidable task of improving evaluating techniques in physical education.

Evaluation means more than testing. It includes subjective judgment on the part of all concerned in the learning process. The most important aspect of all learning is the purpose of the learner. Learning any skill is done best if the learner has a sense of need and when he has a genuine desire to learn. If he does succeed in making progress he is apt to persist, even in the face of subsequent difficulties. It seems logical that any scheme of evaluation must help the student in his efforts to achieve his purposes. With this concept firmly in mind the teacher is better prepared to choose wisely the tools of evaluation which will make a contribution to the learning process.

As one appraises any specific task of teaching in terms of its effectiveness to produce authentic results the six principles discussed here are intimately involved. Indeed, they merge into one another continually, for they are merely different ways of looking at the same process, the process of meaningful learning.

Selected References

Brownell, Clifford Lee and E. Patricia Hagman, *Physical Education—Foundations and Principles,* New York: McGraw-Hill Book Company, 1951, Chapters 15 and 16.

Teachers Guide to Physical Education for Girls in High School, Sacramento: California State Department of Education, 1957, Chapter 12.

Cowell, Charles C. and Helen W. Hazelton, *Curriculum Designs in Physical Education,* Englewood Cliffs, N. J.: Prentice-Hall, Inc., 1955, Chapters 3 and 8.

Davis, Elwood C. and Earl L. Wallis, *Toward Better Teaching in Physical Education,* Englewood Cliffs, N. J.: Prentice-Hall, Inc., 1961, Chapters 11-16.

Jaeger, Eloise M. and Else H. Bockstruck, "Effective Student Leadership," *JOHPER* (December, 1959), pp. 32-34 and 52.

Knapp, Clyde and E. Patricia Hagman, *Teaching Methods for Physical Education,* New York: McGraw-Hill Book Company, 1953, Part III.

Mursell, James L., *Successful Teaching: Its Psychological Principles,* New York: McGraw-Hill Book Company, 1946.

———, *Developmental Teaching,* New York: McGraw-Hill Book Company, 1949.

Oberteuffer, Delbert, *Physical Education,* New York: Harper & Brothers, 1956, Chapter 11.

Price, Herbert C. Jr., "A New Kind of Report Card," *JOHPER* (February, 1961), pp. 18-20 and 38.

Shepard, Natalie M., *Foundations and Principles of Physical Education,* New York: The Ronald Press Company, 1960, Chapters 12 and 14.

Vannier, Maryhelen and Hollis F. Fait, *Teaching Physical Education in Secondary Schools,* Philadelphia: W. B. Saunders Company, 1957, Chapter 4.

Williams, Jesse Feiring, *The Principles of Physical Education,* Philadelphia: W. B. Saunders Company, 1959, Chapters 11, 13.

THE POSER

GO ON AND BOWL
WE'VE HAD OUR LOOK
CUT OUT THE POSE
LET'S SEE A HOOK!

Walt Ditzen, Courtesy of National Bowling Council

The Future and Physical Education

Look not mournfully to the past—it comes not back again; wisely improve the present—it is thine; go forth to meet the shadowy future without fear, and with a manly heart.

Henry Wadsworth Longfellow

17

Many facts, principles, philosophies and trends relating to physical education as a profession have been placed before you in these chapters. Other materials have been cited to help you become more familiar with historical backgrounds and basic concepts. A careful study of the material presented herein should help you (1) to be sure you are headed toward a career that offers challenge, opportunity, and individual satisfaction, and (2) to be aware of the nature and scope of the work that lies ahead in professional preparation and on-the-job service.

257

It has not been possible in this introductory text to penetrate as deeply into the many problems and solutions as will be possible in later more advanced courses. Before closing this first adventure into the profession we shall now take a final look ahead in this concluding chapter.

EDUCATION IN TRANSITION

The past two or three decades have been characterized by dramatic changes in educational practice, and by a growing public awareness of its significance, its methods, and its needs. All of these influences have similarly affected the field of physical education.

Oberteuffer[1] reflected this effect from critical public evaluation as follows:

To estimate the effect of current re-examination of American education on the field of physical education is a challenging task. It is intriguing because it is so speculative. Who knows what impact modern pressures will have upon us? And if physical education changes in the next ten years, will it be because of these modern pressures or because the redirection of physical education was inevitable with or without the sober recommendations of Conant or the frenetic irrationalities of Rickover and Bestor?

One thing is certain about physical education. There are always trends! We are always on the move! We may be forging ahead or stepping sideways. Or we may actually be reversing our field and going back to the ancient philosophies and activities of the nineteenth century. An examination of our literature and observation of programs around the country would show that the status quo is not one of our sacred cows!

Abernathy expressed it this way:[2]

If current popular literature is accurate in reflecting critical opinion, crucial problems of education in the United States might

1 Delbert Oberteuffer, "What Will Be The Impact of Modern Pressures?" *JOHPER*, January, 1961, pp. 21 and 73.

2 Ruth Abernathy, "Implications for Physical Education in the Current Reexamination of American Education," *JOHPER*, January, 1961, pp. 19-20.

well be identified as centering around conformity, mediocrity, selfishness, and softness arising from political and economic pressures and consequent dichotomies.

The increasing public interest in education has been largely productive of desirable change, although all change is not desirable. Certainly, educators have been forced to band together to study their purposes, their current methods and procedures, and to seek quality while always forced to contend with quantity.

These pressures have caused school boards to be alert to best practices, to drive toward better facilities, more ample equipment and supplies, and to put their trust in the selection of better prepared administrators and teachers.

One of the significant forces for desirable change in education has been the series of pronouncements of the Educational Policies Commission. In one article[3] the point was made that

the current debate (assessment of public education) is animated by a new spirit of urgency due to an unprecedented foreboding about the future and an unprecedented awareness of human potential for progress. Man's destiny appears to depend upon his acquisition and use of knowledge. Public concern is based, in short, upon a new sense of relationship between the quality of education and the future of America.

Many new trends are causing redirection of education. Some are strongly advocating a national curriculum. Conant points out the divergencies that make it impossible to develop nationwide standards, yet the effort gathers momentum, particularly in physical education. Education is often castigated because it has failed to change with the times, yet there remains a persistent clamor for a return to sound education of former years.

The published studies of James A. Conant have left their impact on educational operation. The increasing cost of school facilities, rises in teachers' salaries, the rapid increase in tax rates, all combined with a hunger for improved educational opportunity have conspired to impel close scrutiny of education's directions.

[3] Educational Policies Commission, "An Essay on Quality in Public Education," National Education Association, 1959, p. 5.

Some states and local school systems have moved ahead to meet all challenges, regardless of the cost. Others have tended to lag behind, a fact that has prompted recent efforts to secure Federal support for education. The debate continues on the matter of local-state operation versus Federal support.

It is believed that public pressure for excellence in American education will continue and become more audible. All these factors will have a profound influence on physical education in the future. We are moving toward substantial progress and recognition provided the profession can take all necessary steps to prove its indisputable place at the "educational table."

PHYSICAL EDUCATION IN TRANSITION

An examination of the history of physical education in this nation reveals many shifting tides. It was natural that we borrowed directly from much of our European heritage. We have moved from era to era with formalized patterns of mass movement, emphasis on the gymnastics of Germany and the Scandinavian countries, an effort toward the British concept of sports and games, a meager beginning into the medical-educational attempt to meet individual physical needs through remedial, corrective, adapted and modified programs. The dance as a medium for group and individual expression has grown in acceptance. More recently a trend toward coeducational instruction and recreation in secondary schools has gathered momentum.

Through the past fifty years a preponderance of trial effort has been translated into our stadiums on each week-end where thousands sit and watch while a few reap the real values of competitive athletics. Our smaller high schools have made a fetish out of interscholastic basketball as the *summum bonum* with little attempt made to meet the needs of all students.

National survival has prompted a periodic revival of emphasis on physical fitness. Recent years have brought a realization that this need is basic and should not be subject to threats from abroad. But with frenzied efforts to meet fitness needs there is a growing danger of losing sight of the total health and physical education needs of children and youth.

All these and many more forces are causing changes in the kind of physical education we will have in future years. Accumulating research evidence is providing the profession with more accurate guide lines to direct their efforts. Our group of research-trained leaders are gaining respect among all disciplines in education and social progress.

FORCES SHAPING DIRECTIONS IN PHYSICAL EDUCATION

We are affected by swirling tides and pressures. Perhaps all or most of these forces could and should become determining factors in the development of a truly American pattern of functional physical education. As a future potential leader you have an opportunity to help shape ultimate directions.

We are forced to consider these forces constantly. Moves may be made through serious and thoughtful study of an evolving philosophy. We may be goaded into certain kinds of effort because comparative test results alarm and motivate. Shall our efforts be concentrated on physical ends or have we the vehicle which can make significant contributions to social, emotional and intellectual growth which cannot be gained elsewhere? Do we need to seek one without the other? Must we always stay safely "on shore" with traditional methods, or do we dare venture toward or beyond the "three-mile limit"?

As the movement grows to strengthen the total program of education, so must physical education marshall its best resources to do likewise, or even exceed the efforts of other disciplines. Our curriculums and programs must be shaped accordingly or we will feel the consequences.

The quest for skills which will better prepare youth to live constructively grows in emphasis, threatened somewhat by those who see only a saturated program of vigorous exercise as our purpose. Learnings which come through physical education besides skill in activities and strength and coordination must be recognized. Many of our leaders push for greater emphasis on the intellectual content of physical education while others ignore its potential. Some say the intellectual and verbally expressive content of physical education is just as significant as motor content.

Mediocrity and poor leadership, a lack of graded and sequential patterns of learning, skewed emphases, lack of homework and preparation, poor marking procedures, and unequal attention to the highly skilled performer all have conspired to cause many administrators to relegate physical education to a peripheral rather than a central part of education. Good programs in many places have reversed this trend. This is a real challenge for the future.

Automation, the space age, and the trend toward "life on wheels" is having a real effect on the future of physical education. Thinking people are becoming aware of basic needs for movement which must be met in the school or be lost forever. A deteriorating physical fitness index threatens our national security. Values of individualized and mass fitness activities are now abundantly recognized. Attention to individual weaknesses and needs will increase in importance.

Social scientists recognize and accept the social values that are possible through physical education more than do our physical educators. The impact on our culture of American sports is better known by them than extolled by our own profession. What a vista of promise this area holds for you and other future physical educators! Yours is indeed a golden opportunity.

The powerful influence of the White House in recent years has caused profound changes in physical education emphasis. Couple this with the threat of Russian competition and domination and physical education has a tremendous task in the future. We have recently witnessed the effect of presidential pressure on state superintendents of public instruction who in turn have exerted unusual pressure on school administrators. Will this be boom or bust? Will our leadership be able to utilize these assists to professional status and indispensability and at the same time use them to forge a kind of physical education which will stand as a monument to professional acumen? Never before has physical education faced such challenges, had so much going for it, and had greater need for clear vision and staunch, vigorous leadership. The future is bright and full of hope.

Those who push for greater emphasis on skills instruction, those who promote interschool athletics as the great hope, those who propose a new "movement kick" as basic to progress, those who stump for social competency or intellectual status, those who propose physical education largely as a preparation for an increased era of leisure, and those who see our unique contribution as physical fitness all must work together to produce a physical education that will merit respect and continuing support. This will not be an easy task.

THE CRYSTAL BALL

Many factors combine to cause optimism and enthusiasm for the future of physical education. Several states are on the move. State units of AAHPER are rapidly growing in strength and power. The national professional organization (AAHPER-NEA) has rapidly matured and is growing steadily in status and strength. Its expanding services are significant. Some state legislatures have recently enacted favorable laws to protect and strengthen physical education requirements. State departments of education are adding new staff personnel in our allied areas of education each year. Should Federal appropriations become available, and possibilities are good, further gains in state leadership are assured.

Opportunities are increasing for assignments in many foreign countries for leaders in health, physical education and sports, and recreation. The United States State Department program, the Peace Corps, and various teacher exchange programs are all utilizing specialists who wish to work abroad. The work of the World Health Organization (WHO) has become significant. The universal desire to improve sports skills and introduce community recreation programs is attracting American leaders in quantity. AAHPER has in recent years worked successfully to strengthen the International Council for Health, Physical Education and Recreation (ICHPER), which has become one of the strongest links in the World Confederation of the Teaching Profession (WCOTP). In the future physical educators with international aspirations will have increased opportunities for service at home and abroad.

Teacher shortages will continue, accentuated by the population explosion. Women physical educators will be in tremendous demand. Many of the above mentioned trends will add greatly to the demand for professionally prepared men teachers, coaches and school recreation leaders.

Salaries, tenure and welfare benefits, and working conditions have improved greatly in the last few years, and the trend will continue. New positions will add to job opportunities with the growth and spread of the community school concept. The trend toward the use of physical education specialists in elementary schools will be accelerated, thus providing the need for large numbers of prepared teachers. This fact plus the need for help for classroom teachers creates many more opportunities for placement and professional growth.

The tug of war for curriculum time, particularly in secondary schools, will not succeed in substantial curtailment of physical education scheduling. More school districts will provide more days per week for more students. Increasing public awareness will demand greater attention to the physical and health needs of children and youth.

The growing harmony and cooperation between physical education and medicine will increase. Their objectives and their efforts are too closely parallel to suggest a lessening of a trend which is desirable and holds much promise. The identification and correction of remedial defects will receive increasing attention.

Movements are in process which will produce greater numbers of sports and fitness clubs. More attention will be paid to motivation and recognition of individual achievement. Improved efforts in public relations by physical educators will continue to yield substantial gains in acceptance and expanded programs wherever these efforts are made.

The role of physical education in adult education and in providing skilled leadership for post-school youth and adults will increase in stature. Efforts in this direction by some leaders have met with great respect and appreciation. This is an area of service which has hardly been touched and which has great potential.

Status and recognition of our areas of education will be greater in coming years. Yet all of these predictions are based only on the fact that professional maturity is being achieved but cannot be maintained or increased without positive effort.

Professional status is something which our profession must win for itself. Nobody can confer prestige and status upon us. We ourselves must earn them through professional dedication and achievement, through competence and a sense of confidence in our own abilities.

We have succeeded in obtaining a seat at the educational table which took decades to achieve. The chair, however, is not permanently endowed. Our seat at the council table will be available as long as we continue to merit respect and confidence.

Physical education has contributed to the betterment of society since antiquity. It can do a much better job; it can be a greater profession. Its contributions to enrich living for the total population can be accelerated.

THE FUTURE AND YOU

You have become more familiar with the great possibilities in physical education as a career. It is not too late at this point to change to other career preparation if you do not at this point look ahead with eagerness and anticipation to a life of service and work in this profession. Only those who are strongly moved to prepare for this kind of educational leadership should proceed further toward its realization. Careful thought and deliberation are suggested.

The physical education profession is proud of those qualified students who are now preparing for this professional opportunity. It is confident that its institutions of higher education will give them the best possible preparation for this specialized work.

Unmet needs of American youth everywhere—inadequate facilities and undeveloped programs—beckon an annual added group of young leaders. Will you be ready and equal to the task? Our great issues and unsolved problems await your best efforts. The profession wishes for you the best of success and great happiness as you proceed toward a field of endeavor which has no equal for personal satisfaction derived from conscientious efforts.

Selected References

Abernathy, Ruth, "Implications for Physical Education in the Current Re-examination of American Education," *JOHPER* (January, 1961), pp. 19-21.

Bucher, Charles A., *Foundations of Physical Education,* St. Louis: C. V. Mosby Company, 1960, Chapter 24.

Coughlan, Robert, "A $40 Billion Bill Just For Fun," *Life Magazine* (December 28, 1959), Vol. 47, No. 26, pp. 69-75.

Cowell, Charles C., *Scientific Foundations of Physical Education,* New York: Harper & Brothers, 1953.

Duncan, Ray O. and Helen B. Watson, *Introduction to Physical Education,* New York: The Ronald Press, 1960.

Educational Policies Commission, *An Essay on Quality in Public Education,* Washington, D. C.: National Education Association, 1961.

Esslinger, Arthur A., "Yesterday, Today, and Tomorrow," *JOHPER* (September, 1959), pp. 19-21.

Jenny, John H., *Physical Education, Health Education, and Recreation,* New York: The Macmillan Company, 1961, Chapter 18.

JOHPER Feature, "Focus on Facilities: Planning Space for Physical Activity," *JOHPER* (April, 1962), pp. 33-51.

Metheny, Eleanor, "The Third Dimension in Physical Education," *JOHPER* (March, 1954), pp. 27-28.

Oberteuffer, Delbert, "What Will be the Impact of Modern Pressures," *JOHPER* (January, 1961), pp. 21 and 73.

Oberteuffer, Delbert, "The Years Ahead," *JOHPER* (September, 1959), pp. 36 and 37.

Powers, Harold, "The School with the 'Plus' Program," *JOHPER* (November, 1960), p. 29.

Romney, Golden, "Creative Teaching," *JOHPER* (October, 1961), pp. 17-19.

Snyder, Raymond A., "Images of the Future in Physical Education," *64th Proceedings CPEA,* 1961, pp. 1-7.

Trump, J. Lloyd, "An Image of a Future Secondary School Health, Physical Education and Recreation Program," *JOHPER* (January, 1961), pp. 15-18.

Index

Index